D0179703

Choosing You

SEAL PRESS

Choosing You
Deciding to Have a Baby on My Own

Copyright © 2008 by Alexandra Soiseth

Published by
Seal Press
A Member of the Perseus Books Group
1700 Fourth Street
Berkeley, California 94710

All rights reserved. No part of this book may be reproduced or transmitted
in any form without written permission from the publisher, except by reviewers
who may quote brief excerpts in connection with a review.

Some names, identifying details, and places have been changed to protect the anonymity
of the author's family and friends.

Library of Congress Cataloging-in-Publication Data

Soiseth, Alexandra.
Choosing you : deciding to have a baby on my own / by Alexandra Soiseth.
p. cm.
ISBN-13: 978-1-58005-222-1
ISBN-10: 1-58005-222-3
1. Soiseth, Alexandra. 2. Unmarried mothers--Biography. 3. Single
mothers--Biography. I. Title.
HQ759.45.S65 2008
306.874'32092--dc22
[B]
2008004014

Cover design by Tabitha Lahr
Interior design by Amber Pirker
Printed in the United States of America
Distributed by Publishers Group West

Choosing You

Deciding to Have
a Baby on My Own

By Alexandra Soiseth

SEAL PRESS

To Kaj, the daughter I always wanted

contents

Deciding to Have a Baby on My Own

I'm in my ob-gyn's office, feet in the stirrups. Dr. Bakas peeks up over the paper sheet draped across my knees and pulls his gloves off with a snap. "So? Do you want a cigarette?"

My friend Bev laughs, as does the nurse, and I chuckle a little, because it actually is funny. But something snags inside of me, a little hurt of some kind, nothing I can pay attention to just then because I'm too intent on not moving or jiggling. The tiny sperm Dr. Bakas just injected are making their long journey up through my uterus to my little waiting egg, and I don't want to do anything to disrupt them.

They've already had to do a lot of traveling. I bought them from the

Scandinavian Cryobank, which shipped them from Denmark. They are from Olaf—whose real name isn't Olaf, thank God. Though it could be worse, I guess: Stig or Thor or Anders. He's a masters student at a university in Denmark. He is twenty-two, blond, and blue-eyed, and he's six feet tall but weighs only 140 pounds.

FedEx delivered Olaf's swimmers, packed in dry ice, seven days before I actually ovulated. The container sat for a time in my kitchen beside its American cousin, the midsize garbage can. There's a strong family resemblance—they're the same width, and they both have a domed lid—but the garbage can is a little taller, standing a full three feet high.

Olaf (or his sperm, at least) hung out with me as we waited till I ovulated. He was my dinner companion. I set him up in his large, round container on the chair across the table from me. As I ate my steamed vegetables and George Foreman-ed meat (I've been dieting for three years and am hoping to lose another two pounds before I ovulate—so far I've lost 107 pounds and counting), I told him about my day. Part of me thought it would be lovely if I didn't have to drink both glasses of wine and Olaf had more to contribute to the conversation. He kind of just agreed with me all the time, though what could I expect? He's only twenty-two.

As I sat there each night, I couldn't help comparing him with other men I've had dinner with over the last four years—many men over many plates of steamed veggies in the midst of many pounds lost.

I was on a mission.

"You see, Olaf," I said one night, "I wanted to get married. I wanted babies. Lots of babies."

I looked for a long while at Olaf's routing bills and thought how it was about more than just wanting babies. It was about needing babies. A deep, physical craving.

It was about waking up sweating after a dream where I am old and alone on an empty beach, sitting in an old-fashioned lawn chair and thinking it's impossible that I'm still this way: partnerless, childless.

About this one thing I have always been certain: I was born to be a mother.

Through my twenties and thirties, all around me, friends paired up and married. A little while later, they got pregnant. But not me. I was off to school and then grad school. I was traveling. I was thinking I had time. Lots of time.

And then I turned thirty-five.

ONE

Getting Ready

At thirty-five, I am just finishing grad school. It is spring break, March 2000—the slivery edge of a new millennium. I have taken a month away to finish my thesis at my best friend's lodge in Canada.

School's ending has made me stressed about the future. I left Toronto to go to grad school three years ago (at Sarah Lawrence College, just outside New York City) to broaden my horizons, meet new people, and strengthen my writing. Hoping a change of scene would also bring me a change of luck, I imagined a whirlwind romance somewhere in there too. But that didn't happen. Instead, I did what I always do: I found myself a best friend and then built a community around myself. We had big parties, ate Thanksgiving dinner together, talked about writing and theater, and read each other's work. As the three years passed, I slipped further and further away from a relationship and scurried deep inside, hiding in writing. I can't even really say why. All I know is that I wrote and ate, wrote and ate: Cheez-Its and chips and KitKat bars, all possible types of junk, as long as I was at my desk writing while I ate it.

So here I am, with school almost over, with lots of friends but no lovers, and fat, fat, fat, feeling like crap. I'm in no place to go forth and get what I really want: a family of my own.

In the bathroom of this lodge is a scale. I notice it on the first day, then pretend I don't see it. I have not weighed myself since I began grad school, but the scale's presence pulsates through the lodge, and one morning before I'm really awake, I disrobe and look down at it. It's one of those old scales with an arm that swings around, and when I step on it, that arm shimmies all the way to the tippy-toe edge, where you can't get any fatter because there are no numbers left to record your weight.

I'm 274 pounds.

Holy crap! Sweet Jesus.

I leap off, remove my watch, my gold studs, and the scrunchy holding my hair in a ponytail.

Stepping on again, I close my eyes until I know the needle is still.

275. Off again. Pant a little. On again, this time with my feet curled around the sides of the scale. This time it says 272.5 pounds.

EFFFF. YOU. SEE. KAY.

274 pounds.

Conscious of the mirror behind me now, I put my long nightgown back on and slowly turn to look at myself, front view then side view.

It strikes me that I am the shape of a refrigerator—the same width sideways as frontways.

My rather small head looks like a bowl someone has left on top of the refrigerator. I blink at myself. I look pale. This is not the first moment of reckoning in my life about my weight, but it feels like the most momentous. I have never been this heavy before. Of course, I've kind of known I'm heavier than ever—the lethargy, the puffing when I walk very far, the gasping as I climb stairs. But I haven't had an actual number, hard evidence, before.

And here's the thing: To me, being fat has always meant being alone. *You better lose the weight, or no one is going to want to go out with you!*

We could stand here and argue about whether that is true (I've come to understand, in fact, that it *isn't* true—there are plenty of fat men and woman out there having relationships), but in my heart and head, in that moment, it's the truth.

To me, 274 pounds means a lot of aloneness.

I shake myself loose to walk into the kitchen, make myself a cup of tea, and stare out the window at the snow and the evergreens. The constant, brutal cold has kept me inside this lodge for two weeks. But today is sunny and windless, and there is no frost on the windows, so I'm guessing it's not as bad as it has been. Maybe I can go for a walk.

I take a sip of tea. *Sure, that's an idea,* the optimist in me thinks. But another part of my brain says, *What's the point?* What good will a 10-minute walk do me when I have 150 pounds to lose and a whole life to rearrange?

The tea is good, the perfect temperature and strength, and I lean forward over the kitchen table to enjoy it, still staring out these second-floor windows across the sparkling snow. The light and the bright snow and the perfect tea want to make me happy, even as the dark pressure of that number moves about in my skull.

Dropping into my brain is an image of the pound of butter in the fridge, and the flour and powdered sugar in the cupboard. As I stretch my aching back, I imagine the shortbread cookies those three ingredients could make, and my tea grows cold as they take over my thoughts. Once the thoughts are there, I can't get them out. I look at the sparkling snow, think about pulling that cold lovely air into my lungs and throat: *Go outside, go outside, go outside.* I force myself to imagine the outside world, but I can't make myself go there. Instead, I am moving toward the fridge, pulling out the butter and softening it in the microwave.

I have no thoughts in my bowl-like head now as I beat the butter, add powdered sugar and flour, beat until it's too thick and all the flour and sugar is incorporated, sweating a little at the hard work. I roll out the dough on the floured surface of the counter and cut out the square cookies. I nibble the dough. I am focused and single minded, snow and tea and that dreadful number forgotten. As the cookies bake I clean the dishes, put on water for more tea, and wait.

This is the best time. The cookies are still only a smell, an imagined taste. This lovely time—before I'm too full to think, too sick and corroded with heartburn to move.

When the first batch is done, I put a few on a plate and take the plate, with my new tea, to the kitchen table and wait a moment as they cool. They are perfect and golden, and when they are cool enough to bite, they snap in my teeth.

Oh, that first bite—not too sweet, but rich and smooth. I roll the crumbling cookie between my tongue and the roof of my mouth. This is worth waiting for. Dreaming about. This is Christmas and my mother still living with us, baking cookies, letting us eat as many as we like. It is a really good romance novel, in which the heroine is fierce and feisty and the hero is angry and tragic, but ultimately and inextricably in love with the heroine, who is, of course, really me.

I take the next bite and it is almost as good. I savor this one too, breathing through my nose to fully capture the buttery taste. The third bite is just slightly more diminished. I eat the four cookies on my plate and drink a little tea. I think, *Okay, that's enough. I enjoyed that. I'll save the rest for later. Like a normal person.* But I'm up and putting four more cookies on my plate even as I say these words to myself. I sit at the table, eat them, get up, take six, sit, and eat them more quickly, little taste to them now, my stomach feeling ever heavier. Finally I just stand at the counter and eat the whole first batch as the second one finishes baking. Out they come, and I put one in my mouth that's too hot. I feel it sizzle against my saliva, and I have to spit it out in the sink.

I eat until I can eat no more. I eat until the rest of the cookies are gone. Then I lie on the couch and wait for the nausea and pain to pass. The smell of shortbread is overwhelming now, and if I could move I would open the patio doors, despite the cold. At least there is no one for forty miles to see me this way, my nightgown up around my neck, my panties rolled down because even the lightest fabric on my belly hurts.

I'm 274 pounds. And when I graduate in May, I'll start work in the community partnerships office at the college. I'll help run trips to Nicaragua and Mexico and other hot, humid places. I fret about that now too; I imagine the sweat, imagine trying to fit into a plane seat.

I keep looking in that direction, toward graduation and the drop into emptiness on the other side. How am I ever going to build a life for myself when my usual tendency is to make shortbread cookies when I feel bad?

What a stupid thing to do. This is exactly why I haven't weighed myself in years. The news is never good, or good enough. And in this case, it is *terrible*. So I eat, making the news next time even worse. I'm upset that I'm fat so I eat. Making me fatter. I've done this my whole life. How crazy am I? I force myself to think about my novel to take my mind off the rising heartburn and pressure in my belly. I wiggle myself back inside the story, back to the end, watching my heroine in the hotel where I left her yesterday. *So, Lee,* I ask her, *what are we doing now?*

I get myself outside later that day. After dozing on the couch and drinking a bottle of club soda, I feel a little better. The road hasn't been cleared since the snow two nights ago, so I go the other way, down to the lake. The snow is hip deep in places, so it's slow going.

Before I'm even at the lake, I am sweating and lurching about, losing my footing and toppling, then pawing the snow for something to use to heave myself back up. It's the landscape's fault. I've only been down here in the summer, when everything makes sense. But where does the lake end and the land begin now? Where are the landmarks, the docks, the curving beach? There's only blinding white snow from here, where I wobble, all the way to the rise of rocks at the end of the lake, three miles away.

I am alone here. I am alone. How is it that I haven't felt it like this before?

Suddenly I can't handle the sweating or the whiteness or the hateful snow, so I follow my own messy trail back up to the lodge and fall asleep on the couch, totally chilled with sweat but too beaten up to have a bath or build up the fire.

On Friday night, my best friend, Margaret, and her husband, Jim, arrive for the week of their kids' spring break. They have a medical practice in Ottawa and own this lodge. I don't often admit this to myself, or allow myself to even think about it, but it feels terribly obvious to me here and now: I envy her life. Her husband. The money she and Jim have, this lodge, a big house in Ottawa, two kids, two cars, two cats, two dogs. I envy the volume of her life—next to her, I feel young and singular, a reed next to her forest.

On Monday, Margaret's brother Ken, who is the caretaker here, will get back from visiting his girlfriend in Toronto, so my total solitude is over now, and I am relieved.

Before long, everyone is in bed but Margaret and me, the banked fire behind us and the utter darkness outside. I'm at the table, picking at dessert crumbs from the Costco pies Margaret brought with her from Ottawa.

"Mrs.," Margaret says over her shoulder from the stove, "more tea?" Margaret started the "Mrs." thing long before she was a Mrs., long ago when we were growing up in Porcupine Plain, Saskatchewan, two blocks away from each other, her dad the veterinarian in town, my dad the Sask-Power guy.

"I'd love some green tea." I'm uncomfortable in the kitchen chair. I'd like to suggest that we go to the living room, but that's not what we do. We hang out in the kitchen, and Margaret sits cross-legged or pulls her feet beneath her. When I'm skinny, I do the same. But when I'm fat, I lean on the table or put my feet up on another chair. I pull my sweatshirt away from the rolls of fat on my belly. I watch Margaret make the tea; I watch how she doesn't notice the rolls of fat on my body. She has never seemed to notice them. She never talks about my fat unless I bring it up, and that is not very often. She is the one person in the universe I get to be weightless with.

"Sooooo," she says, sitting at the table, "what's happening?"

"Writing writing writing," I say, sipping my tea, deliberately not thinking about the shortbread cookies, or the brownies the next day, or the piecrust rolled with butter and brown sugar two days later. "Went out for walks." Well, walk. That one walk to the lake, which was more like a clumsy stumble through the snow. I should correct this lie and say, "Walk, I mean. I went for a walk." But I don't.

Margaret says, "Did you go across the road to the Ski-Doo path?"

"No, I didn't know there was one."

"We'll go this week. It's beautiful. It's like a magical land, like Bambi in winter."

I have such a hate on for the snow and the cold that I begin to plan my excuses right now.

"Margaret," I say, after a bit of silence. "I've been thinking about this for a while. . . . " I pause. "I want to ask Ken to be my Just-in-Case Guy."

"Your what?"

"My Just-in-Case-I-Don't-Get-Married-and-Want-to-Have-a-Kid Guy."

I watch as she sits back in her chair to take me seriously, sipping her tea, thinking about it. "I don't know. It might kind of freak him out."

"It's just the idea of it right now. I feel like I need to have something real arranged. Just in case. And it would be great to have him as the father."

She nods her head. "It could work."

"I still want a full-on family, you know, a husband, lots and lots of kids.

But if that doesn't happen, I don't want to miss having kids. I really love kids and babies."

"I know." Margaret smiles at me and says, "Remember in university when I thought I was pregnant?"

I do remember. We were in my studio apartment, a basement apartment, supposedly studying, but I was teaching myself to French braid my own hair, and Margaret was counting the days since her last period. "I've been so irregular," she said to me. "It's hard to know if I'm really late."

"And you keep forgetting to take the damn pill," I said from under my craned neck, resting my arms on my head as I tried to visualize what was going on with my hair. It seemed far more important to me that I figure out how to do this French-braid thing than study for my chem test. (I did, in fact, go on to fail chemistry that year. I also got a 54 in biology, dropped physics, and scored a 95 in English and a 94 in sociology. Go figure I didn't become a doctor. Margaret, however, was already in med school at that point. She went to university a year before me because I had to stay behind to make up for the year I spent in Denmark during grade ten. She then did the unthinkable and got into med school after only one year of undergrad.)

My Mrs. is, and was, a very smart woman—except when it came to taking her birth control pills. "But what if I'm pregnant?" She had said.

I remember looking over at her, sitting with her feet tucked underneath her in the cute black vinyl chair that Dad and I bought at a garage sale before I moved to university. The two chairs and tiny matching table fit perfectly into the corner made by my deep closet across from the kitchenette. I was sitting on the brown upholstered rocking chair I stole from my dad's house (he and Mom had separated three years earlier, although Mom came back for my high school graduation in May and said that she was not going back to Denmark again afterward). This wonderfully comfortable chair had always been my TV-watching chair, but Dad thought that perhaps I shouldn't get a TV in my apartment—way too distracting when I should be studying.

Beside me was the daybed. I loved my little studio apartment. It was mine, all mine, even though, truthfully, I was never alone in it. Either Margaret was with me or I stayed at her place. Which was part of what made us best friends: We had the same intolerance of being alone.

"If you're pregnant, I'll take a break from school and look after the baby, and then, when you're finished with med school and have more money, I'll go back and finish."

Margaret looked at me a long time. I could see the stress drain away as she thought about what I had said. "That could work, right?"

A part of me wondered if I really meant what I said, or if I just didn't want her to worry anymore. But really, it did seem like a good idea—in fact, it was irresistible. How great to not have to study for chemistry, but to do something so much lovelier.

Over the next few weeks, we waited—no period. Then her doctor sent her for an ultrasound, where they asked her to drink tons of water ahead of time. ("Oh my god!" she said, as I handed her cup after cup of water in the waiting room. "I have to pee!")

But she wasn't pregnant. And I think we were both disappointed. I certainly had started to like the idea of stepping off the train I was on and going somewhere else completely unexpected. I think about it now and wonder why I didn't just try to make another life for myself. Change directions. Find a boyfriend (I had not actually had a boyfriend yet, not a real one, just some hookups in high school), get married, have a kid if I wanted one so badly.

But that all seemed so prosaic to me, so expected. It was what almost all the girls back in Porcupine Plain did, and I wasn't going to be that. So ordinary. I wanted to do something extraordinary in my life.

Margaret smiles at me, and I say, "If I did this with Ken, just think—you would be my baby's aunt."

She laughs. "That would be cool!" We laugh together at the idea, liking it very much.

"It wouldn't hurt to ask, right?"

"Right."

In the morning the kids are up first, watching a video. I stop and watch them for a long moment before going into the kitchen. They are beautiful children—well behaved, smart, and thoughtful. I know Christian best, probably because he is the oldest and my godson. He surprises me with his understanding of things, even at eleven. I imagine for a moment they are my kids. I close my eyes and think about how that feels. But it's too abstract; I can't really feel it. They are so much Margaret's kids.

As I enter the kitchen, Jim turns on the coffeemaker and I stand still, waiting. Then it comes—that gorgeous smell of brewing coffee. I stand close to the machine for a whiff or two more before sitting down to finish waking up. Margaret stumbles in, scratching her scalp luxuriously, her thick, wiry hair standing straight up off her scalp. We mumble "Good morning" to each other and she yawns, which makes me yawn. Out of the corner of my eye, I can see Jim yawn too as he stares out the window over the sink, waiting for the coffee.

"I'll make pancakes," she says, and I'm happy. She makes the best pancakes in the known world. She whips egg whites and uses buttermilk. They are the right mix of dense and fluff.

She pulls out the eggs and a bowl, the mix master. From the cupboard she takes down the baking powder and salt, then stands still, with her hands on her hips. "I thought for sure I had some flour here," she says, to herself really, as Jim walks by her to pour some coffee. He makes her a cup too, and puts milk and sugar in both. I look past her to the cupboard. Past Jim *clink clink clink*-ing the spoon against the edge of the mugs. . . .

Oh, shit. I forgot to replace the flour.

I went to town as soon as the road was cleared, and I remembered to buy more butter and margarine, and I refilled the sugar bag so there was the same amount in it as there was when I arrived. But I forgot to get more flour. I feel my face flush, and a sick nausea and a kind of spotlight on my brain, and I want to say, "I baked bread!" Or, "There was a flour emergency!" But what can I say? What possible reason can there be for a whole bag of flour to be gone?

Margaret goes into the closet in the master bedroom, which she uses as a pantry. She has a smallish Tupperware with her when she comes back.

"There's not really enough for pancakes here," she says to me as she walks by. "So I think I'll make bacon and eggs. Sound okay?"

"Sure," I say, glad that the burning is out of my cheeks now. I watch her put the pancake stuff away, and I wonder if she suspects that I've used up the flour, or if she thinks she was just wrong about having some here at the lake. I can't tell, but, looking down at my red plaid slippers, I feel sick and sad and I hate myself. I wonder if she thinks I am now silently lying to her, letting her think she's crazy.

"Coffee, Mrs.?" Jim asks me.

"No thanks," I say, jumping a little. "I'm drinking tea these days."

I get up to boil water. I feel exposed walking between them, waddle-like, to the stove—self-conscious in front of Jim because he's a man (a handsome man, a Bon Jovi–type handsome man), and in front of Margaret now too, because I think she's going to look at me, suddenly realize how fat I am, think about the flour, and go, "Oh! Look how fat she is! It must have been *her* who used my flour! I bet she baked shortbread cookies and brownies and ate herself into oblivion, right to the point of bursting. And now she's lying to me about it."

I watch her peel bacon into the frying pan and think how, even with my shame, I feel terribly disappointed there'll be no pancakes.

I am quiet during breakfast and don't let myself eat much in the way of bacon, as penance for the flour and the lies. When the dishes are done, Margaret says, "Let's go for a walk up the Ski-Doo path. I want you to see it."

"Let's do it later today," I say, hoping that by then the idea will be forgotten forever. "I'm feeling so much pressure to get this novel done right now."

"Come on, you'll work better once you've been outside."

"I really don't feel good."

"Come on, Mrs.," she says in a jolly voice, the voice she uses with her kids when she is telling them to eat the broccoli *and* the carrots. She gets dressed, and so do her kids, and I feel stupid and enormous and hulking.

I put on my jacket and hat and gloves. Margaret and the kids march up the cleared drive and across the road to a path I have never noticed before. I struggle to keep up. There's an abandoned cabin deep down this path, and she wants to show it to me. It seems all uphill, endlessly uphill.

Back at the lodge again, an hour and a half later, my legs tremble as I climb the stairs. I think about the fit person I used to be in my twenties, the fit person who had lovers, who ran in races (never to win, of course—just for fun and the funky T-shirts or hats they give you), who rode her bike everywhere around Toronto. I think how now I worry about a coronary as I walk up these steep stairs.

After a short nap, I retreat into writing. I write and write, earplugs in, locked in a bedroom. Lee takes my hand and pulls me toward the end of her story and away from mine.

The next morning, I wake up stiff. It's early, still dark, long before anyone else is awake, but I'm too sore to sleep. I look up at the dark ceiling and think about Nicaragua and the trips I will lead in my new job—which I start in two months. About the Habitat for Humanity projects we'll do, about Mexico, and heat and humidity and tiny seats in planes, sitting with my arms clutched over bounteous breasts and my tummy cinched tight by the short little seatbelt.

And it all feels so *bad*.

So instead I think about yesterday, walking in the snow against my will. But once the path leveled off, I caught my breath and found myself standing in the white light, dizzy but suddenly really happy. The sky was brutally blue above the flat, even snow that stretched off beside us as we walked, through trees and what in summer must be swamps. There were birds singing in the bare trees, and it seemed as though they had sprung up whole from the bare limbs that very morning.

Christian and Chloe pushed each other into the snow and Margaret told me a joke and I loved them with every single sun-drenched, spring-anticipating part of me.

It was hard to believe this was the same place I had been living in two weeks before, with the bitter wind leaking through cracks in the walls, the ice covering the windows, and the need to keep the fire large and stoked day and night to keep the cold away.

As we walked, we could hear the rushing sound of melting snow on the move, icy water hurtling down the hill toward the lake, and it felt like the revved-up blood inside me, coursing through me as we hiked.

Later that morning, still stiff and creaky, I go outside again while Margaret makes breakfast. I'm not sure what I'm looking for, but I can't get the sound of rushing water out of my head.

I make for the lake, and before long I'm out an immeasurable distance, panting, heaving, and snorting like a horse. It's kind of funny—great, actually—feeling like a horse, big and strong and loud and coarse. I stomp and snort and swing my arms. Snot and spit and sweat drop onto the snow, making little black holes. I yell toward the dark bare trees circling the lake and laugh at the hot blood pulsing inside me. I march faster, breathe harder, chanting under my heaving breath: "Let's go, Alex, let's go. Let's go, Alex, let's go."

On Monday, Ken gets back from Toronto, happy that the days are getting warm enough to work outside. He's been dying to start work again on the big deck they've been planning since last summer. Before the first frost, they got the posts down and cemented, and the frame nailed in, and now he can finally put in the floor and the base for the Jacuzzi.

From the moment he drives up to the lodge, I am tense. Margaret and I have mulled over the idea of Ken as the father a few more times, and we get more excited each time.

I go out for a walk again that afternoon, and when I get back, I find Ken outside on the skeletal deck. I go out to join him, hand him a beer, and sit with my back against the warm outside wall of the lodge. I have made myself a cup of tea.

"How was Toronto?"

"Mucky," he says, and holds up the beer. "Thanks."

Ken and I have known each other since we were in our early teens and I became friends with Margaret. He and I were even in the same class when I came back from Denmark and lost that year of high school. We graduated together in 1983. We were two of a handful of our graduating class of thirty-three students to go on to university. We joined Margaret at the University of Saskatchewan as she was starting med school. Ken went into engineering; I, into premed.

As I watch him drink his beer, I think about those years at university, about how cold and hungry we were. Winter in Saskatoon had a brittle, bone-chilling cold we hadn't experienced in Porcupine Plain.

He and Margaret and their older sister Angela and I used to go to the biggest and cheapest Chinese buffet in Saskatoon—carrying Tupperware containers in our knapsacks—and load up on food for a few days. We drove around together, the four of us, in Margaret's Dodge Dart, which we would have to push for half an icy block until Margaret popped the clutch to get it started.

It seemed that first year was always dark—dark when we woke up, dark when we left the library after studying. Dark and overcast even during the day.

"Ken," I say, putting my empty mug on the plank beside me, "can I ask you something?"

"Sure," Ken says, smiling at me in his lopsided way. He is a handsome man—Japanese, tallish, around five-foot-eleven. He's even more handsome when he smiles like he is smiling now—kind of embarrassed, expectant. It makes his face crooked, probably because of the fall he had when he was really little that broke one of his cheekbones. It's a little higher than the other cheekbone, and when he smiles, it makes him look sort of impish and playful.

Why haven't I fallen in love with Ken? Wouldn't it have been lovely if that had happened? A romantic tidal wave washes over me: *What if Ken and I connect over the baby? What if we begin to see something in each other that was hidden before? What if we fall in love, live together, and raise our child together?*

I take a deep breath and calm myself.

Still. Our kids would be beautiful, the way Christian and Chloe are beautiful.

"I've been thinking," I say, then pause. I actually don't know how I'm going to say this. "I turned thirty-five this February."

He looks at me with a little frown. He knows exactly how old I am. Half a year older than Margaret. A year and a half older than he is.

"I've been thinking about having kids."

He lifts his eyebrows.

"Later, I mean. . . ." I sigh. Make myself stop talking. Give myself a chance to regroup.

"I have always thought that if I got close to forty and wasn't married, I would have a kid on my own."

Ken nods. He has heard this before. It is one of the things I have talked about ever since I can remember. "The thing is, I want to ask you—when the time comes—would you consider being the father?"

"Oh."

"For some reason, right now I would like to have that planned."

Ken nods. He runs his calloused hand along the thigh of his jeans. He looks up at me and says, "I'm flattered."

I laugh, realizing I had assumed all along that he would just say yes. I don't know what to say to "flattered."

He takes his time. Has another drink or two of his beer. And then it is empty. The birds are out again, and in this corner, no wind can reach us, so it's all about the sun. I am warm. I close my eyes for a moment to feel how wonderfully warm I am.

"Okay," he says, and I open my eyes. "Sure. I'll do it."

"Really?!" We both stand up.

"Really."

Ha!

"I'm very happy," I say to him, and we smile at each other.

"The one thing is, though, we'll have to clear it with my wife if I'm married by then. That sort of thing."

I look at him for a moment and think again, *God, I wish that could be me.*

"Of course." I say. Then, feeling awkward, I add, "Well, we've both got work to do." I go back inside to my novel. As I sit at the little table I have put in front of the open window, I look down at the sheets and sheets of paper and see just the paper for a change. And the black letters on that paper. This project feels more like a novel suddenly, and less like a refuge. I look out the window and enjoy the unexpected feeling of having a life that I am living. Something real and hopeful to hang on to. Something I can control.

TWO

So Many Men, So Little Time (Left)

I don't know what it is about me, but I find it easy to create a circle of support and love around myself, no matter where I go. A family of sorts. This is my thing. Perhaps it's because I've had a lot of practice. Maybe it's because Mom left the first time when I was young, seven years old or so. Dad felt he couldn't take care of my sister and me (baby Glenn went with Mom), so he set us down in the midst of his brother's family, back on the homestead where he had grown up. Linda and I slipped into the midst of our four cousins; five of us girls slept together in one room.

When Mom left us the second time, I was a teenager, and I attached myself to my next-door neighbor's family. Mrs. Poniatowski became my second mom. I baby-sat her kids, went there and baked cookies for the Christmas cookie exchange. I got so good at making bread, she would have me come over and whip up a batch for her.

Later, at the end of my fourth year of hobbling through university, I looked up from the couch where I'd been sitting for weeks, doing nothing but eating chips, I looked up at the crack between the curtains that was letting a drop of sunlight fall onto the brown shag rug at my feet, and I thought, *I have got to get out of here or I am going to do something very bad to myself.*

Toronto came to mind, for some reason—as the gateway to Europe and the world. So I decided to go there, to live there perhaps, or in Montreal or London. Somewhere far from here. Somewhere exciting. Within two weeks, I had sold or given away everything I had. I bought a one-way train ticket to Toronto. (Why a train? It wasn't really cheaper than flying. Was it because Saskatoon would feel extra far away from Toronto if it took two days and two nights to get there?) I packed two changes of clothes, my Walkman and some tapes, and the doll Margaret's mom had made me, which I loved. I was twenty-two and I had $900 in the bank.

I know my parents worried about this move, though they didn't say anything. I went home to say goodbye a week or so before I left. Margaret and Ken and their older sister Angela saw me off at the train station. I felt like the oldest son, heading out into the world to seek his fortune. *I'll send money when I find work in the New World!* And off I went.

In Toronto two days later, we pulled into Union Station at 8:00 PM and I called the youth hostel, figuring I'd just stay there the first few nights. The guy who answered the phone said, "It's August. We're full." What he meant was, *Are you nuts? How could you think there would be room?*

That was when it hit me: What had I done? At $100 a night for a hotel room, I would burn through $900 really fast. I knew not even *one* person in Toronto.

The guy at the hostel must have heard the panic in my voice, because he suggested I try the YWCA, which I did. They had a bed available in a dormlike room in their basement with nine other beds, about half of which were used in the week I stayed there.

And that was where I felt like my true nature revealed itself.

I met two women that week. One had just returned from Israel and Palestine. I told her I had been thinking more and more about going to journalism school to become a writer/reporter. She told me, "Don't do that! Just get on a plane and go to Palestine and write about what's going on there. Papers are always looking for copy. You can make a living, and you don't have to go to school for that." That was what she had been doing for two years. She was in Toronto for a conference; then she was going to Africa to see what she could write about there.

God, I loved that idea. It was *exactly* what I had been craving: to get far away from my problems and find adventure instead of depression and endless eating.

And I have to say, my belief that radical and immediate changes will fix my problems is not without precedent or merit, really. The year I spent in Denmark when I was fifteen saved my life. I had been miserable, friendless, and lonely for two years since we'd moved to Porcupine Plain. Then I had the brainwave that if I went off to Denmark as an exchange student, I would be special and new, and would have no trouble finding friends. My parents, bless them, arranged for me to live with my mom's sister, which was more of a cushioned adventure than I had been imagining, but that was okay. Now I think how even while running away, I end up with family.

And it's obvious to me now, of course, that I ran away to the place my mom ran to when I was a child. I think I had come to see Denmark as a magical place that could fix people, make them happy. Deep inside my mind, I knew that if it had worked for my mom, it might work for me. And it did. Living there, I found much more than friends. I came to understand that there was a whole world beyond the boundaries of Porcupine Plain, and that while I might be forced to finish school and grow up there, I didn't have to stay there.

And so it came to pass.

Here I was, far away from Porcupine Plain, alone this time. Free. In a YWCA in Toronto, dreaming about Tel Aviv, with my new journalism friend sleeping three beds down from me. What a gift I had received in meeting her; how possible she made it seem for me to have a great and exciting life.

The second woman I met was an Irish girl who was on her way home but was spending a week or so saying goodbye to friends. She had been working as a caretaker for an elderly man. She earned a thousand dollars a month, plus room and board. She had many friends who did the same thing but took care of children.

"There are tons of people looking for nannies," she told me. "Just go to one of the placement agencies, and they'll set you up in no time."

A nanny. *Babies,* I thought. *Children.* For a second, I remembered Margaret's pregnancy scare and the disappointment I had felt. There would be a room, so I wouldn't have to worry about renting an apartment, or about first and last month's rent. I would be safe there.

I would like to be able to say that I grabbed my two changes of clothes, my Walkman, and my doll and got on a plane to Israel. That I leapt without a net into a country where I knew no one, where I had very little money and no experience writing newspaper stories.

But I didn't. I chose the nanny route, cushioned my entry into the grown-up world of full-time work, and struggled with the knowledge that I wasn't the brave person I wanted to be.

For a year I lived in the Hanley-Johnson household. I took care of Katherine; I worked with her mother, Carol, to cook and do laundry; I helped pack and move their household twice. And almost every evening, I baby-sat at Carol's sister's house for $10 an hour.

Within a month, I was going to all their family functions as myself, not as the nanny (I don't know that I was ever *not* the nanny, but it felt very familyish). I got to know Carol's mother. I went to their Christmas celebrations, their Easter dinners, and all their birthday parties.

And it was cozy. I had time to settle into Toronto, apply to journalism school (taking the safe route into the world of journalism after all), and get some money for my own apartment. And then I got into journalism school, and I did it all over again: I developed a tight-knit circle of girlfriends who stayed with me until I moved to New York for grad school. It was super cozy.

And, of course, there were the Hashimotos (Margaret and Ken's family), with their weddings and holidays (I split my holidays between their family and my parents)—although part of me never felt completely like part of their family. I was close, but not blood, and I know now that at least part of the attraction of having Ken be the father of my baby was that we would finally have a blood tie. The irony is that it still would have been an *almost* thing, in the sense that it would have been my baby who was blood related, while I would have been an almost-in-law. Another back door, a safe route to family that didn't involve the messiness of marriage.

I had a couple of boyfriends during that time and went on numerous dates. But nothing serious ever came along. Or perhaps I was never serious about finding someone. I did think it would be nice to pair up like all my friends, to have someone love me exclusively like that. But really, I wasn't lonely. I had so many friends.

Now it is March.

I'm back from the lodge, and I look to my future and think, *This time I'm going to do it differently. I'm starting a new branch of my life. I'm not going to do what I did in Toronto, or what I did when I moved to New York. I'm not going to focus on friends. I'm going to focus on finding a* boyfriend!

I am convinced that the solution to all my problems lies there.

I move into my own apartment, away from the house of Sarah Lawrence where I made a new best friend (who lived upstairs) my second day there. For the next three years, we were inseparable. The whole house held parties and *Absolutely Fabulous* marathons and we spent long evenings talking about art. But now school is ending and everyone is moving and leaving our cozy family, my new best friend included. It is a natural break, an opportunity to do things differently.

This time, I say to myself, *I am going to strike out on my own and find a boyfriend,* not *another best friend. This time I am going to make my* own *family happen.*

The most essential thing to do, in my mind, is to lose weight. I can't see myself dating anyone feeling the way I do. So when I get back to New York from the lodge, I go to the gym almost every day. I join Weight Watchers. I go to the doctor and start on antidepressants to help pull me out of what I realize has been a low-grade depression these last few months. Slowly but steadily, I lose weight.

I don't even have to fight off overwhelming thoughts about food; they just don't enter my head anymore. It's like a switch went off at the lodge and hasn't gone on again. I say to Margaret on the phone one evening, "It's easy. I don't know why, but it is."

"Well, that's great," she says, happy for me in a health-conscious way, but sort of mild and distracted. As I said, she has no vested interest in my being fat or thin.

We talk about other things; then she tells me that she and Jim are training to do a marathon the following May. She wants to quit smoking, so she has started to run. I remember running with her when we were in high school. My dad and I used to run too.

Wouldn't that be cool, if I were ever thin enough to do that again? It would be so normal. Normal, of course, would also include being married, having kids. Being someone who brushed her teeth every day without having to force herself to. It might even be more than normal, better than normal, if I were really skinny and really fast. I could be beautiful and special and married to someone amazing and fabulous, and we would have spectacular kids together. I could be like the heroine of the romances I grew up reading: someone with white teeth and long blond hair.

After I've lost about forty pounds, I join Match.com and begin emailing with a guy named Shawn. This is in the early days of my Internet dating, before I become efficient—exchange an email or two, talk on the phone once, then meet. It takes about six months from the start of my Internet dating career to realize that I know nothing about a guy until I am in his presence and can look him in the eye.

Shawn sends me a picture. He looks like a pale Paul McCartney. He has kind eyes. For weeks we email, and he resists my hints about actually meeting, until I come right out and say, "It's time to meet."

He writes, "Yes. But first I have to tell you something. I have a stutter."

I get this email and look up at the ceiling. *Well, that doesn't matter,* I think. There was a guy I worked with once who had a stutter. The hardest thing about it was not jumping in and finishing his sentences—something I have a problem with anyway. If he's a nice guy, who cares?

I write back, "I don't care."

Part of me is relieved, because I can also add this to the email: "And by the way, if you're into skinny chicks, I'm not for you. I'm a big girl."

He writes back, "I don't care about that."

We arrange to go out to dinner.

Shawn and I have a lot in common. We love a lot of the same movies. He's my age and ready for kids. He writes about his niece and nephew a lot, how he longs for kids of his own. *Great,* I think. *Great.*

He picks me up in his very clean, very cream Toyota Camry. He is dressed in an off-white button-down top and khaki pants, and I almost can't distinguish him from the cream interior of the car—there's just a vague outline where he ends and the car begins. His skin is pale, his hair graying. He holds in one hand a cream-colored handkerchief, which he uses to wipe his eyes. They tend to water, I notice.

He has a severe stutter, probably compounded by the stress of this date. But I'm not going to judge. I'm stressed too, and our conversation in the car is strained. He opens the car door for me when we get to the steak-and-po-tatoes restaurant he has chosen. He helps me take off my coat, and he pulls out my chair at the table. He asks me questions as we wait for the waiter. He listens as I talk, nodding and waiting to wipe his eyes until I look away. I don't really know how I feel about him, because I'm so intent on not being judgmental about the stutter. I don't want to ask him too many questions, either, and put him on the spot.

I order steak, which turns out to be a bad idea. I realize halfway through the meal that I left my Advil and my tampons on the kitchen table. I can see them there in my mind's eye, waiting to go into my purse. Throughout dinner I feel the previous Advil I've taken wear off, and the heavy steak presses down on my burning menstrual cramps, making me nauseated. I get distracted and excuse myself to the bathroom to be sure I'm not bleeding all over my clothes, and to set up reinforcements with toilet paper.

Neither the waiter nor the hostess have ibuprofen. None of the staff, it appears, have ibuprofen.

I tell Shawn I'm not feeling well and that I have to go home. I'm pale now too; I can feel it and I have to focus on my breathing to not throw up. About halfway back to my place, he says quietly and clearly, "I make you sick, don't I?"

"No!" I say. "No. Really, no." I breathe and say, "It's just that . . . I have my period. I forgot my drugs, and my cramps are really bad."

I can see that he doesn't believe me. Even to myself I sound overly com-pensatory, trying way too hard. His face is clear to me now against the black night behind him in the window. In the dark his body is more substantial too, illuminated by the dashboard light.

"This happens to me," I say. "I get really sick with my period."

He nods and wipes his eyes.

He doesn't look at me as I get out, doesn't acknowledge me when I thank him for dinner. He just waits, staring ahead, for me to close the door. When I do, he peels away from the curb and down my street.

Added to my nausea now is something else, something deeper and more painful. I make my way to my apartment slightly bent over; I take four Advil and a large shot of scotch and go to bed. I struggle to fall asleep, troubled by the evening, by myself, by the idea that I operate sometimes on the surface without looking deeper inside. *(Did he make me sick? Am I that person?)* I am troubled by the feeling that I am not nearly as nice a person as I think I am.

I can now see certain tendencies of mine, certain ways of being, that I was blind to then.

In my head I had no doubt that I wanted to be in a relationship, that I wanted my own family. The whole picture—husband, children, a house. A newer version of what Margaret had. And in the months that followed, I went on date after date, looking for He Who Would Bring Me All.

And a pattern emerged. A discounting.

There were many first dates, no second dates. There was always a flaw, something wrong. I can see now that for me then, nothing short of a Harlequin Romance hero would do. A man who stuttered would not do. An ordinary, kind man was not enough. He had to be something special and spectacular.

Then I meet someone who I think might actually be that spectacular man. I've shed over eighty pounds by now and feel beautiful. I am fit and strong. I do two hundred situps and fifty pushups at the gym in the morning. I do

20-20-20 with my running partners: twenty minutes on the strider, twenty minutes on the rowing machine, twenty minutes running.

He is French. His name is Claude. He owns his own restaurant. He appears to be rather rich as well. And he is seriously handsome. We email a fair amount, more than I usually do, mostly because it takes some time to actually meet, because he has been traveling in France for a few weeks.

When I meet him at his restaurant in Greenwich, Connecticut, I am a little frightened and intimidated. For the first time since I started this husband search, the guy I'm meeting is actually more handsome than his photo. This is to be just drinks, but after two hours of laughing and my getting quite drunk, we move into the dining room, and he orders dinner for us both, and more wine.

Oh my god, he really is something. Lovely square jaw. Black hair with graying temples and an expansive sense of humor—very broad humor, involving many arm gestures and hand motions. Under the influence of feeling pretty, and several glasses of wine, I am myself quite witty, and I *love* it when he throws his head back to laugh at something I say. I watch his Adam's apple quiver. I want to touch him.

Hours later, I have sobered up and calmed down, but when we kiss and kiss and kiss at my car, I feel drunk again. "I'll call you," he says, pulling away slowly, catching his breath.

"Please. Do," I say.

I drive away feeling witty and pretty and bright. Over the next few days, I relive that date and feel flushed and happy, terribly hopeful.

At last, the dream.

But then, well, he does not call. He emails me.

He emails me a week later to tell me that he and his ex-girlfriend have decided to try to work things out. He enjoyed meeting me tremendously, he says. *C'est la guerre,* I think.

I take one last look at his picture and think, *He could have been the one to fall in love with. He could have been the one.*

In the months after Claude, I enter a new dating phase. I was so close, I feel. There is a new urgency. I am normal (perhaps even better than normal). I say this to myself in the morning as I dress in clothes that are ten sizes smaller than they were at the lodge. I am so close to being all that I have ever wanted to be. I can find a husband and a father for my children. I can have what I've always wanted, because I have worked very hard.

In the post-Claude months, I meet:

1) Sex-Talk Guy—we meet at Starbucks and happen to sit next to a student who is enrolled in the writing program I help run. Right off the bat my date says, "A nympho and a lesbo enter a bar . . . " I close my eyes and pray that the Sarah Lawrence student is too distracted to hear what he is saying. I burn the roof of my mouth finishing the cappuccino he has bought me, and I skedaddle outta there.

2) A week later, I have a date with I Teased Him about Being Gay and Consequently Never Heard from Him Again Guy. He is also Worried about Women Stealing His Money Guy.

3) Then there is Preppy, Just out of Undergrad Guy who lives in Brooklyn— we meet at a café he chooses. He is cute in a boyish, I'm-just-out-of-undergrad kind of way. I want to jump his bones. I flirt madly, but at the end of the evening, outside the café, he just shakes my hand.

But then there is also:

1) Went for a Hike Together and He Was Really Nice and I Was Going to See Him Again Guy, but then in the meantime I focus on his unspectacular job and rebuilt fifteen-year-old truck. I don't pick up the phone when he calls to arrange our second date. I don't call him back, either.
2) College Professor with Bad Hair Guy, who seems smart and kind. But I can't get past the Prince Charles side part and checked shirt.
3) Visual Artist in Brooklyn Guy, successful too, but he's fifty years old and has never been married. What does that say about him?

So, not a Harlequin hero among them. No captain of industry. No prince. No yacht owners or country club members.

But now, looking down the long telescope of time, I can see what the hero search was all about: Despite what I thought, I didn't really want a man, which is to say, I didn't really want to get married. Didn't want to be a partner to someone, didn't want to compromise, to give in.

Didn't want to fall in love.

I mean, even that phrase, "*fall* in love." Who wants to fall, get hurt, be left crying alone? I had never fallen in love in my life, and I can see now that I wasn't ready to fall in love then, either. So I used the idea of a prince and perfection to be sure I didn't actually find anyone.

Even at the time, I wasn't totally clueless about all this. What I was focused on, though, was my weight. I couldn't get over the fact that at last I was thin (well, thin*ner*). At last. And I *still* couldn't find a partner, no matter how hard I tried. I had assumed for many years that my fat kept me alone, but I began to wonder if my persistent singleness could just be a function of being too picky and judgmental. I thought about my previous months of dating and realized that I had certainly discounted a lot of men.

So I give up for a while. I focus instead on working out, doing my job, and hashing though my issues in therapy. I tell my therapist I think I have intimacy issues and he says, "Duh!" We start to meet twice a week.

Then a guy named Juan emails me to say that he likes my picture and my profile. In his picture he is at Yankee Stadium, looking happy in a red T-shirt that I will come to know quite well. His profile says he wants kids. He lives in and loves New York City.

We meet, and he tells me, as we sip cappuccinos, that he doesn't have a job. And since I am a newly self-aware dater, conscious that I am too picky and dismissive, I let it slide. For the old me, no job meant no second date. Period.

We have a second date, then a third. Then we get together a couple of times a week. I grow fonder of him. There is something compelling about his matter-of-factness about our relationship. There are no games, no hide-and-seek. He calls me the next day, always.

I also like that ours is a New York relationship. I always go down to his apartment near Times Square because he doesn't see the point of Westchester. We talk about writing a lot, since he's a screenwriter. Someday, he tells me, he will have a screenplay or two produced, and then he'll have money to do what he wants: direct. "This is the most important thing in my life," he tells me on one of our first dates. "Until I get a screenplay produced, I can't do anything else with my life."

Weeks slide by.

That July, as usual, New York is hit by a heat wave. Day after day of ninety-degree temperatures and unbelievably high humidity.

Sleeping at Juan's is a trial. Most of the windows in his apartment are poorly placed or painted shut, so there's not much ventilation. At night, as I try to sleep edged away from him below the sealed window in his bedroom, I pant like a cocker spaniel and dream about cross-breezes. I won't let even the sheet touch me. I sweat through the night, despite the relentless fan, and I wake up with a sharp, itchy thirst that only seltzer can scratch.

On Saturday morning, Juan runs out for breakfast and seltzer and coffee, which, happily, I'm drinking again. Since I've lost weight, the stomach issues that made me quit seem to have passed.

I crawl over the bed to the window. His bedroom is so small that there is only room in it for the queen bed and a chest of drawers facing the bed. It sits so close, you can't actually open the drawers all the way. There's no room for a nightstand, so his alarm clock sits on the floor.

The window is indeed painted shut. I go to the kitchen and grab a steak knife with a strong wooden handle. I stab and saw at the paint between the frame of the window and the frame for the glass. All the way around, I ease the edges away from each other, then strain to lift the window. I am, of course, saturated with sweat by now, smearing years of black city dust from the window all over my clothes and the sheets.

By the time Juan gets back, I have given up and am lying on his bed, arms stretched out like Jesus, staring at his ceiling. There are stars up there, the kind that glow fluorescent green after you turn off the lights. I wonder, not for the first time, if he or the last tenant put them there.

"What are you doing?"

"I'm getting some air in here."

"Air? You look like you're waiting to be taken back to the mother ship."

I smile up at him. He's upside down because of the way I'm lying on the bed, and looking up at him, I see how perfectly round his face is. Really great. I reach up and touch his cheek with my dirty fingers.

"I mean the window," I say.

He looks over and sees the steak knife, bent at the tip now, on the windowsill. "I told you. It's painted shut."

"Well, not anymore. But it still won't open. It must be painted shut on the outside, too."

I sit up and let the head rush pass, then say, "Let's go see."

I take his hand in my dirty hand and pull him out his door and down the hall to the front door.

I see, once we are outside, that his bedroom window is unfortunately just over the corral of garbage cans for the building. The sharp, organic smell of rot rises in the summer heat. I shove my way through the cans to look at the window and see, sure enough, that paint has sealed the window tightly.

"Well, that's why I couldn't open it."

"Hang on," he says. "I'll get something."

I expect him to get a sophisticated tool from some red toolbox he has hidden in his tiny apartment, but he comes out with the same steak knife I used.

I step aside and let him wiggle his way through the cans to the window, because my arms are tired now and I really don't need to sweat anymore. The breeze is wonderful. I wish now that I had paid more attention to the coffee Juan brought back from Starbucks. Maybe I could go inside and bring it out. I turn to ask for the keys, but he is so into the scraping that I leave it alone for a moment and go sit on the other side of the garbage corral, on the stone steps of the apartment building.

Did he put the coffees in the kitchen? Did he leave them on the chest of drawers in his room? As I watch Juan work away at the window, I try to envision his bedroom.

That reminds me—"You know," I say to him. "We need to do something about your bedroom."

"Hmm?" He leans into the window, pushing up now, grunting with the effort. I see the window move a little and stand up.

"Hey!" It moves a little more, then gives suddenly, with the sound of wood scraping against wood. "Wow!" I say, jumping up and down. I watch as he moves the window up and down a couple more times.

He turns to me and grins, and we laugh, and now he is covered with black city dust too. I come around as he emerges from the corral, and I give him a big sweaty hug.

We run back into his apartment, and I throw myself down on his bed and laugh as a wind tunnel–like breeze blows in through the window above me. I pull Juan down beside me and kiss him and laugh at the same time. We roll around on his brown and cream–colored sheets and kiss and wrestle a little. "This is *great!*" I say, throwing myself onto my back, and we lie quietly beside each other in the breeze.

"I was worried we'd get the smell of garbage, but it's okay, right? I don't smell it."

"No, it's good." He rolls on his side, resting his head on his arm. "Thanks," he says.

I smile and say, "You know, I'm not quite done yet."

He raises his eyebrows.

"I think we need to change this room around. I think we need to flip the bed around, put the head of the bed on the other side. Then there will be room to move the dresser over by the door, and you can open the drawers all the way and use it like a night table, so you don't have to have your alarm clock on the floor."

He looks around the room. I jump up and demonstrate with my arms where I imagine the dresser going.

"Just a sec," he says, running into the living room and coming back with a small red toolbox. He pulls out a measuring tape. I lie back and watch him measure his way to some kind of reassurance.

"You might even have room to bring your bookcase in here from the living room," I say, thinking how it sits awkwardly in the corner, jutting out beside the sofa. "You could put it over there, where the dresser was."

"Yeah," he says. "Yeah."

I grab my cappuccino from the dresser (it *was* on the dresser) and lean against the headboard while he measures away. *This is really nice,* I think. I'm happy with him, sweaty and dirty and not self-conscious. So he's no captain of industry. But I can be dirty and messy with him, and that's okay. I can still have thirty pounds to lose and that's okay too. I couldn't imagine being this way with Claude, my French restaurateur. Besides, having kids is a messy thing, so perhaps Juan could handle the chaos.

I stand up and go to him. I put my hand at the base of his neck and kiss him seriously. I wrap my arms around him for a moment, my cappuccino warm against his back. "This is great," I say.

He laughs and squeezes me tight. "Yes, this is great."

"What did you do today?" I ask Juan on a Friday night, flopping onto his couch after driving down straight from work. It is August, and we have been together for almost three months now. There is a languid feel to our relationship, an understanding that we are together without really defining how.

"Nothing much," he says, turning off the TV. "You?"

I sigh. "Well, school starts up again at the end of the month, so there's lots of stuff to do."

He nods a little distractedly.

"Are you okay? You seem a little down."

"The production company in L.A. that asked for the baseball screenplay emailed today to say they're going to pass."

"Oh, Juan, I'm so sorry."

He nods. "That screenplay is only out at one other place now. And that's a long shot anyway. I thought we had our best chance with these guys. They seemed so enthusiastic."

I put my arm around him and give him a hug. "Really, I know how hard this stuff is."

"I thought it was good!"

"But you know how it is. That doesn't matter sometimes. Sometimes it's just not what they're looking for."

He nods, but I can tell it doesn't help to know that.

"Would you do me a favor?" he asks. "Would you mind taking a look at it for me? Tell me what you think."

"Sure," I say, though I realize I am scared. I have deliberately stayed away from reading his work and haven't given him any of mine. A lot rides on these screenplays in terms of his life, but a lot rides on them for me. I don't think I could attach my life to another writer's if I didn't respect his writing.

The next day, we go to Central Park, and I watch him play softball. I bring his screenplay with me but only glance at the first pages. I roll down the straps of my sundress and catch some rays.

I spend the day trying to cheer Juan up. I treat him to a movie, and we hold hands walking back through crowded streets, something expectant between us, all repressed desire and suggestion. We fall into his apartment and kiss with a wild urgency as the door closes behind us. We move only a few steps to the hall, and he pushes me against the wall. This time it is like a movie kiss, and we rip at each other's clothes. We do not actually make it down the hall to the bedroom.

One Saturday later in August, we are, for a change, up at my apartment. I cook us dinner, and we sit and play cards, and he drinks beer—a fair amount of it, I notice—while I have my usual single beer, then switch to seltzer. "Kiss me," I say as I pull him up the stairs. He kisses my neck. In my hot, dry attic bedroom, I turn on the air conditioner, but it is a while before the room cools off. We slip over and under each other like wet eels, and I am amazed, as always, by how good our sex is. But then Juan loses focus, and things get tense. When he falls asleep, I lie angrily beside him and have to pull my vibrator out of the drawer in my night table. The little sound it makes is masked by the air conditioner's loud rattling.

I wake up in the middle of the night naked and chilled, and I pull the feather duvet over both of us. It enters my mind, as I try to fall asleep again, that Juan likes to drink. I think back on our time together and realize that there is always beer around. He isn't always drunk like tonight, but he is often tipsy, his edges softened even more than they are normally, his smile milder than usual. I am thinking about this as I fall asleep, and I have unsettled dreams for the rest of the night.

In the morning I drive us back to the city for a Sunday softball game. While he plays, I plan to read the *Times,* but instead sit and wonder how I feel about him. I watch him play ball in the red T-shirt he wore in the Match.com photograph, the T-shirt he wears every time he plays, and I wonder: *What do I think about him, about us?* I like that he likes my body, which is, let's face it, still almost 190 pounds. I like our sex (well, except when stuff like last night happens). I like how we hang out in Central Park like I'm in a movie.

But even after all these months, I know I'm not in love with him—at least I'm assuming I'm not, because I don't have all those "in-love symptoms" I've read about or seen in friends falling in love, and that's all I've got to go on. I take a moment to scan my insides.

Nope. Not in love.

He waves to me from the outfield, feeling my eyes on him, perhaps.

Does he love me?

He bends his knees and rests his hands on his thighs, waiting for the batter, and I think, *No, he's not in love with me. Not yet.*

Maybe that doesn't matter. I like a lot of things about him, not the least of which is how kind he is. He likes me too. And he would be a great, loving father, I'm sure, like my own dad. Not a brutal, yelling father, which is a terrible fear of mine.

"So why do you have two guitars?" I ask him a week or so later. I've wondered about this for a while but have never gotten around to asking him.

"Well, one's acoustic and one's electric."

They are quite pretty. I've seen him take them off their stands to dust them, but I've never heard him play.

"There's the amp," he says, pointing to a black box covered in papers.

"You used to play?" I ask.

"I'm learning now."

"Oh. How?"

"I have a program, a tape, and . . ."—he goes into his room to the bookcase and brings back a black binder—"this."

"I see," I say, opening the binder to notes and lyrics and instructions on hand positions.

"Here, let me play you something."

With care and love, he pulls the acoustic guitar over to the couch and runs his fingers over the strings, which squeak slightly. He opens the binder to a Sheryl Crow song and starts singing.

"This house is full of lies . . ."

He moves his fingers smoothly along the frets, and I know the song, but when Juan starts to sing, it is so off key that I almost don't recognize it. I should have told him not to sing to me. I can't stand having someone sing to me. I look down at my feet as he sings and feel myself shut down. I crawl inside myself. Spots show up behind my eyes, and there's a rushing sound in my ears. A long, long time ago a guy sang to me, and it was bad. I didn't want to be there with him, but I was too young to know how to free myself.

"Can I try?" I ask, cutting him off by putting my hand on his.

He's a little surprised, but he gives me the guitar and leans over to show me how to make a C chord. It is rather awkward, and the strings bite into the pads of my fingers.

"Ow. Wow, this is hard."

He laughs. "I know, but after you do it for a while, you get calluses on your fingers and it doesn't hurt as much." He shows me the tips of his fingers, and I notice little wartlike pads. "I haven't played much lately." He smiles at me. "They're getting all soft again."

I wonder if he knows how tone-deaf he is. Maybe he doesn't know, or maybe he does and loves to play so much that he doesn't care. Well, it's a good thing he doesn't want to be a rock star.

"So, what do you want to do tonight?" he asks. "You want to go out, grab a couple of drinks?"

"Nah . . . let's stay in."

"Okay." He pulls my foot onto his lap and starts to massage my aching arch. "You okay?"

"Tired."

"Hard week?" He continues to rub my feet.

"No, it was okay." I feel strange tonight, and that singing didn't help. I feel all poised, like I'm ready to leap somewhere.

I've been thinking lately that I have been fine this summer with not knowing where we're going. I am comfortable with Juan, and many things are good about how we are together. But with summer winding down, I have started to feel my age. I've become aware that another year has passed and I'm soon going to start another school year. I don't feel like I can drift anymore. I'm thirty-eight, for God's sake.

"Juan," I say, and he stops the massage and raises his eyebrows.

"Yes?"

"Do you remember when we first started dating, we talked for, like, five seconds about kids and stuff?"

"Yes."

"You want kids, right?"

"Sure. I love them."

"Hmm." I wiggle my toes so he'll remember to start massaging again. But he gives my foot a pat and says, "Do you want a beer?"

He gets up and I say, "A seltzer, please."

"Sure."

I scroll through the channels with the sound off while he is in the kitchen. "I rented a movie," he says, padding down the hall toward me in his bare feet.

"Do you think it's weird that I'm asking about kids?" I ask, taking the seltzer from his hand. It doesn't seem too early to me, actually. In fact, I'm amazed it has taken this long. But part of me hasn't wanted to know.

"Um, I guess not."

There's a Pond's cold cream commercial on the silent TV, of a woman splashing her face with water and smiling at the same time. Her smooth, lineless face glistens.

I look at him watching the TV, and I think about his determination to be a director, about the times he's said it was the most important thing in his life. "You're nowhere near ready to have kids, are you?"

He takes a moment, then says, "Well, I don't want to be distracted."

"Right." I think about all the things he's not saying, all that I understand him to mean by "distracted": obligations, money worries, someone else to consider before quitting a job you hate, making money to take care of a kid. "But, you see, I am. Ready, I mean."

He takes a long drink from his Bud. I bring my seltzer up for a sip, too, but I bang the glass against my front teeth. The blue light from the TV flickers over us. The water in my glass looks blue, then clear, then orange.

"I know. You've said that. It's just," he pauses, "I think I've been honest with you."

"Yes, you have."

He's finished his beer and puts it on the floor underneath the lip of the futon.

"So, really. What *do* you want to do tonight?"

I feel deflated and lean my head against the back of the futon. I look up at the ceiling and strain my eyes as wide as I can to dry the tears I feel building. My limbs are heavy, and my fingers feel like they can't even hold my glass of seltzer anymore. "I don't think I'm up to much. Why don't we just watch the movie you rented?"

He nods, gets up, puts it in the DVD player, and goes to the kitchen for another beer.

That night in his bed, I can't sleep. He runs his hand over my belly when we first lie down, but I discourage him, because he's had quite a lot to drink tonight.

This alcohol thing—I wonder if it's a real problem, or if I'm making it a bigger deal than it is. Am I following my usual MO and looking for a wedge to drive between us?

I don't want to admit that my doubts about him are related to the fact that I looked over his screenplay this week. It has been almost a month since he gave it to me, and, although he has not asked about it, I finally sat at my dining room table and began.

I couldn't finish it.

It wasn't that the screenplay was terrible. It was just flat, and not only because I'm not interested in baseball. It didn't seem impossible that it might get produced. Nevertheless, I found myself being hard on the screenplay as I read it. I yelled inside my head: *Why can't you be brilliant?*

I fall asleep looking at the faded fluorescent stars on his ceiling. I remember the day we unstuck the window, and I feel sad.

The next day, I flip through a magazine while Juan showers. I notice a full-page Baby Gap ad with a blue-eyed, crazy-cute kid in a bunny suit, white hair curling up and around the bunny hood. I rip out the picture. It feels significant, somehow, that the picture has popped out at me today.

After his shower, we sit on the couch to talk about the day, and I find myself saying, "Juan?"

He looks at me like he knows something bad is headed his way.

"Juan, I'm thirty-eight."

"I know." He frowns at me.

"All that's left now is thirty-nine and then forty."

"So?" he says. "I'm forty-two. It's not so bad."

I smile and even laugh a little. "You're a guy, Juan." I pause, then say, "I think I need to break up with you."

"What?" Juan leans away from me, and I think about the drinking, about his soft smile, about his not wanting kids for a long time yet.

"This is a little . . . out of the blue." There is something odd about his face, a stiffness to his half smile. He looks hurt and surprised.

I blush and look down at my bare toes. I can't take back the words now, or the feeling of certainty that bubbled up behind them.

"I'm sorry. I feel a lot of pressure about the kid thing," I say.

"You've never said anything like that." He waves his hand like he's gesturing toward something behind us. "Sure, I've known you want kids. You've said so right from the beginning. But do you need to have them right now?"

"No, not right now, but soon. And I feel like soon is too soon for you."

He sits in silence, looking across the room at the space where the bookcase used to be. "I don't know when I'll be ready, Alex. I just know that I'm not now."

Juan puts his hand on my arm and tries to get me to look at him. His hair still wet, he smells fresh and clean, like Herbal Essences. I can't look at him because the heat is in my eyes, and I can't see. I feel like I'm going to cry.

"Come on, we don't have to decide this stuff now. Let's just wait a little bit. Take a moment." But I'm shaking my head as he talks. I am done. I know I've made up my mind. To stay would just prolong things.

THREE

Now What?

I miss Juan and often wonder if I've made a mistake. But when he emails me around Thanksgiving to say how thankful he is for the time we spent together, I think how grateful I am that he said he wasn't ready for kids. Because if he had said, "Let's go," I might have overlooked the drinking and gently nudged him into a job, pushed him to move in together, get married, have children.

In the months after Juan, I rest. I do more therapy and lose more weight. I change from Weight Watchers to a low-carbohydrate, high-protein diet. No sugar, no flour, and plenty of meat. Altogether, since my time at the lodge, I've lost 109 pounds. I run four times a week with my good friend Pat, including a long run on the weekend, ten miles or so, as she and I train for a half marathon—totally inspired by Margaret and Jim's recent half marathon.

In early May, Margaret's sister Susan calls me to say that her oncologist has suggested that she and Jeff push their wedding forward. They have an August renaissance wedding planned, but the doctor thinks they might not want to wait that long. They might even want to think about getting married this month.

Susan has cancer in her lungs. It started in the muscle of her leg ten years ago, when she was twenty. She has been in a pitched battle with it ever since. Now, it would appear, she is losing. But we have thought that before, and she has always bounced back. I have tremendous faith in Susan's will to live.

When I drive to Ottawa two weeks later for the family-only "shotgun wedding," as Susan calls it, I arrive late Friday night to see her in the center of her six siblings, her right leg stretched out straight and far thinner than her left because of the aggressive surgery nine and a half years ago that was meant to seize all the cancer cells before they spread.

"Mrs.!" Margaret calls out, getting up off the floor beside Susan, where she has been weaving small white flowers together to make a crown.

"Mrs.!" everyone calls out to me. It looks like everyone has arrived; the house feels bursting with people. I hug Margaret, then walk to Susan and kiss her on the cheek.

"Congratulations! This is so exciting," I say.

"We got our renaissance dresses!" she says, pointing to the dresses hanging from the doorframe by the kitchen. They are beautiful, in gold brocade material with bronze corded trim. They lace up tightly in the back. "We'll wear them again in August," she says.

I smile at her but wonder if she will live that long. I see a real change since I saw her at Christmas, which she and Jeff hosted at his country cottage south of Montreal. It was a tremendous three days, with sleigh rides, ringette on the lake, and mulled cider each night. At the center of it all was Susan, directing everyone about where to go and when, her usual social self. But now she is breathless and pale and, if at all possible, thinner. But she looks happy—among family again, making wreaths to wear in her hair, with daffodils and tulips everywhere, ready for the reception tomorrow.

The irony of that wedding, when I think about it now, is how I spent each moment telling myself, *Don't forget this. Don't forget a single thing, because this could be the last time everyone is together like this.* Yet I don't remember very much at all. I have a quick impression of the very grand church, of taking pictures in the park covered end to end with daffodils and tulips. But Susan's May wedding is totally overshadowed in my memory by the full-on renaissance wedding that she did live to have in August, when she was actually still quite well and indeed got to wear her renaissance dress again.

Of course, the only other thing that sticks out in my mind has to do with me. Me, me, me, me, me. I remember noticing that I wasn't asked to be in as many pictures as everyone else, like that was a measuring stick of belonging (this was not the first time I've noticed myself keeping score like that). *Do they really love me? Am I really like a member of the family?*

Now it is July, and I'm heading up to the lodge for a week of rest in the sun, the first week of my three-week vacation. On the way there, I decide to drop by Jenn and Dave's place in Massachusetts. I get there just in time for dinner, and Dave cooks a steak dish he's been wanting to try. (He knows about my no-sugar, no-flour routine, so he is catering a little to my carnivorous ways.) We sit out on their screened-in porch to eat. He and I were roommates during grad school in the big, happy Sarah Lawrence house. His girlfriend, now wife, was there most of the time too. Sophie, their daughter, joins us for about ten minutes, but she's two, so she's more interested in her toys than in food. Jenn is just starting to show—she's five months pregnant with their second.

I can't take my eyes off Jenn's belly, or off Sophie when she joins us. I love the house they live in and the mountains that surround them in this old mill town. We were all together only three years before, but their lives have changed so much, and mine so little. I think about watching Christian and Chloe at the lodge, and yes, I'm a much healthier person, much thinner than I was, but I'm no closer to having the real and deep things I want.

As Jenn passes me the steak for a second helping, I say, "I'm going to have a baby." I take a piece of steak and look up at them. "On my own."

"What!" Jenn jumps out of her chair and claps her hands. "Really?" She leans in to give me a hug. Jenn is like that: enthusiastic, loving.

"That's great," Dave says, in his more laconic way.

I smile at them both and think, *I'm almost as surprised as they are.*

"But how did this come about?" Jenn asks.

"Well, I've been thinking lately—I'm thirty-nine." I ponder that for a moment, then say, "That's it, really—I'm thirty-nine."

"This is great. Have you told your parents yet?" Dave asks. He's Canadian too, and I think he feels connected to my parents because they live not too far from his.

"You're actually the first people I've told."

"Who's going to be the father?" Dave asks.

"Well, I've asked Ken, Margaret's brother."

"And he said yes?"

"I asked him years ago, and he said yes. We're all going to be together for Susan's real wedding in August, so I think I'll ask him then."

Of course that's what I'll do. That's the plan I set in motion years ago, for just this moment.

"No way!" Margaret screams when I say to her, "I'm going to do it. I'm ready to have a baby." She looks at me through the falling evening light. We are running up the driveway of the lodge to go for a three-mile run, now that the heat of the day is over. As we pass the Ski-Doo path across the road from the lodge, I can't help but think about how endlessly uphill that walk felt three years ago, how hard it was to climb the stairs afterward, my breathlessness. I look at Margaret and feel suddenly like I can do anything. If I can become who I am after who I was, I can do anything.

"I'm going to ask Ken at the wedding."

"Well, he's single right now, so that's one problem dealt with."

We run a little more.

"You know," she says, "the more I think about this, the more I think it's a great idea."

"Really? Why?"

"Well, it seems risky to me to wait for the right guy to come along. There's no guarantee you'll find him, especially before you run out of baby-making time. This way, you've got the kid taken care of, and you can be more relaxed about finding a guy. Right? No desperate searches."

Good point, I think. "And like you said, I'm never going to marry a guy who doesn't want kids anyway—this way I'll already have one."

Later that night, as I laugh and dance crazily around the room with Chloe and Christian, I think for one intense moment how wonderful it would be to have a child like them—a child who is beautiful and funny and smart like they are. *Asking Ken is a stroke of genius,* I think. *A way to be connected to this wonderful family by blood. Then there will be no doubt about my being part of the family. There will be a true blood tie.*

My sister Linda and I are close now. But when we were kids, I remember beating on her like I meant it. When Mom left the second time for Denmark, when I was sixteen, she took Linda with her. Linda was fourteen then, and we didn't live with each other again until my third year of university, when she came to Saskatoon too. We moved into a basement apartment together and got to know each other all over again (this was the same apartment where, two years later, the sunlight on the brown rug would make me move to Toronto).

We are very different, Linda and I. When we were little, she was the pretty one, and I was the one with a lovely personality. Now that we are older, although it is hard to shake these myths, it is clear that Linda is both pretty and has a nice personality. She has three kids and a husband named Glenn, which creates confusion sometimes, since our brother is also named Glenn. To distinguish our brother from Husband Glenn, I've taken to calling him Brother Glenn, which has led some of my friends to ask if he is in the priesthood. Brother Glenn lives in Edmonton with his wife, Eva.

My parents now live in North Battleford, a medium-size city an hour and a half north of Saskatoon. They have been back together since Mom came home for my high school graduation. Now that I'm in my thirties and have left some baggage behind, I visit every summer—the loveliest time of year to be there. I say "baggage" because during my twenties, I did some fairly passive–aggressive things—the abrupt move to Toronto, for example, then not going home again for years. Never phoning home, sending cards or presents during the holidays, or acknowledging birthdays.

This summer I will fly to Saskatchewan from Toronto but will spend a little time with my sister first. She lives in a suburb just outside the city. I am bursting to tell her my plans, but I wait until we have a moment alone. Given her kids and husband, that finally happens the second day, when we go out for a run.

"I'm going to have a kid on my own," I say after we've been running for a good while and are well into our stride.

"Really?" She has always counseled me to think long and hard about this when I've brought it up before.

"Yes." As we talk, I realize that part of my talking about this with Jen and Dave and Margaret and Linda is testing out the idea of having a baby on my own, pulling it into the open to see what it looks like and how people react.

"I sometimes think you don't realize how hard that would be." She says this kindly and, I know, from experience. But I can't help feeling bristly. I want everyone to be ecstatic about this idea, to say, "What a brilliant idea!" I want all the positive energy to push me into action and make me brave.

"I know."

"I have Glenn, and it's still really hard."

"Okay, what's so hard?" I hear how this sounds and add, "I mean that, really. I'm not being sarcastic. I really want to know."

Linda takes a deep breath and doesn't say anything for a little while.

We are running through the winding streets of her suburb, and I am totally lost. If she left me now, it would take weeks for me to find my way back to her house.

"Well, what is hard changes all the time. At first it's never sleeping. Then it's all about time and money; there's never enough. And then there's the kid, wanting, wanting, wanting. It never lets up. And if you're alone, all the wanting would focus on just you. It's intense."

"Wanting toys and stuff?"

"Sure, toys, but sometimes it's just to make you mad, to push you until you explode. It's 'Mommy, Mommy, Mommy, Mommy.' Endless."

I think about her three kids and what it's like when I visit her, or visit Margaret, especially when Chloe and Christian were little, and I see what she is saying. It's hard to do any real talking until they are in bed, and even then, we're all so tired, we rarely do. *Then again, I'm only talking about one kid here,* I think. *It won't be that bad.*

"And the worrying, and then they're sick, and to go through all that alone seems impossible."

We say nothing for several blocks, and I stew quietly. I feel a need to convince her. Much later, when things are hard, I will remember this moment—how irritated I was by her lack of enthusiasm, how I didn't want to hear what she said. But of course she was right: Parenting alone is terribly difficult. And sometimes only your biological family is brave enough to speak the truth to you.

She leads us around another loop of houses and says, "The dating's not going so well?"

"It's going, well, you know. It's just late. What if I have trouble getting pregnant? I'll have no wiggle room." We run out onto a main road, and suddenly I know where we are. It's not far now back to her house. "It feels like the kid thing has taken over the husband thing. It feels way more urgent."

"I see."

We cut across the road and some grass, and we are in the loop where her house is. We walk the last block to catch our breath.

"Why do you want a baby so badly?"

"You know I've always wanted kids."

"I know, but the rush, suddenly. Now."

"I don't want it to be too late."

"Yes, but is it a baby you want? Or is it just that you don't want to be alone?"

My sister is not very psychological. She has not been in therapy for a million years like I have, but she does have a knack for getting down to the heart of things. I feel like saying to her: *I'm not alone! I have millions of friends! I have a rewarding job! I'm happy!* But judging by how defensive I feel, this merits more thought.

"You know, Alex," she says when it's clear that I'm not going to answer, "I'll support whatever you decide." I look at her, and we smile at each other, and I know this is true. I give her a big hug, and we pat each other on the back and continue toward the house. "Keep me posted on how it goes."

"I will." We get into the house and I say, "I still have to tell Mom and Dad."

She laughs a little and says, "Yes you do."

Back in journalism school, as I was emerging from the coziness of nannying and defining who I was, away from Margaret and my family, I decided I was a writer. And journalism, which I had already been thinking about, was going to be my way of supporting myself in this career. To solidify my new identity, I decided to change my name.

My father named me Donna Marie Soiseth when I was born. I think I came to see that name as linking me too closely to a Donna Reed–type life, to the idea of never leaving the place where I was born, to marrying and having kids. And perhaps it was that kind of conventional life that I resisted in my twenties. I wanted to travel, to live in other places.

At twenty-five, when I changed my name, I was still in the midst of that idea, so I renamed myself the person I wanted to be: Alexandra Abildgaard Soiseth. Alexandra was for me. Abildgaard was for my mom; it was her middle name, which had come to her through many generations of her family. By taking that name, I felt I was connected to those generations too. It also honored my aunt who took good care of me the year I lived in Denmark, and all the love I have for that country. And I kept Soiseth because that's who I was—my father's daughter.

My parents have tried over the years to call me Alexandra, but for the most part, they call me Donna. Linda made the switch no problem, and Brother Glenn does pretty well too.

I see this whole name-change thing now with different eyes. I see how it must have hurt my parents' feelings, especially my dad's. I know I was trying to change my destiny, assert a new self in the world, but there was a lot of anger toward my parents in the change too, and for that I'm sorry now.

I wonder, though, if my life would be any different now if I had kept the name Donna.

When my flight to Saskatoon lands early, I walk out of the gate looking for Dad, because he's the kind of guy who's usually early. Mom, I'm sure, has stayed home. She prefers, above all other things, the comforts of home (followed closely by cigarettes and golfing).

But I don't see Dad. I think that perhaps I just don't recognize him. It usually takes a second or two, because he doesn't look the way he looks in my mind—like he did when I was eighteen and he was fifty, when I lived at home and he worked for SaskPower, doing physical work that gave him bulk. Now he is completely gray, and smaller. Or maybe that's just what happens when you grow up.

I wander over to the luggage carousel and compare this shiny, renovated Saskatoon Airport to the smaller, older one from my childhood. How it looked thirty-five years ago is the real airport to me. In those days, you weren't as close to the planes, though the glass windows still looked out over the runways. I think about Linda and our run together a few days ago, and what she said about being alone. I've thought a lot about it, and, although it's a little hard to admit, I am lonely. With many friends, it's easy to ignore most of the time, but when I think about being old, the idea of being alone terrifies me.

Maybe that's what Mom was afraid of when she came back to Dad, especially the second time. Maybe that's what I'm trying to avoid by having this baby. A baby is less terrifying than an imperfect husband who will leave me. Hmm—somewhere really deep inside, I think I'm afraid of being left.

This airport has been the setting for many departures—a natural thing, of course. Me leaving for Denmark when I was fifteen. Mom and Linda leaving for Denmark when I was sixteen. Dad on various vacations over the years: Mexico, Cuba, Venezuela. And that time way back, when Mom left for Denmark the first time.

Maybe because that was the first serious leaving, I have written about it many times. I watch my mom walk through the gate and away, with my brother in her arms. Winter static makes his blond hair stick out from his head like porcupine quills. I lean against the glass, wanting to suck my thumb. It's late winter, and ice glistens on the plane that holds Mom and my brother. I am seven. My father, sister, and I watch the plane rock a little from side to side as it pulls away from the gate and creeps off to its runway.

When the plane is out of sight, Dad leads us from the airport into a new life. My sister and I go to live with his brother, Uncle Ralph, and his wife, Aunty Alice, on the homestead where Dad was born and raised, a two-hour drive from where our family has been living in Meadow Lake.

There are immediate and obvious changes. I sleep in a bed with my sister now, not on my top bunk; I have one drawer for my clothes, not a dresser; I take the bus to school instead of running the two blocks to Martin Gran public school. I have real chores, like feeding the chickens, doing dishes, cleaning the house, and dusting and vacuuming—not just picking up my clothes and dropping them down the laundry chute. On weekends, my sister and our four cousins and I play for hours. Linda plays mostly with Barb, who is just two weeks older than she is. They are like twins. We all say so. And though I have found Linda to be a pest most of my life, I miss her here on the farm, where so much else has gone missing for me.

"Is Dad coming this weekend?" I ask Aunty Alice one Saturday morning. It is hair-cutting day, and Linda and I are in the kitchen, awaiting our turns. Aunty Alice is talking to my oldest cousin. Uncle Ralph is busy at the sink. Neither of them turn to me, so I've probably said it too quietly.

Dad usually comes on the weekends, though he misses many because of work. When he is here, I am happy. He doesn't even do anything, really. He isn't the kind of father who plays with his kids. He helps Uncle Ralph on the farm. He talks to Aunty Alice in the kitchen. I decide to ask again later, without everyone listening, but Linda pipes up beside me in her clear, high voice. "Um, Aunty Alice?" Aunty Alice looks up. "Is Daddy coming today?"

"This afternoon sometime. I don't know when."

"Yay!" Linda claps her hands and bounces up and down. I wiggle around too. Maybe he'll take us into town for a treat or something. Maybe he has a letter from Mom, although that's too much to hope for. But Dad is coming today! Dad is coming!

Waiting all afternoon, Linda and I bounce around the house in our new light shag haircuts. I'm jealous of my oldest cousin, Carol, who is thirteen and gets to grow her blond hair as long as she wants. All us younger ones, we get our hair chopped.

"Is he coming *now?*" Linda asks every time she passes the kitchen. Aunty Alice shakes her head. Later, as Aunty Alice sits at her sewing machine, Linda follows her, jumping from foot to foot.

"Soon," Aunty Alice says through the pins in her mouth, not looking up.

"Daddy! Daddy! Daddy!" Linda screams when he finally pulls up in the big brown car, ages and ages after lunch. She bounces up and down in the doorway as he stomps the snow off his boots on the rubber mat in the mudroom. I hang back a little. There he is, tall and handsome, with a brush cut, dark sideburns. I can see that he is a little overwhelmed by our excitement. We leap on him as he comes into the house from the mudroom, wearing his socks. His face and hands are still tanned from last summer. He's always brown from working outside.

I realize too that he was still a young man then. He was thirty-nine years old. What were his nights like during the week in that big, empty house? All our rooms dusty. Sorting laundry, stuffing his clothes into the dryer (the same dryer he uses to this day, repaired and repaired over forty years), folding his socks with his big brown hands. Frying potatoes in the square electric frying pan. All alone.

It's crossed my mind since becoming an adult that he might have started to see someone during that time. But somehow I don't think so. He's not a wildly outgoing guy, and that separation was only a year.

When everyone sits to watch the news at night—the kids on the floor because there isn't room on the furniture for everyone—I try to sneak onto his lap, even though I know I'm too old for that. He laughs and fends me off with his hot coffee, pushing it toward me like a shield. But later, during Hockey Night in Canada, when hardly anyone is left and there is room beside him on the couch, I can sit, his arm around me, pulling me close. Sometimes I lie with my head on his lap and his hand on my hair, and I fall asleep to the sounds of hockey.

But then there is the leaving on Sunday. After church, and into Sunday afternoon, the dread begins. I watch Dad. Linda watches Dad. From our separate farm worlds—Linda beside her cousin-twin, I in the shadows of the hall—we watch. We wait for him to put his hands on his knees, push himself up from the vinyl kitchen chair, and say, "Well." And sigh.

I hold Linda's hand. We follow him to the door. Our quivery silence is shaped by the story Aunty Alice told us one day, several months into our stay here: When Carol had her tonsils out, she cried and cried when everyone left her after visiting hours. Aunty Alice told her that if she made such a fuss when everyone left, they just wouldn't visit. Was this what we wanted? For Dad not to visit?

So the early Sundays of wailing and pitching fits and hitting the floor are over. We stand, gulping air, and watch Dad leave, holding hands at the door until his big brown car makes its way down the long driveway, turns left at the road, and heads toward town and on from there to our home in Meadow Lake. The place where all my friends still live, where all my toys still are. Then we turn and slip into the bathroom to sit beside each other on the hard edge of the narrow tub and cry together into towels.

"You're early," Dad says. "Good flight?"

I look up from dropping my bag onto the luggage cart. "You're here. I was starting to worry." We hug. I say, "The flight was fine, but they don't feed you anymore, just, like, pretzels."

He has stepped back to look at me. I look at him. It really is a shock to see how he is no longer the big, strapping father of my memories. I know I don't look like myself either, and I can see he's holding himself back from saying something about my weight loss. He pats me on the back before pushing my cart out the door. "You look good, kid."

Years ago I made it clear that there was to be no talk of my weight, good or bad, up or down. So now we are restrained, which is perhaps a little disappointing, given the accomplishment of losing 109 pounds. But overall I think it's a good thing. Besides, my weight feels like old news. I'm all consumed with this I'm-soon-to-be-forty-so-I'm-thinking-about-having-a-baby thing.

It's an hour-and-a-half drive to North Battleford. We drive for ten minutes or so, until I can't take it anymore and say, "What would you think about me having a baby, on my own?"

"Well, you mentioned something like that to Mommy a while ago," Dad says, keeping his eyes on the road. All our big conversations happen this way, either in the car or walking, both facing forward, turning to each other when we are ready.

"Would you use AI?" he asks after a long silence.

"AI?"

"Artificial insemination."

"Oh." I'm not totally comfortable talking to Dad about this, but I decide to play it cool. "I asked Ken years ago if he would think about being a father for me, if it should come to that."

Another silence.

"Have you made up your mind that's what you're going to do?"

"I did ask him."

I'm aware of CBC radio mumbling between us through our extended silences. It's not loud enough to make out actual words, but unconsciously I strain to understand. AI. I realize that to Dad, this means sperm banks and anonymous donors, and that it reaches back to his farm days. It is the language of impregnating cows.

"Having a child is complicated. Knowing the father, but not being married to him, could be . . . hard."

Well, there's one good thing to be said about what's going on here: He's jumped right ahead, without even blinking, to my having the kid.

"But it would be nice for the baby to know its father." I pull the fabric of my dress out from my body. I suddenly feel monstrously fat.

"But who would he be to the baby? Would he help with money? Does he want to visit, take the kid during the summer?"

The short sleeves of this dress are choking my arms now; I tug at them to cover the hideousness of my loose, quivery upper arms. I pretend to consider what Dad is saying, but I angle the sun visor down to check, in the little mirror, whether they look as revolting as I imagine.

"Well, that's up to him. I'll ask him what he wants."

"Oh, Donna," he says. "This is very complicated. What if he says today that he wants nothing to do with the baby, but then changes his mind? Or the opposite. What if you start fighting over the kid?"

"We won't, Dad." I clasp my hands together in my lap to stop fidgeting. "I just think it would be wonderful if Margaret could be the baby's aunt, and Christian and Chloe could be cousins. That whole Hashimoto family would be the father, really, is what I was thinking."

He sighs. "Listen, it seems to me that when you have a choice. When . . ." He stops and says nothing for a little while.

"It's hard enough in this world . . ." he starts again.

"What are you saying?"

"Ken is Japanese," Dad says finally.

"What?"

"I just think, it's not like you're marrying Ken. You're just having a baby, and a half-Japanese baby is going to find it harder in this world."

"Oh, Dad." What I think but don't say is, *Come on, Dad! This isn't a hundred years ago.* I want to fight with him about this, tell him he is wrong, wrong, wrong.

"This baby is already going to be different. A single mom, no father."

"Hmm," I say, hoping that if I just drift away from this conversation, it will go away.

"You don't know what Ken is going to do with this baby. You won't be married to him. He'll go on with his life. What happens when he gets married and has a family? How is your baby going to feel about that?"

Oh.

"How is your child going to feel at Christmas when his or her father is there with another family altogether? When he's too busy with his other kids to pay attention to yours?"

I don't like these questions. They are messing up the cozy family vision I have been harboring since I asked Ken about this.

"Besides, you'll have a baby that won't look like our family. It won't even look like you."

I glance at Dad, then down at my fingers still pulling at my dress. *That's okay,* I think. *Ken is handsome. And underneath all the weight issues, I've got some pretty stuff going on. Our kid will look great. Besides, the baby may not look like my biological family, but it would look like my Hashimoto family. And that's as real to me as anything.*

"Well," I say, wanting to be done with this conversation, "I haven't even talked to him about it again. It's been years and years. Maybe he's changed his mind."

But the worm is in me now; I feel it wiggling around. I can pretend I'm an adult who's capable of doing whatever I want. If I want Ken to be the father, Ken can be the father. For God's sake, I'm thirty-nine-and-a-half years old. But shit, it still matters to me what Dad thinks.

Mom and I go to the café the next morning in the Territorial Place Mall after shopping at the grocery store. The café opens onto the hall of the mall, so you can see everyone's comings and goings. It's 10:00 AM, prime Coffee Row time, when plump and sensible women sit clustered with their rugged, deeply creased husbands to talk politics and grain prices. Walking by the café, I see an ocean of blue hair and John Deere caps.

Both North Battleford and Saskatoon are officially cities, but Saskatoon revolves around its university and businesses, while North Battleford's heart still belongs to farming. There are more pickup trucks than cars in the parking lot, and around the corner is an enormous farm-equipment dealership and several Seed and Feeds. We go through the cafeteria line to get coffee, and I look away from the lovely crusty bread and almond pastries. I'm still firmly in a no-sugar, no-flour phase, but being home has put a strain on this way of eating. Honestly, it would strain any eating pattern of mine. My parents aren't even saying anything. I just want to eat.

My relationship with my mother is complicated. If the family myth about me is that I have a lovely personality, then implicit in that is my tendency to *not* make waves, to be the family mediator, joker, and overall cheerleader. I've always carried the weight of that role, both emotionally and physically. I rarely say what's really on my mind, especially if it's negative.

"So," I say as we sit down, "did Dad tell you what I'm thinking about?"

Mom smiles at me. "Yes," she says. "I think it's a great idea, dear." If my dad and I have all our important conversations in the car, facing forward, my mom and I have ours like this, drinking coffee across a table from each other. Two years ago, when the whole family was at Linda's house for the birth of her youngest, Mom and I went out for coffee, and for the first time in our lives, we talked about when she left us the first time to go live in Denmark. It felt very present to both of us, I think, because Linda's oldest child was about the age Linda and I were when Mom left—still babies, really, just starting school, still needing our mom so much.

"I can't believe I left you kids that way," Mom said, looking down at her coffee.

I went rigid with not knowing what to say. There had been years of therapy, yelling into pillows, role playing to tell her I hated her, that I would never forgive her, that she had broken my heart. But with the real thing, I was speechless, then sad. Mom looked brokenhearted herself, and I found myself saying, "It's okay, Mom." In a way, I meant it. I didn't want her to be hurting. I didn't forgive her or even understand her, but I didn't want to punish her.

Today, talking with her over a different cup of coffee, I look across the blue-haired ladies to the buffet line and the huge basket of crusty bread, and I want a piece more than ever. It's almost like my old obsessive wanting at the lodge. Like long ago on the farm, when I fell in love with everything that had to do with bread: the smell of it rising and baking, and the warm, white feel of a slice in my hand, cut just out of the oven.

On weekends at the farm, my aunt always made bread. All morning, as we played, I could smell it rising, and I was happy knowing there would be fresh bread for lunch, soft and fluffy and wonderful. It was all I wanted to eat that year. I took a slice as it passed by me at the beginning of the meal, and then I watched through my feathered bangs where the plate went, hoping desperately that someone would put the plate down near me. *Near me, near me!* When it was placed within reach, I relaxed a little. I looked at the plate of bread as I slowly chewed the piece I had; when it was this fresh, I never put butter on it, because that ruined the sweet white taste.

I thought about Mom's bread, about watching her mix dough in her big blue plastic bowl. I could see the hollow of her underarm as she went up onto her tiptoes to get over the dough as she kneaded it. I would stand close enough to smell her and the dough's yeasty warmth. Sweet and sharp together—Chanel No. 5, cigarettes, sweat, and coffee—this was Mom. On the farm, I went back again and again to the memory of standing near her, feeling her move up on her toes, down on her heels, up on her toes, down on her heels, over and over, grunting a little with the effort, scraping the side of the bowl with her floury dough–covered hand.

Today, turning away from the bread basket, vowing, *No sugar, no flour,* I say to her, "I'm glad that you're glad. I think it's right for me."

"I know you've always wanted kids," she says. "Are you worried about getting married someday?"

"You mean if I have Ken's baby?" I sigh, push the undrinkable coffee away, and lean back in my chair. Something unpleasant is happening in my stomach. "I sometimes feel like I'll never get married. I've never even been in love. What does that tell you?"

"Oh, honey," Mom says, reaching out to squeeze my hand.

"Something is broken, I think." Sitting here with my mom in the midst of Coffee Row, I know this to be true, though I'm not sure what to do about it. Years of therapy have brought me to this understanding, and if I'm honest, I know that having a baby is at least partly about trying to make myself whole. And I worry that that's not such a great idea. Linda's question about my not wanting to be alone rattles about in my head again too.

Mom and I sit and look at each other for a long moment. There's nothing to say, really.

"So, should we go home?" I ask, believing that walking and moving around will help my stomach.

As we walk out to the car, I think about how I still don't feel entirely comfortable around my parents. I love them both, even though I'm not fully myself with them. My real thoughts stay with me and get between us, and until I can actually tell them the full truth about myself and what I think, I'll always be on guard around them. I'll always feel like the little kid who had to cheer them up and hide herself.

I leave my parents' house after a week. I land in Toronto, pick up my car, and drive an hour south of Montreal for Susan's big renaissance wedding. She has pulled it off, our wonderful Susan, exceeding everyone's expectations again.

One of the things I did with Mom during my visit was sew myself a Maid Marian dress to wear to the medieval ceremony, but she did the hard stuff, and when I sewed the sleeves on backward, she spent an entire evening fixing it for me.

I park on the road as I was told to, walk up the drive with my suitcase, and see all the Hashimotos raking gravel from the garage all the way across the flat area where we usually park. This is where the reception is going to be, apparently.

"Mrs.!" Margaret and Jim shout.

Margaret stops for a second and leans on her rake. "You're up in our room again," she says. "Drop your stuff in there. We'll be done here in a second."

"Great. Should I make some tea?"

"Perfect," Margaret says.

I go in to say hi to Susan, who is in the kitchen supervising Jeff's two daughters as they arrange bouquets of wildflowers for the banquet tables. Jeff's oldest daughter, Nicole, who is only eighteen or so, is pregnant—

about-to-drop-any-second pregnant. She and I sang karaoke together last Christmas when she and her boyfriend visited for a few days. I have always thought of her as a child, so seeing her pregnant is a little disconcerting. I look over at her boyfriend in the living room, playing a video game beside Mr. Hashimoto, who is angling his newspaper toward the bright window and squinting at the print. I wonder if his cataracts are coming back.

"Hey Susan!" I kiss her on the cheek and give her a hug. "Wedding number two!" I decide not to make a big deal about Nicole's baby in front of Susan. Aside from this being her day, she doesn't need anyone making a fuss about something she will never experience.

I sit down beside her. "So," she says, "we bought a house!"

"You didn't!" I give her another hug. She has always wanted to own a home to decorate any way she wants. "Where is it?"

"It's in Hull, only a few blocks from our old apartment, actually. Are you coming back to Ottawa after the wedding? You can come by and see it."

"That would be great," I say. "I'll call and see if I can take a few extra days." I smile and nod at Jeff's daughters. My eyes get caught on Nicole's enormous belly again. It seems like another sign that this idea of mine is right.

"So, anyone for some tea?" I say. In the end, I will not be able to take the extra days, and only after Susan dies will I see her new house. There will be snow everywhere then, and dark curtains on the windows, but all around will be pictures from both her weddings—tulips in some, wildflowers in others.

That night we sing karaoke again, and everyone joins in on "I Will Survive." We sing at the top of our lungs, but the song has a bittersweet feel that becomes obvious to me only as we finish. It's not just about Susan's surviving until the wedding, which is, in a way, triumphant. Ten months ago, when we were here singing this song at Christmas, we thought Susan would survive forever. She had just come through another surgery brilliantly. They had removed cancer clusters from her lungs, and she was up at the mic, singing with everyone else. I have pictures of her with her head thrown back, laughing and singing to the stars.

But tonight she sits and watches, and after a while she moves with her dad to the kitchen to keep working on the oral history project she has started, capturing her father and mother on tape, telling the story of their lives.

In the morning Margaret and I run together, both hungover, with Gatorade hanging from our water belts. I tell her that somehow I have to get Ken alone. I've tried again and again, but the cottage is so small, and with all the people staying there, I've barely seen him, much less talked to him privately.

"Maybe I can send you two on an errand or something," she says. We run a little more, and suddenly she stops short. "Hey! Should I have another baby? Maybe I should have another baby!"

I stop too, and feel the Gatorade bouncing against my hip. What a great idea! This is a total *bonus!* Margaret and I used to talk about getting pregnant together and raising our kids side by side. And the babies would be cousins! "Will Jim go for that?"

"He says he'd rather take a bullet to the brain, but I think I might be able to turn him around." I have a fleeting thought that the one good thing about going it alone is that there's no one I have to "turn around."

We say together, "Imagine! Pregnant together!"

The next morning, the day before Susan's wedding, Margaret arranges for

Ken to ride in my car when we all go to the village to pick up chairs. We make idle chitchat and talk about how surprised we are that Nicole is so pregnant. "Does that mean she was pregnant already last Christmas?" I ask. We both count on our fingers.

"Yes! She must have been, right? January to August is eight months. She was probably pregnant but didn't know it yet."

We look at each other and I think, *Hey, this is the perfect opening.* "So, do you remember a couple of years ago, us talking on the new deck at the cottage?"

Ken says nothing for a moment, as he tries to figure out what I'm talking about. Then he smiles. "Okay, yes, I do." I can see out of the corner of my eye that he's flushing slightly, and I feel my own face warm up.

"Um, I'm ready now," I say, louder than I intended.

He says nothing.

"We can talk about the specifics now," I say. "Now that it's real."

"What do you mean?"

I clear my throat and slow down as we enter the village and turn toward the church. "Like, how much of a role you would play in the baby's life. That sort of thing. I want you to know that this wouldn't be a financial burden for you."

"Okay." Ken looks away.

"I'm easy about whatever you would like," I say. "Whatever you feel comfortable with."

Now he is looking at me, but I focus on my driving. "This is a big decision," he says, cracking his big knuckles. "When we talked about this before, it seemed much simpler."

"Yeah, for me too." I glance at him and smile. "I guess it was just an idea then. Now, you know, I need to buy a crib. And a car seat. And all that kind of stuff."

"Right. I guess so."

I slow down to a crawl through this small Quebec village, mindful of families on bikes and couples walking toward the lake, holding hands. I don't want to reach the church just yet.

"I want you to feel sure about this, so take as much time as you need," I say, but I'm terribly disappointed. How could I have thought he would just say yes, like at the cottage? This is different. This is real. I want to ask him straight out how long he thinks he needs to make up his mind, but I'm as feeble at being straight with non–family members as I am with Mom and Dad.

As we get out of the car at the church, I stop him before he walks in to start loading chairs. I say, "Listen, just think about it, and we'll talk in a couple of weeks. Is that okay?"

He nods, and we look at each other for a long moment before going inside. As he goes on ahead of me, I watch him walk away, and think that I'll get Margaret to press him a little. Get her to explain all the things I've been too embarrassed to say myself.

Susan's wedding day is bright and sunny. My dress is green. The sleeves are made of a gauzy material that flows all the way to the ground. The waist is nipped in a little, and then it flares out like a bell with a crinoline. I love this renaissance idea. I love this dress. I feel lovely and would wear the dress every day if I could. I embody the heroine I've thought so much about during my recent dating life, and I'm struck by how easy it is to feel that longing again.

The church is old and hazy with incense, and my feeling of otherworldliness is compounded by the fact that everything is in French and I don't understand a word. There are more than a hundred people here, knights and ladies and princesses with crowns. Jim and Christian are carrying swords. Even Nicole has found a velvet maiden dress to fit over her large belly.

Susan's voice is soft and breathless when she says what I assume is "I do." Jeff's voice booms. The organ plays softly, and the priest motions for us all to stand. He proclaims something in French, and we all clap and cheer thunderously as they walk slowly down the aisle.

Taking pictures out on the lawn, I think, *I have been foolish. I have been wasting time. Why have I been dillydallying, testing out the idea over and over again, waiting for permission? This is it, girl. You're fucking thirty-nine. Have a baby! It doesn't make any difference why I want this baby. I just do. I do, I do, I do.* And I can't wait even a moment longer, not even for Ken and the chance to be a bona fide member of the Hashimoto family.

FOUR

Baby, Baby

On Monday, the day after I return from the wedding, I Google for sperm.

I don't know anything about how to do this, other than what I've seen on TV and in a play where a lesbian couple used a gay friend's sperm to get pregnant. There was much talk of turkey basters, much rushing about with sealed Tupperware containers from bathroom to bedroom, their friend slipping away after providing his contribution.

I guess the first thing to do is get the sperm. Since Ken isn't ready to go just yet, I'm going to see about sperm banks. There are, I see on the web, a lot of sperm banks, especially in California.

And one in White Plains, just twenty-five minutes away. I click through the website until I get to descriptions of the donors. I look at profiles of white men, Hispanic men, and African American men.

I lean back in my office chair and stare out the miniature window over my desk. How in God's name does a person choose?

Pat stops by my office on her way to hers. We work on the third floor of a building that used to be a home but is now the graduate studies office. We have the only two offices up here, and because we are way up at the top of the house, we don't get a lot of visitors.

"What are you working on?" she asks, glancing at my computer screen.

"I'm doing some research," I say.

She flops down in the visitors' chair with a sigh. "Research on what?" she asks.

It feels odd that I've made this big decision in the month since I saw her last. Pat is usually in on all the details of my life. She is my BFF, in addition to being my workout partner and weight-loss buddy; we have promised each other to walk together through life without sugar or flour. Pat has become, in fact, the very best friend I vowed I would not find as I was graduating with my MFA.

"I'm looking at sperm banks."

She nods slowly. "Oh." We look at each other for a long second as she digests this information. "So you're going to do this on your own? No more Man Search?"

"Right."

She nods and smiles at me, shaking her head a little. "Well, that's totally brave of you."

I laugh and shrug my shoulders. Bravery was what I was hoping to find all summer as I talked and talked and talked about the idea. What I have now is simply determination and a certainty that I *have* to do this. "Actually," I say, pointing to the computer screen, "I'm totally overwhelmed."

I turn to the Google results again and begin to scroll down. "I mean, look at all the sperm banks. How am I supposed to decide?" I ask, scrolling down the list.

Then I notice it: "Scandinavian donors. Worldwide delivery."

"Aren't you Danish?" she asks as I click on the website.

"My mom is. My dad's Norwegian."

"Very blond," she says, looking at a picture of a mother and baby on the homepage. I glance at her, because I catch something in the tone of her voice.

"I'm blond," I say, but I'm distracted now by the picture, and I'm thinking, *Wow, I want that.*

I'm not sure where this surge of desire comes from, but I totally want one of those white-haired babies I can buy a Baby Gap bunny suit for, one of those babies that look exactly like my sister's babies. And I feel suddenly how very jealous of Linda I have been. Linda and her three beautiful babies. I've always felt a little competitive with her, but we've been on such different tracks. We've had such different goals and different lives. How could I have been competitive? But I know I was; I just didn't want to feel it. I love her little babies, and all along I have wanted some of my own.

I am reminded too of a photograph of my mom and me when I'm a year old. I'm pulling off her glasses, and she's throwing her head back, laughing. My hair is white and a little curly, like the baby's in the photo on the website, and my mother is happy. I've come to think of that as a golden time for me—before my sister was born, when Mom and Dad were pleased with their lives. Mom was relaxed; Dad wasn't too busy at work. They took me to fastball games where Dad was the catcher and Mom cheered in the stands with me.

"Well," Pat says, standing up, "it looks like that narrows your sperm-bank search."

"I guess it does," I say. I hear that little something in her voice again, and I feel defensive and say faintly, "I would like my baby to look like me." But I think of the fierceness of my wanting just a moment earlier. I'm reminded of Dad in the car, saying a baby with Ken wouldn't even look like me.

"Okay," she says, laughing just a little. "I didn't say anything."

"I just want the baby to look like my family," I tell her as she leaves my office. "This is about family!" But she is in her office now and doesn't answer.

And I don't blame her. I feel like a madwoman. "This is about family!" What is wrong with me?

When Mom gets back from Denmark, we move to the lake. This is what we do in the summer. Day after day, I get to live in my bathing suit. There's sand in my hair and under my nails.

In the car, Linda and I count the months she was gone. There are eleven.

Mom moves her cigarette from her left to her right hand as Dad drives us the last three miles on the gravel road to the cabin. Inconspicuously, from the back seat, I reach over to put my hand on Mom's right shoulder. Her skin is warm beneath her white cotton shirt, and she reaches up with her right hand to put it over mine. I am so happy she is home. I am so glad to be in my own room with my own things.

I can't stop touching her.

I lean my cheek against the vinyl seat back, and we stay like that awhile, the washboard road jiggling us inside the car.

Kimball Lake is clean and clear, and the air is dry. Silvery wild blueberries carpet the ground from the cabin to the lake, just a few steps way. Our dock bobs in the little waves, just ripples, really. The sun is hot, the sky big and pale blue.

In pictures from that summer, my eight-year-old self is as brown as a farm egg, and just as speckled, with freckles across my cheeks and nose. There's that belly everyone was worried about, but I'm knock-kneed and bony-armed. The mandatory farm shag is growing out.

Linda and I play War and Go Fish when it rains, but mostly it doesn't, and we swim at the public beach where there is a lifeguard and we wait an hour after we eat, biking up and down the path in front of our cabin and around the lake to the store, with a clutch of coins between our palms and the soft plastic grip of the handlebars.

There is a guy. A teenager guy. His family rents a cabin down the lake in the opposite direction of the public beach. Today we are in the boathouse together.

Hot, dry air pulses down from the ceiling where the sun presses hard against the black-tiled roof. There is a smell of gassy rags and wet oars and life jackets. There is no drywall or insulation, just the studs and the outside walls. Nails as hooks stick out here and there to hang the puffy old life jackets, orange and bloated, looming like monstrous spider bellies in the dim light. There are only a couple of tiny windows, because this is just a boathouse. This is where we keep the boat, silver and red aluminum, leaning against the wall.

The tiny outboard motor hangs from the frame Dad built near the wall, its butterfly blades facing away from us.

This isn't the first thing between me and this guy, here in the hot boathouse smelling of gas, on the bed our infrequent guests sleep on. We have done fun things before this time under dark wool blankets. Itchy, dusty-smelling blankets. Hot.

I came to this moment okay. I like that he plays with me. He's older than anyone I have ever played with. He is going to be a singer in a band. Maybe he said he is already a singer in a band. I'm not sure, because he starts singing to me then, and I feel embarrassed for him. Can't look at him. "See you . . . in September," he sings, a little wobbly.

Before, he taught me a game: kissing underwater. Linda is with us there, swimming too, and I'm happy because it's *me* he wants to play this game with. Not Linda. Because I'm older and more grown up. It is fun and a little ticklish. It reminds me of sitting off the dock, legs in the water very still, late in the day as the sun goes down. Sitting still until the minnows come and kiss my calves and the soles of my feet a thousand soft times. So ticklish I have to stop my squirmy self from moving and scaring them away. That's what it's like kissing underwater. Feathery touch like the fish, and I can't help laughing, and I burst from the water snorting.

He says let's try again, and I look through the clear lake water into his green eyes. His red hair waves like fish fins as we drift back and forth under the water. I don't laugh.

Then I show him somersaults underwater. How I can do five in a row. Linda can only do four.

But now we are here in the boathouse, and even though before, in the water, it was fun and fluttery in the stomach, now I'm just shivery, and hot too, and I feel like the bouncing minnows are in my head, bumping around in my brain, saying, *Out, out, out, out, out.*

Come here, let's kiss under the blanket. Come. He pulls me from the edge of the bed. I just hate these hot itchy blankets. He pushes my shorts down, and his too. My tank top is at my neck. His breath smells like Tang. I'm breathing fast, because I don't like this. I don't like this. I don't like this. He takes my hand and puts it on his body. His white and red squishy body. And there are hard places and he has long bony fingers.

I have a headache, I say. Please. I have to go in. I have a headache. And this is not a lie. There's a heavy hot pounding like something too big is in my head, growing and growing and wanting to burst out through my eyes.

He says go inside, get an aspirin.

In my head I'm chanting, *Please just let me. Just leave me alone.*

Get an aspirin. Come back. I'll sing for you.

I pull up my shorts and tug down my top. Outside it is so cool under the trees. I walk around to the side of the cabin. I delay and delay there, leaning against the rough pink side of the cabin.

I need an aspirin, I say to Mom. I have a headache.

I stand on one foot by the door. She will know what is happening just a little way over in the boathouse. She will know because I have never had a headache. She will be able to tell by my face that something terrible is happening next door. *Please. Please help me, keep me here, ask me what is happening, ask me what is really wrong.*

She gives me a look. Dad is in the kitchen doing something, I don't know what. She puts her hand on my forehead. You're sweating, she says.

I nod.

She goes to her purse and pulls out the baby-aspirin bottle and gives me two. I chew them, not enjoying them the way I usually do.

"You better stay out of the water until you're better," Mom says, and I stand there waiting for more. *Stop me. Tell me to go to bed. Make me stay inside.*

My stomach is twisting and rolling, and I go outside and delay, standing in the shade near the cabin.

The heat is like a wall when I go back inside. I stare at the butterfly blades turned away from us, down on the other side of the boathouse.

There are burning points on my head where his fingertips press. I am choking on the heat and really, really, really I want to die.

My memory is so crisp sometimes, it's just like I'm standing there again, just outside the action, watching myself, feeling everything. Like in the boathouse. The itchy blankets, his long fingers. The aspirin, my dad at the sink. Gas.

But then I worry about certain details—the outboard motor and the boat, for example. I don't think we actually kept the boat in the boathouse. And why would the blades of the outboard motor face into the wall like that? That doesn't make sense when you think about the shape of an outboard motor. It would want to face out, the way it faces out from the back of a boat. Any frame Dad would have built would have had the blades face out. Maybe he made it that way so it was safer with kids around.

So I call him to ask. I'm at my kitchen table, taking notes. He struggles to remember. He too thinks the blades faced in, but after a moment says, "No, the blades faced out."

"It sat over in the left-hand corner, right? If you're standing with your back to the lake."

"Right."

I let him remember. "I kept the gas tank in there too, and dammit, during the winter all the gas leaked out. You know an outboard motor uses an oil-gas mix, right?" He clears his throat. "After that winter, the whole floor had a slick, oily surface. That happened the very first winter, and dammit, the smell never went away."

"We didn't really keep the boat in there either, did we?"

"No. When it wasn't down by the water, I kept it against the outside of the boathouse."

We don't talk about it now, but he understands why I'm asking, because I told him the boathouse story a couple of years ago. We were driving back to Kimball Lake during a visit in the summer of 2002.

"I remember the boy," he said, keeping his eyes looking ahead.

There were thick trees beside us on each side of the road. A power line ran between us and the trees. He remembered the boy because he wondered why this teenager would be interested in playing with an eight-year-old child.

"But those were different days," he said.

We were quiet after that for a while.

"I always thought we were so lucky," he said finally, "that nothing bad like that ever happened to you kids."

He sounded so sad that I wanted to say it was only that one guy, that one summer. It wasn't so terrible. But then I thought about my life since, and I knew how that summer left its mark. I thought about all the dating but never falling in love. How I've kept myself safe behind fat. How only perfection would do, to make up for everything.

I also knew, in that moment in the car, that what Dad was really saying was *I'm sorry.*

When we drove up to the cabin (I hadn't been back since I was thirteen), it was unrecognizable, renovated and made larger. They'd moved the boathouse too, out from beside the cabin and angled toward the driveway. As we approached the boathouse, I wished I had waited until we were on our way home to tell Dad. I felt sick about seeing the inside of this place, and now that Dad knew about it, too, I felt self-conscious and scared.

But I needn't have worried. As we peered inside, I realized that it too had changed beyond recognition. But when the wet, gassy smell hit me, I had to step away.

In the car again, Dad asked me, "But why did you go back in?"

I shrugged and looked out my window at the passing power lines. "I didn't know I could say no."

I have thought many times since then about having a child of my own, and about how I would make sure she *never* got into a situation like that, that she would always know how to ask for help.

But when you actually have a child, it's more difficult to be confident, and you become afraid every day, because it is so easy for trouble to find you. The world is full of danger, and I can see how my mother could never have known anything bad was happening just because I came in saying I had a headache.

I understand something else now too, something that I didn't really get before. I see now how painful it must have been for Dad to hear me tell this story. I understand now, in a way I never could before, how your child's pain is your pain, like a knife through your stomach.

I've only been home from the wedding for a few days, and already I have a dark brown manila folder full of printouts and notes.

There are a bunch of things I need to decide and arrange right away if I want to catch this cycle, but there is still so much I don't understand. On each website, I notice a distinction made between IUI and ICI. I have no idea what these are. I don't know where I'm going to have the insemination done. (Thinking about this thing, I get a weird feeling in my stomach. I decide that I don't like this word at all and will use "injection" instead.) I have no idea how much this is going to cost. I don't even know if my medical insurance will cover any of it.

Also, school starts up again in a couple of weeks, and I have a ton of work to do, so I feel jittery every time I get diverted from work to do more research.

Pat suggests I call my ob-gyn for advice, and I talk my way into an appointment that afternoon. Ilona, who works in the office, asks if I want Dr. Bakas or Dr. McGroary, who is new. I'm tempted to go with the stranger, thinking somehow it will be easier, but in the end I stick with the familiar.

While I wait in the little examination room, clothes off, paper gown on (I'm getting an overdue Pap test while I'm here), I step on the scale and am pleased to see I've lost a couple more pounds.

There's a little knock. I call, "Come in," and Dr. Bakas enters, looking down at my file. He's very handsome, Dr. Bakas is, which was almost a problem for me in the beginning. Somehow I thought it would make these potentially embarrassing visits even harder. But he is so gentle, understanding, and kind that after my first visit I couldn't imagine going anywhere else.

"So, a Pap test today, right?"

"Yes," I say. "And some advice, if you don't mind."

"About?" He looks directly at me now, clicking his pen open and closed.

"I want to have a baby. Myself, with a sperm bank and stuff."

"Okay," he says, looking back down at the file. "Great. You're . . ." He shuffles through the papers. "You're thirty-nine, right?"

"Yeah."

"And you've never been pregnant before."

"Right."

Shuffle shuffle. The top of his head is all I see over the file; his black curly hair is gorgeous. "No reasons to suspect a problem, though."

"Well," I say. "I've done some risky things. What I mean is, I've had unprotected sex at risky times but have never gotten pregnant. Which worries me."

He shrugs. "Could mean anything."

"Should I get some tests done? Should I go on any drugs to help? Where should I do it? And how is it done?"

"Wait, wait, slow down." He looks at me directly again. There's an appealing shyness to Dr. Bakas. But when he looks at you, he really focuses on you. "I don't think we should assume there'll be any problems unless they arise. I suggest low-tech first. No drugs. The only useful test right now is an HSG to be sure there's no blockage anywhere, no obvious issue."

"Okay." I have no idea what an HSG is.

"Then, well. . ."—*click click click* with the pen—"let me do some research. Maybe we can do it here."

"Do what? The HSG?"

"No, that has to be done at a hospital. No, I mean the insemination."

I *hate* that word.

"Really? You could do it here? That would be great." I had imagined some cold, strange clinic somewhere.

"Anything else?"

"Well . . ." I hesitate.

He waits.

"I'd really like to do it next cycle, I mean this cycle." I clear my throat, feeling impulsive, but I want him to know so he'll do the research soon, even today. "Like, in a couple of weeks, when I ovulate again. I just finished my period."

"Oh," he nods. "Okay." He nods some more. He looks a little strained, or maybe I'm just projecting. "Okay." Nodding. Clicking. "I'll get Ilona and we'll do the Pap."

I leave the office with a prescription for the HSG test, and instructions to start taking folic acid to help prevent things like spina bifida. Wow, *now* this is starting to feel real.

I don't think I can overestimate how much losing all that weight made it possible for me to do all I was doing to try to make this pregnancy thing happen. Or, even more profoundly, to think that I could do this at all: have a baby on my own, get pregnant, be pregnant alone, have the baby, and then raise it by myself.

I have struggled with my weight all my life. Back in university, part of what made me so depressed just before I moved to Toronto was the fact that at the beginning of that fourth year, in September, Dad paid for me to go to the Diet Center, and I lost sixty pounds. Hurray! I weighed less then than I have ever weighed, before or since, in my adult life. But by January, I had fallen off the wagon and I quickly gained it all back. By that day at the end of July, when I was eating chips on the couch in front of the spot of sunlight on the rug, I was ten pounds heavier than I had been when I started the Diet Center the September before. I wanted to die.

The backdrop for the rest of my life—through all my adventures and travels, school endeavors and various jobs and friendships and lovers—was a constant and bitter battle with my weight. Up and down. Up and down.

But here I am at thirty-nine. *Finally* I'm a normal weight. (I could still lose a few more pounds, but what the hell?) But more importantly, I have been in control and healthy for over three years. I realize this is longer than ever before. I am certain I have it all licked.

I have wrestled most of the other parts of my life into shape too. I floss my teeth every night. My finances are in good shape. My apartment is usually neat and clean with very little clutter, though probably still too much furniture. I am a good person with a solid life—and yes, I'm a normal, healthy weight.

I deserve to be a parent now.

Over the next few days, I squeeze in some calls to fertility clinics to see about getting it done there if it doesn't work out with Bakas. And to surreptitiously get more answers. I also find out what IUI and ICI are. IUI, or intrauterine insemination, involves "washed" sperm—once the sperm are thawed, the dead sperm and the fluid that the sperm live in are "washed" away, so all that are left are the happy sperm. They are injected directly into the uterus through a long, thin tube, the idea being that the sperm are through the cervix and a lot closer to the egg. It's supposed to have a higher success rate than ICI, which means intracervical insemination and is pretty much the same as sex. The upside of doing the ICI is that you can do it yourself at home. Somehow, though, I have no interest in doing this. It is clear to me right away that I want to do the IUI.

I'm not quite sure, but I think I've got my insurance company on board to pay for some of this, up to three tries. The sperm cost more or less the same everywhere, around $200 or $300, and the cost of delivery is almost as much, I guess because the sperm have to be kept frozen in dry ice.

I mention to one nurse at a clinic that I'm thinking of having my obgyn do it, and she is silent for a moment. Then she asks, "Do you really want to do that?"

"What do you mean?"

"Well, I just think that you'd want to go to a specialist. If I had cancer I wouldn't go to my family doctor, if you see what I mean. I'd go to an oncologist, right?" This talk of oncologists makes me think about Susan, and I am seized with a panicky feeling of being rushed.

I'm in a rush, and now I'm doing it wrong.

When I talk to Dr. Bakas a few days later, he says if I help pay for the equipment to wash the sperm, he can do it there. "So, you've done this before?" I ask, wondering how I couldn't have asked before.

"It's nothing," he says. "I saw it done when I was a resident. There's really nothing to it."

"Okay," I say slowly. "Let me see. How much is the equipment?"

"About $500, so you could pay half and we'll pay half."

I'm having doubts now, but my inner voice is like, *You have to do this with him now; he's done all this work. And $250 is a drop in the bucket.*

"Okay," I find myself saying.

"Right. I'll order it then."

I have a crisis of faith.

It's all suddenly too much. All these decisions to make, and I don't feel able to make even one of them. How can I think about having a kid when I can't even navigate getting pregnant?

I find myself crying in the office kitchen. Pat is not around, and when Crystal walks in I can't stop. I don't know her very well, but this will be the beginning of our becoming friends. I say to her, "I'm doing this all wrong."

"Doing what?" she asks.

"Trying to have a baby."

And I tell her about Bakas and the receptionist, and how I shouldn't have agreed to do it with Dr. Bakas. How the insurance company is a nightmare.

Crystal stands beside the coffee machine and nods sympathetically. As I cry she comes over to give me a hug. She is a single mother herself, with two kids. "This is big stuff," she says. "Very emotional stuff."

Then I find myself telling her about my HSG test that morning. How the room was freezing. How I was placed, virtually naked as usual, on a cold x-ray table. No one explained what was going to happen, though the nurse turned a TV screen toward me so I could watch my x-rayed uterus as we went along.

The radiologist came in and sat down between my legs, which the nurse had put in stirrups. When he jammed that speculum in to inject the dye, I froze up. I went rigid from head to toe. He persisted so roughly, I began to feel nauseated.

"Please," I said. "That really hurts."

"Just try to relax," the nurse said.

I thought, *Are you kidding me? Relax?*

He pushed even harder. I felt myself heaving and closed my eyes. *Please don't throw up.* The dye burned as he injected it, and even though I tried to watch what was happening on the TV, I couldn't tell what was going on.

"I can't do this," I say to Crystal as she pats my back.

"Yes you can," she says into my hair, and I cry harder. "I'm sorry about this morning. That sounds just awful."

I finally stop crying, and I can see that this morning has colored my whole day, tainted my feelings about all I am doing. Part of me was feeling punished, like I wasn't supposed to be able to have this baby, and the receptionist and the violent radiologist were signs.

"Listen," Crystal says, "you just have to go with your instincts. If your first reaction was that you wanted to do this at your doctor's office because it was more familiar, then that's the right decision. Don't let some cranky old bitch-nurse in some expensive clinic make you feel bad."

I laugh out loud at hearing her swear. Crystal is usually a very refined Southern woman, and the cursing is a surprise.

"Thanks," I say, reassured and befriended.

Crystal's talk helps a lot, and I go back up to my office with a little more energy. I'm still not quite up for thinking about sperm, but I know I have to. I just don't want to face that person who lusted so greedily after a blond baby. I am finding that choosing a father is a strange and somewhat creepy process of separating out all other factors and just thinking about which ingredients I want to use in producing a baby. I've never been married, but I can't imagine that people marry for these ingredients—for the kind of children they will bake up.

I imagine when you fall in love, you decide to have children together as an expression of your love: a little of me, a little of you, left forever in the world.

So what does it mean for me to make this child on my own, when it's just me deciding?

Frankly, as I go from donor to donor, characteristic to characteristic, my most prevalent feeling is one of sheer consumerism. I feel like I am buying a baby.

FIVE

Torn between Two Donors

On Monday, home for a week now and feeling fresher and stronger, I give myself a couple of hours in the morning to straighten out the sperm situation.

Work presses hard against my closed office door, but I'm going to ignore it for a few moments. I pay $100 to the Scandinavian Cryobank website to get access to the detailed donor profiles. Holding both my consumerism and my judgment of my consumerism in check, I look over the list of men and their attributes.

I feel that greed again, and this is what I want: blond, blue-green eyes. Creative. The parts of me I like. And I want to fix the things about myself that I've felt uncertain about: how I've never felt smart enough, how I've always felt short and fat. So I look for tall men. Thin men. Men with more advanced degrees than me.

I notice that the bank has a photo-matching service. I sign up for that, too. I'm on a roll and determined now, so I email a rather glamorous photo of myself from my time with Margaret at the lodge, sitting on a log with the wind blowing my blond hair away from my face. I am fit and thin and tanned. *Match this*, I think. *Make a match with the very best of me.* As I do it, I think about how this feels like the complete opposite of my dad's saying in the car that a baby with Ken wouldn't look like me.

I think about my time in Denmark too—the cobbled streets, the churches and castles five hundred years old. How that placed saved me, helped me grow up.

I call Claus, the director of the sperm bank, to be sure he got the photo and to explain that I want someone who looks like me.

"It's pretty subjective, you understand."

"Of course," I say. "Whatever you can do."

It's only later that I realize the photo-matching service probably isn't meant for this, but is rather for matching the donor to the parenting father, so the baby can look somewhat like him, or perhaps for lesbian couples, so the baby might look a little like the nongestating mother.

While I wait for Claus to get back to me, I take a closer look at the profiles and find Boris, who lists himself as both a student and a writer. In his profile he talks a lot about creativity and art. But he's five-foot-eight and 170 pounds, which seems kind of short and stout. He has brown hair and brown eyes. There's a handwritten note scanned into the end of his profile, and I stare at it for a long time. It is short, just a couple of sentences. He writes that he is anxious to help families have children, that he had such great parents and such a happy childhood, he wants other loving couples to be able to have kids.

This strikes me as beautiful.

He has a master's in Danish and is working on his PhD. I dream about him that night, I see him walking toward me across the main square in Copenhagen as I buy a *rød pølse* (like a hot dog, but longer and thinner, with red skin that snaps when you bite into it) from a street vendor. Boris's brown hair is long and tied back into a ponytail. His brown leather jacket is open and reveals a little paunch, just above his belt. When he reaches me he cracks a joke about my *rød pølse,* and even though I'm only dreaming, I feel myself blush.

When I wake up, it's not lost on me that I'm eating in this dream and he thinks it's sexy. The dream resurfaces several times during the day, and it is only late that evening, as I'm showering before bed, that I remember: *Oh, right. I'm never going to meet this Boris guy.*

I go to bed feeling a little deflated.

A few days later I speak with Claus again, and after he forwarded my photo to the head office in Denmark, the girls working there told him they thought I looked a lot like Olaf.

"They say he's very nice," Claus says. "And handsome."

"Hey, that's great." And I think about Boris in my dream and how he was nice too, and took me to Tivoli. But he wasn't handsome at all. Then I think, *Wait, I don't know what Boris looks like; he's not even real.* Well, Boris is real, obviously, but the person I think of as Boris is not.

It strikes me then how safe it is to dream about a guy I'll never meet, who will father a child for me without our ever having sex. I can't get hurt or left behind or any of that messy stuff. Having a baby this way fits right in with my tendencies toward safety, despite my dreams of adventure.

I hang up the phone and pull up Olaf's profile.

There he is: six feet tall and 140 pounds. Blond as a kid and blond now. Left-handed! Cool. I like that. I've always wanted to be left-handed. All the most creative people I know are left-handed. But as I read through his profile, I'm kind of disappointed. He's a masters student, not a PhD, and he's a little . . . what's the word?

Boring.

He's into psychology. He likes German shepherds. He stopped his PhD studies to continue working in business.

I think, *I like Boris better.*

I'd like to hang out with Boris. Olaf, well, Olaf seems very staid and straight and earnest and right brained. He wouldn't be interested in the fact that I'm a writer. He might not even be a reader.

There I go again. *What am I doing?*

It's like a flashback to the days when I was dating online. Checking out Boris' and Olaf's profiles, I'm reminded of looking at Teased about Being Gay Guy, and Claude's profiles, how I assessed their dating potential, always thinking about them as lovers and possible fathers—having romantic dreams and fantasies about them—before we even met.

Now I'm looking at Boris' and Olaf's profiles and thinking about their dating potential while forgetting that I'll never actually meet them. I've confused looking for a sperm donor with looking for a date. Or perhaps, even more profoundly, I'm trying to have it both ways—dreaming about them as lovers whom I'll never meet, yet they'll make me a mother.

There's something very odd about this sequence. Like I'm cheating, avoiding something real and necessary.

I force myself to think about The Baby again. A baby made up of half of me and half of who? Boris? Olaf? Writer, or business guy? Short and stout, or tall and lanky?

I try to imagine the baby I'm hoping to have, who I want that this little person to be, but it's impossible. I can't put the little golem together in my mind and find instead that I'm daydreaming about Boris again. I imagine us walking through the cobbled streets of Copenhagen.

Oh, brother.

I close the browser, because it's clear to me now that there's something I'm not ready to let go of yet. I need just a moment to sort out what feels messy to me now. I want a husband and father, but not really. I have a dream of being loved and cherished for all of me—a dream that I am obviously not ready to let go of.

I need to cry a little about my lost dream. I need to mourn the death of romance.

I go by the hospital at lunch and pick up the results of the HSG test. I walk back out through the emergency exit to my illegally parked car. I sit inside and open the envelope and try to make sense of the three pieces of paper: one white, one pink, one light blue. At the top of a cluster of text are many words I don't understand: "Bilateral fallopian tubes were patent." *Patent? Isn't that what you get to protect an invention?* But by the third line, I totally understand: "Diagnosis: infertility."

Oh my god!

Does this mean what I think it means? I check the pink and light blue pages and they all say the same thing: "Diagnosis: infertility." My hatred for that bastard radiologist explodes in my brain. I look up at the EMERGENCY EXIT sign, then to the ambulance parked there, like I'm going to go find him standing beside it and can bang his head against the hood of his car three times.

I'm infertile?

I forget all about grabbing some lunch, and I drive like a maniac back to my office to call Dr. Bakas. He tells me to fax the results to him and wait for him to call me back.

I sit in my office chair and rock back and forth a little, twirling my hair around my finger, looking for something to calm me down. I think about all the money I was about to spend on sperm. At least I haven't paid for that yet (although this is a bitter thought that doesn't actually make me feel better).

I won't have to choose between Olaf and Boris, either.

I give up on the rocking and sit with my head on my arms over the papers on my desk. I'm reminded of being in university with Margaret, supposedly studying in the library but instead falling asleep at the desk and drooling all over my books. I remember my disappointment about Margaret's nonpregnancy.

God, I'm bad at disappointment. This is so terrible. I feel this right down in my bones. I ache with the idea that I can't have a child.

Why didn't I just run out and get pregnant way back then? I might not have been infertile at that point. Was that the fatal mistake, waiting too long? Thinking I had forever?

Agitation rises up through me and I can't sit still anymore. I stand up and wonder where to go. Pat's not in her office next door. Crystal isn't here either.

Suddenly I hate everyone. It feels as though all the anger I've not expressed throughout my life is rising up inside me, and I try to figure out whose fault this is so I know where to direct it: my parents? The doctor? God? How come I don't get to have a family? Why do other women get to have one without even really working at it?

I think about Juan and the men before him, and I think of all my years of being single, then the years of searching. Then giving that up and moving on to the second plan, the idea of having the baby alone.

And now I'm not even going to get to do that.

Pat finally came back to her office around one-thirty, and I pounced on her and vented for half an hour, so now I don't feel so rageful. I even managed to get a little work done. Dr. Bakas calls me back later in the afternoon.

"What does the form mean? What is this infertility? This polyp?" I ask.

"It's nothing; don't worry about it."

"But . . ."

"There is nothing here to stop us from continuing. The polyp is . . ." I can hear him shuffling papers. "Hmm. We got the results from your Pap." More shuffling of papers. "There are some abnormal cells. You'll need to come in."

It's cancer, I think. I can't help myself. I think about Susan walking with her crutch up the stairs of the little village church a few weeks ago.

"What does that mean?"

"Alexandra," he says, sounding kind, even though I'm panicked, "just make an appointment with Ilona as soon as you can. We'll take a look. At this point it's nothing to worry about."

I hang up and wonder why I can't press him for more information instead of just letting him reassure me. Now I'm mad at myself for not being more assertive, for not being able to say what I mean and think. *What is wrong with me?*

Instead I take a deep breath and call Ilona, who tells me the first appointment they have is with Dr. McGroary, Bakas's new partner, and it isn't until tomorrow afternoon. So I take it, feeling like I don't have much choice.

Dr. McGroary looks twelve years old. He has a different style of shyness than Dr. Bakas. And he's cute in a cute way, whereas Dr. Bakas is cute in a handsome way. Standing just inside the door after knocking, he spends a moment or two looking through my file before sitting down on the low stool in front of the little desklike object in the corner. This makes him look nine years old instead of twelve.

"So, what do you want to talk about first?"

"Do I have cervical cancer?"

He shakes his head as I talk about my concern that I've never had an abnormal Pap. He doesn't interrupt me though. Finally I stop and look at him.

"First, we're going to redo the Pap, and if that test comes back with abnormal cells too, we'll go in and clear them away with a procedure we can do here in the office. Then we'll keep a close eye on things."

He goes on in more detail, and when he finishes he crosses his fingers over my file and says, "So, you're planning a pregnancy?"

"Yes," I say, struggling to switch from thinking about dying to thinking about making a baby. "So the 'Diagnosis: infertility' line on my HSG test doesn't mean anything? Why is it there?"

He shuffles through my file again, and I see the faxed copy of my test results. "That's just the reason for the test. It's not the result."

"Oh." I blink and think about that for a second. Why didn't Bakas just say that? And then I realize he was probably saying the *polyp* was nothing. This reminds me: "What about the polyp on the left side?"

"Well, this is how it works," he says, holding up his closed fist. "Imagine that your uterus is this fist. It's not a hole, just tissue resting together, and nestled inside there is this polyp, or lump, really. If you ovulate on the left side, there's a chance that things may get blocked by the polyp—but then, maybe not. If you ovulate on the right side, it's likely not going to have any effect at all."

"Okay," I say, completely relieved. Then I think of something else. "So the worry with women in their late thirties getting pregnant is that they don't necessarily ovulate every month anymore."

"Right. As you get older, it is less dependable that you will ovulate. Also, since you've had your eggs since you were born, they are getting older as you get older, and they are beginning to be less dependably healthy. That leads to a higher risk of miscarriage; though the egg may be fertilized, there may be something wrong that will lead to miscarriage. Often in cases like this, women don't even know they're pregnant, the miscarriage happens so early. It will just seem like a normal period. Fifty percent of miscarriages happen in that two-week period right after fertilization."

I nod, imagining my old and tired eggs sagging in my ovaries.

"The other thing I'm worried about is my antidepressants," I say. "I heard they can be bad, and they take a while to get out of your system. I don't want to stop them too quickly; I did that before and it was bad."

"Which one are you on?" he asks, flipping through my chart.

"Wellbutrin."

"Wellbutrin's been around for a long time," he says without hesitation. "But it's one of the less studied antidepressants in terms of pregnancy." He leans back and looks at me seriously. "The issue with antidepressants is this: You have to keep in mind that there is also a danger to the baby if you go off the medication and get depressed. Studies show depression leads to lower birth weights, premature births, that sort of thing. Depressed mothers tend to not eat well or get enough sleep, or they get too much sleep and not enough exercise."

"If I do go off, how slowly should I do it?"

"You'd want to do it over six or eight weeks. Have you talked to the doctor who prescribed the Wellbutrin for you?"

"I have an appointment in a couple of days."

"Talk to him. He can help you think this through. It's a very personal decision. The only thing I would caution against is doing anything too rash or too quickly."

I bring the conversation back to the baby. He answers all my questions about getting pregnant, and even puts my mind at ease when I ask him how my mother's gestational diabetes with all of her children might affect me.

After a couple of days off from thinking and doing anything about getting pregnant, I decide to get serious again about the sperm donor, because presumably I'm going to ovulate soon and will need the sperm to be ready to go when I am. The threat of not being able to get pregnant, and the possibility (however unfounded) that I was going to have to battle cervical cancer as well, has had a marvelously focusing effect, and I feel more prepared than ever to do this.

I make a list. What I want in a father for my kid:

1) Super smart with a super-advanced degree, preferably a PhD
2) Creative

3) Good-looking (better looking than me, preferably)

4) Healthy (oops, I guess that should have been first on the list)

5) Funny—wait a second, that's more for a date than for a father. Scratch that:

5) ~~Funny~~

6) Tall and thin, the opposite of me

Sitting back and looking at my list, I feel chagrined to see that what I really want is a Superfather to help create a Superkid—a kid who will have all the advantages I had, which I went on to squander by struggling with my weight my whole life. All the advantages I lost by my mother leaving me when I was young and by being abused in that boathouse.

It seems pretty clear, thinking in this way, that Olaf is the best choice even with his measly masters. But I delay a couple more days before finally ordering his sperm and committing to him. I know this is about something else, even as I sit in front of the computer with my credit card, ready to order, and I let myself be distracted by a work phone call or a bird flying by my window. Once I buy this sperm, that's it. I'm letting go, *forever,* of the dream I had for my life, even though I've come to understand that this dream is flawed and not really what I want, even though I have thought so for a very long time.

When I finally get on the phone with Claus to order the sperm, I tell him I've opted for the left-brain choice and have given up on the creative piece. Claus suggests those are the qualities I can give the baby myself, and I like that idea.

Olaf arrives on a Friday. My wild guess, based on a twenty-eight-day cycle, is that I'll ovulate on Tuesday. But who really knows? Part of me worries that I've taken sperm delivery too early, and that everything will melt before my little old egg pops down into my fallopian tube.

Each morning that weekend, before putting on my running gear to meet Pat and Lyde to do four miles, I use up another ovulation predictor stick to no avail. Nothing nothing nothing. What if, after all this, I don't ovulate?

I've thought a lot about my friend Bev these last few weeks. Eight years ago, she experienced much of what I'm going through and is now the single mother of a two-year-old daughter. She is the one who will come with me when I go for the injection.

A few years ago, we were talking at a holiday party at Sarah Lawrence. She had recently adopted her daughter, and I was thinking again about having a baby on my own.

"What about money?" I asked her. "And all the stuff you need for a baby? Childcare? Being alone?"

"Listen, you have a huge baby shower and get the stuff you need. And what you don't get, you can probably do without. A baby can sleep in a dresser drawer."

I thought about that for a moment. "That's not exactly the dream way to have a baby."

"We've all had dreams about these things." She looked at me long and hard. "When Jane interviewed me about adopting from her agency, she told me that many women who come in to adopt after trying for years to get pregnant have a lot of processing and grieving to do about the loss of their fertility."

I nodded as though I understood what she was saying, but I didn't really. I did know that she had tried a number of times to get pregnant before deciding to adopt.

"It sounds like you have some grieving to do as well," she said to me.

The Monday after Olaf arrives, I take Bev out to lunch. "How did you stand the waiting?"

She laughs. "It's a drag, all right."

"And the predictor kits cost a fortune."

She leans across the table and says quietly, "Do you know about the egg-white discharge?"

"The what?"

"That egg white–like discharge certain times of the month? Did you ever notice it?"

"Well, sure," I say. "Every month."

"Well, that's a sign that you're ovulating."

"Really?"

She nods at me sagely and I think, *That's great!* All afternoon after our lunch, I feel very fertile. The panic I felt over the weekend is gone; now I'm kind of elated. I get that discharge every month. *Ha!*

Meanwhile, Olaf, manifest in the DNA frozen inside his millions of sperm, waits in his beige container. I walk around him as he sits there, old routing bills stuck here and there.

I feel him there as I eat dinner. When I can't stand the silence anymore, I turn and say, "Want to join me?"

I lift the container to the chair across from me and talk about the egg-white discharge, about my day, about the fact that I'm drinking coffee again and am very happy about it.

After I've done the dishes, I take the container with me to the living room to sit beside me as I watch TV. There's not a peep of complaint when I keep changing the channel.

I take tons of pictures.

At work on Thursday I wonder how long I have before Olaf starts to melt. Tomorrow it will be one week since I picked him up. And he was put in that container with the dry ice a couple of days before that.

At lunch I go to the bathroom, and lo and behold—egg-white discharge! Egg-white discharge!

But I have no predictor thingies with me to confirm that I've ovulated, so I get in the car and race to Bronxville to buy some more. When I get back to the office, I make myself pee again on the little stick, and finally, finally, finally! It's a dark straight line!

"Ilona? It's time!" I say over the phone after shakily calling the doctors' office. I hear her call out to Dr. Bakas, "It's Alexandra. It's time."

"Tell her to get here as soon as she can."

Ilona says to me, "He has hospital rounds in an hour and a half, so the sooner you get here, the better."

I call Bev. She's supposed to be in a meeting in half an hour, but she'll get out of it, she says.

I zip home, belt Olaf into the back seat, grab my camera, race back to the school to pick up Bev, and race up to Mount Kisco.

I'm in Dr. Bakas's office within thirty minutes of picking up Bev, even though it's a forty-minute drive. Bev grips the edge of her passenger seat as we streak onto the Saw Mill River Parkway from the Sprain. "Easy does it," she says quietly.

I take a picture of Olaf in his seat belt before lugging the container into the office. Dr. Bakas looks it over and glances up at me. "Do you have any idea how to open this thing?"

"No," I say. "But I have these papers." I pull out the contract I signed with Scandinavian Cryobank and the papers that came pasted to the side of the canister. "You can call Claus; he said he was there to help if you needed it."

Dr. Bakas nods and says, "This'll take a little time; say, thirty minutes?"

We go for a walk, but it's very hot out and I'm impatient, so I drag us back in after twenty-five minutes. Ilona takes us to the back room, where Bakas is warming the sperm. It's a swim-up. As the solution warms, the two million or so happy and healthy sperm that have survived the long freeze will swim to the top. Then Bakas will suction them into a long syringe and inject them into me.

"Nice day to make a baby," Ilona says.

"A little humid, but not bad," I say.

"Supposed to rain tonight," Bev says. Dr. Bakas nods from where he is leaning against the counter beside the swimming sperm. He clicks his pen open and closed.

I shift a little, and the paper gown I'm wearing crinkles loudly. I'm sweating with excitement.

The little sperm-warming machine makes a small *beep,* and Bakas claps his hands. "Okay! Let's go."

I laugh and lean back and reach for Bev's hand because this is supposed to hurt a little.

"Let's make babies!" Bev says.

"Okay, one baby. I only need one baby."

Ilona says, "I'm crossing my fingers and toes."

I assume the Pap test position, and Bakas does his work on the other side of the paper sheet across my knees. Bev holds my hand, and I actually do need to squeeze it a little because it does hurt some, like a menstrual cramp.

When Dr. Bakas snaps off his gloves and says, "So? Do you want a cigarette?" everyone laughs, and I think it's partly from relief, because we had all suddenly gotten very quiet and tense.

But his joke does bring the thought of sex into the room—and the idea, especially for me, that this actually isn't sex. It is technology, not love, making a baby.

I feel very sad for a moment.

Then Bakas says, "It happens very quickly."

"Really?"

"Within minutes, they say."

So I keep myself perfectly still.

I'm home by three-thirty. I grab the phone and lie on the couch beneath my front-room window. This is the couch Olaf lounged on for most of the seven days he was with me. I prop my butt up a little and focus on getting pregnant, just in case Dr. Bakas isn't right about the instantaneousness of insemination.

It was great having Bev there today. It all seems possible when I talk to her. I realize too, as I sit there urging Olaf's sperm up toward my egg, how many of the women I know are raising their kids alone. Crystal has her son and daughter, and an ex-husband in the background; Christina, who also works in my office, has two sons, with fathers there on weekends.

But more important, I think about the poet at our school who went to China to adopt her daughter. She wanted a child and is raising her daughter alone. Then there is the woman I know through one of my community placements who told me one afternoon that she got married fifteen years ago because she wanted a child so badly. They adopted together, but the marriage soon collapsed. "I sometimes wish I could just have adopted on my own. It would have been simpler. But they didn't allow that sort of thing then."

And, of course, there is Bev.

I enjoy the feeling of being in good company.

I pull the phone toward me and phone Margaret first.

"Oh, Mrs.," she says to me. "I'm so excited. This is just the exact right thing to do."

"I feel that way too," I say. "I feel like it took forever to happen."

"It's only been a few weeks since the wedding!"

"I know. But you know how it is—when you're ready, you're ready."

I call Pat and give her a blow-by-blow of the afternoon (and tell her I'm not going to go running for a few days), then sit still for a moment before calling Linda. It is quiet on my street during the day. I'm not usually here when there aren't cars parked in every available space on our road. It is peaceful and lovely.

"Hey, Linda," I say when she answers the phone. We haven't talked about this since our run last month.

"So I did it," I say.

"Did what?"

"I just got back from the doctor. I ovulated today and we did the injection."

"Really? Wow, Alex, you work fast. Did Ken agree?"

"No, that's the thing! I found a sperm bank from Denmark."

"Denmark?"

"The father's name is Olaf."

"Oh, Alex. Your Denmark love rises up again!"

I laugh. "Yes it does." It's strange to me that I love Denmark so much, yet Linda was the one who lived there for three years. She spoke, read, and even learned to write papers in impeccable Danish by the time she came home. My time there seems like a mere flirtation compared with her more serious stay. I never did learn to read or write properly, and the numbers never stopped confounding me. But perhaps it's because I was there for only a year that it's possible for me to sustain my outrageously romantic ideas about Denmark.

"Well, I'm happy for you," Linda says.

"Thanks." I look out my window at the hazy sky. "So, what was the first sign you had that you were pregnant?"

"My breasts! Oh my god, they were so sensitive. I had to wear a bra all the time; I couldn't stand the feeling of fabric rubbing against them."

"And did you get morning sickness?"

"Just with Audrey; with the other two I barely knew I was pregnant."

"You got pregnant really easily, didn't you?"

"Yes. And Mom says she did too."

"Well, I hope that's true for me as well!"

Finally, I phone Mom and Dad. For some reason, I don't remember that conversation. I think Mom called Dad to the phone too. I know they were happy. I also know that I called them last. It strikes me that I always tell my parents last. And I wonder if I just need a number of rehearsals before the main show of telling them, or if it's something more deeply psychological, a kind of pushing away and withholding. Not giving them first access to my fresh excitement.

It's the same way my name change was, on the surface, about reshaping myself into the person I wanted to be, but was also, deep down, a kind of punishment. I wanted to punish my parents by forcing them to take back the name they gave me when I was born.

I can see now that before I was a parent myself, I was pretty arrogant and judgmental. It's amazing what empathy develops once you get a taste of the struggles your own parents have been through.

Two days later, on Saturday, I drive up to visit Crystal. We've done things outside of work a number of times since my breakdown in the kitchen, and I find her Southern demeanor relaxing. Her kids are with their father this weekend; she makes us lunch and we sit outside in the August sun. It feels like the country here, north of Goldens Bridge. After lunch, she takes me to see her garden. As we look at her heavy tomatoes sagging on the vine, I clutch at her suddenly as a wave of dizziness almost knocks me over. I put my hand on my pelvis, where there is a strange pinging. It almost hurts.

Crystal makes me lie down in the dappled sunlight beneath her enormous trees and asks if I want anything. I ask her to bring me some of her fantastic homemade lemonade because there's this awful, weird metallic taste in my mouth that I want to get rid of.

On Sunday, back on Olaf's couch again, I feel the pinging and know for sure that I'm pregnant. Absolutely for sure.

What I don't know is if it will stick.

SIX

I'm Pregnant!

I start running again on Tuesday. We resume our four-times-a-week schedule of running in the early morning. Along with Pat, I run with our friend Lyde, who is a history professor at Sarah Lawrence and a mother of four. Between the three of us, we have lost almost three hundred pounds. I know I've been able to sustain this new me because we've been doing it together—when one of us is flagging, the others pull her along.

"What's your existential question?" Lyde asks. Every run it is either this question or "You left me, you cried," which is our cue to supply her with what we've done since we saw one another last. Lyde is the deep thinker of our little running group—the question-asker, the devil's advocate, the brain.

And if Lyde is the brain, Pat is the passion—a powerful, beautiful, unsettling passion that I envy. And she comes by it honestly. Hers is a Bronx Italian family, with a drop of Irish in there for good measure. At Thanksgiving, Easter, and family birthday parties, I have watched as sudden bursts of angry passion, or loving passion, erupt—screaming fights or screams of laughter. In the beginning, with my cool, quiet Scandinavian upbringing, I found the fights alarming. *That's it,* I thought. *They are never going to talk to each other again.*

By watching them, I came to understand that for me, screaming laughter is fine. But fighting? That's different—I believe if you fight like that, express any kind of anger, it's over. You can't love each other anymore.

I also sometimes think, when I'm at their dinner table, watching the family joking back and forth, how I'm doing it again—insinuating myself into another large family. Wanting to belong somewhere I can never fully be. I'm not family, not blood, and I never will be.

When Lyde, Pat, and I start running again on Tuesdays, Pat talks about her existential issue first, so I can warm up my body and catch my stride. This is our usual routine. This morning Pat tells us about a fight she had last night with her husband.

She leans forward when she runs, and seems a little flat-footed, but she's the fastest of the three of us. And the least in love with running. She ran a pretty fast Mother's Day half marathon in May, and she usually wins in our age category when we sign up to do the races up in our area. She takes her heavy goldlike medals home to her four-year-old son, who tells the kids in his art camp, "My mom's an award-winning runner!"

We cross Palmer Avenue in silence, checking for traffic even though it's five-fifteen in the morning and we almost never see cars.

"What's your existential question, Alex?" Lyde asks as we hit the straight and blessedly flat stretch off the back streets after Palmer.

"I think I'm delusional," I say.

Lyde and Pat laugh, but I say, "No I'm not joking." I feel myself get mad at them and then think, *What's up with that?* "One minute I'm convinced I'm pregnant; the next I'm convinced I'm not. Every twinge makes me stop what I'm doing and try to feel if there's a baby. Sometimes I think I can even feel the cells splitting and growing."

"Oh, Alex," Pat says, "women say that all the time."

Lyde, who used IVF for her first two pregnancies, says, "Pat's right. It's totally normal."

"This morning I gave myself shit for even thinking about going running. What if I *am* pregnant and running shakes it loose?"

"If that worked, there would be no unwanted pregnancies, no Roe v. Wade." Pat says this back to us over her shoulder. We must be running too slowly. She's running ahead and a little faster to pull us along.

Through the whole run, I feel like I never quite catch my breath, but I won't let myself imagine that this might also be a sign that I am pregnant.

That week I scour the drugstores in Yonkers and Bronxville for pregnancy tests that work early. I see the ads on TV that talk about confirming pregnancy *five days earlier than regular tests!* But I can only find tests that tell you you're pregnant after you've already "missed" your period.

My period is still more than a week away. (I think. As I say, I have no clear concept of what my cycle is.)

I feel like I will lose my mind from waiting.

I buy the earliest tests I can find and am shocked by how expensive they are. I stop myself from using one on Wednesday and Thursday, which would be only a week since the injection. But on Friday, even though I know it's stupid and wasteful, I use one in the dark early morning before I meet Lyde and Pat for a run at the Rockefeller estate. The test is, not surprisingly, negative.

My existential question that morning is the very same, and I find myself saying the same words that I've said all week, in the same order, and I'm thankful that Pat and Lyde don't kill me.

At four forty-five the next morning, Saturday, I use my second pregnancy test and think I see, as I peer at the stick under the lamp on my kitchen table, a faint positive line there.

My eyes have deteriorated at an alarming rate since I turned forty—a real blow after a lifetime of twenty-twenty vision—so now I look around, wishing I had a magnifying glass or reading glasses so I could see this stick properly. I squint and squeeze my eyes. Is that a purple double line, or no? I hear the faint *toot* of a horn, put the stick down on a paper towel, grab my water, and run out the door to Lyde waiting in her van. Do I want the test to be positive so badly that I'm imagining a line? Is hoping so hard making me see what I want to see?

During our run, I talk to Pat and Lyde about my wishful thinking, and Pat tells me, "A faint line is totally valid. It still means you're pregnant." She runs backward for a second and looks at me. "Oh my god!"

"Really?" Hope surges up from my belly.

Pat turns around again but says over her shoulder. "This is great!"

As we run through the morning half-light, I think, *What if my half-blind eyes just imagined that faint line?*

This "yes I am, no I'm not" roller coaster is turning my stomach. I feel queasy.

"It's true," Lyde says. "They work by detecting a hormone that's only there if you're pregnant, HGG or HCG or something. It takes a while to build up. That's why they don't work right away."

"Really?"

Pat says, "Really! Go to the doctor on Monday and get them to do a blood test."

I'm dumbfounded and scared and excited now. This could be it. Couldn't it?

That Saturday afternoon, I have a date.

It is with Michael, a friend of Pat's who lives in Massachusetts near Jenn and Dave. We've talked a few times. He's smart and funny—at least on the phone.

As I get ready, I think how twisted and torn I felt calling Claus and ordering Olaf's sperm. How I felt as if I was letting go of romantic love and the white picket fence and life in the normal lane—thin, married, with children.

But the fact that I jumped all over the idea of calling Michael when Pat mentioned it makes me think that I didn't *really* give up on the idea of having it all. That the normalcy-seeking romantic in me wasn't going to sacrifice that easily.

Today Michael is coming almost halfway to Yonkers for a huge annual Labor Day weekend party at a friend's house near Poughkeepsie. It is only an hour's drive for me. When he suggested that I come up for the party and meet him there, I agreed, even though it made me nervous.

As I pull on my short black skirt, I check out the running muscles along my thighs, suck in my stomach, look at my profile. I'm wearing a black flowered gauze shirt over a black camisole. My hair is newly high-lighted and cut in long, flowing layers. I even blow-dried it, so it's fluffy.

I look at myself and think, *It's all good.*

The run this morning boosted my mood, and I feel more stable and solid than I have all week. The idea that a faint line is still a line buoys me too, though a worrisome little voice in the back of my head wonders, *Did you really see it?*

The party is outdoors, and Michael said to bring a bathing suit for the pool, but I'm not ready for that. I feel great about my new body, but not *that* great.

I pull up to the house and am a little alarmed to see forty cars parked across the large driveway and on the lawn. I get out of my car in the warm afternoon. I hear voices to my right, but I head left toward the house and through what seems like the front door. But it takes me into a cavernous, ancient room with nothing but a fireplace and the smell of ancient smoke. It is a sad, oppressive room. The ceiling is low and the windows are small. I notice stairs in the far corner and skedaddle over there.

Upstairs, I wander around until I find the kitchen. Sitting on a stool is a very pregnant woman (also wearing a gauzy black top, I notice), drinking a tall glass of water with ice. The condensation on the side of the glass drips down onto the lap of her long, gauzy black skirt.

"Hi," I say, and she jumps.

"I didn't hear you." She is annoyed.

"I'm sorry; I didn't mean to scare you." She has a light sheen of sweat across her face, and she looks tired.

"Must be hard to be so pregnant in August," I say, feeling a kind of kinship with her. *Hey,* I think, *that could be me in eight months.*

She gets a look across her face—irritation, I think. Like she hates that people talk to her about her pregnancy. She shrugs. "It would be hard anytime."

My arms and hands feel enormous suddenly, hanging at my sides. I can think of nothing to say.

"Everyone is out by the pool." She points to the back door.

I nod and leave quickly.

It is only as I step outside and look back that I realize how very large the house is. Granted, the kitchen alone is the size of the whole first floor of my apartment, but as I walk to the pool, I see how section after section has been added over time. The original stone house is still discernible at the center, with the newer parts sort of bubbling up and around it.

Michael's friend Reggie, the host, is very rich. This house has been in his family for generations. Someone way back had it built as a summerhouse. He is the great-grandson or great-great-grandson of some industrialist (I wasn't really listening when Michael explained it to me) who owned something like General Electric or the Transcontinental Railway. But Reggie himself is into politics, the backroom kind. He's also a philanthropist—his job is doling out charitable gifts. Most of the people here would be like that, Michael said. Rich, powerful. He became friends with all of them when he was at Harvard. He is the poverty-stricken, leftist thorn in their side, he says. But he loves them all like brothers. The pregnant woman in the kitchen, it turns out, is the wife of his best friend from those days.

As I pick my way across the uneven grass in my high-heeled sandals, I say to myself, *I am pretty, I am witty, and I am normal. Hey, perhaps I'm more than normal.* I think about the way I looked this morning in the mirror: the blond hair, the slenderish body. Perhaps I am finally the heroine of my own romance story, just like I have always wanted to be, and here is the kind of party I always imagined the heroine going to. *Be happy,* I say to myself. *You belong here.*

At the pool I look around and wonder which one of the thirty or so men is Michael. Some boys and men are in the pool. No women, I notice, though on the other side I see a couple in bikinis on loungers, their faces shadowed under large floppy hats. A kid right next to me cannonballs into the pool. I jump back and watch as water splashes up onto the cream-colored tiles of the patio. I wonder for a moment why the pool is so far from the house—a good hundred yards. I like it, though. It goes with the house's randomness. I see a tennis court even farther from the house, and opposite us, on the other side, sprawls an apple orchard.

Right next to me is a table of crudités and crackers and cheeses and dips and chips and such. There is a drinks table over by the lounging bikini women. A blond and carefully tanned woman comes up to the table and puts what looks like Rondelé onto a cracker. She smiles at me and I smile back.

"You don't happen to know who Michael Drake is, do you?" I ask her, then feel bad because her mouth is full and she can't talk. But she nods amiably and points to the other side of the pool.

"I'm supposed to be meeting him here," I say. She gives me a look like, *You're meeting him here but you don't know what he looks like?* I add, a little breathlessly, "It's kind of like a blind date." But I don't continue, since I'm not sure how much Michael would want people to know.

"That's brave," she says after swallowing her cracker. She has a fabulous, thick Swedish accent. She sounds just like my Aunty Rut, who was married to my mother's brother, and I look at her fully now and resist the urge to hug her. I feel I have suddenly found a friend in this party of strangers. She calls out across the pool, "Michael!"

And a blond man, medium height, wearing a tan shirt and khaki shorts, starts walking toward us. My first thought is, *He's not bad looking. He's kind of handsome in an animated sort of way.* My second thought is, *Here's a man who never sleeps, a jumpy and jittery man, ready to laugh or tell a joke.*

"You made it!" he says and shakes my hand. "This is Anya," he says, putting his arm around the shoulder of my new Swedish friend. "That's her husband, Anders, over there, and their two kids in the pool." It isn't hard to pick out any of them—one a whiter blond than the other. Anders is just as tanned as Anya is. When he sees us looking at him, he waves his empty drink glass at her.

"Uh," she says to us, "I promised him a refill. Nice to meet you . . . ?"

"Alexandra," I say quickly, and we shake hands.

"Enjoy the party." (En*joy* the party!) I laugh with delight.

Michael turns to me and says, "Welcome. I'm glad we could arrange this." We look at each other and wonder what to say. Michael looks back at Anders and Anya and says, "He, by the way, is the Swedish ambassador to the United States." He points out men and women all around the pool, telling me they are the CEO of this, the president of that, the chairman of the board of whatever. None of the names stay with me, because they don't mean anything. I don't even recognize most of the company names. That doesn't stop me from being impressed, though. I've never been in such exalted company before, and all I can think is that they look like anybody else I've known. Maybe their clothes and their haircuts are a little better, but even that's hard to tell when everyone is wearing khakis and T-shirts or has just come from the pool.

Michael and I chitchat for a while, continuing conversations we have started over the phone in the last two weeks. Reggie, our host, comes by, and Michael introduces us. He's a big, jovial guy whose eyes slide over and past me as he smiles and says, "Nice to meet you." He turns to Michael and says, "Hey, can you give me a hand with the tables? It's time to set up for dinner." Michael looks at me and I say, "Of course." I'm pretending to be cool and okay. I stand for a while, wondering what to do with my hands, trying not to eat too much even though the table is right beside me.

Before long, the handsome Anders comes by for veggies. He points to one of his kids in the pool and says, "I took him into the pool to teach him to swim when he was six months old."

I nod, remembering films I've seen with mothers dunking their infants in the water, and how their little arms and legs automatically do the dog paddle. When Anders looks at me I have trouble deciding which eye to look into because his left eye moves all over the place, independent of the other.

"Look in this eye," he says to me, pointing to his right eye. His accent isn't as strong as his wife's, just soft enough to be charming, and his voice is melodious. "This other one is a little wonky." He laughs and so do I, and I feel like I've fallen in love.

I tell him about my uncle who sang in the Gothenburg opera, and his wife, Rut, who was famous in her day. He says he thinks he remembers hearing her sing, but a long while ago, and I say yes, she has been retired for years, just teaching now. And your uncle? he asks. "He died a few years ago," I say.

"Oh, I'm so sorry."

"Thank you." I look in Anders' good eye, feel his engagement with me. I find myself saying, "The one thing I feel good about, though, is when he turned sixty—you know what a big deal that is in Scandinavia—I decided at the last second to fly there for the weekend to surprise him." I laugh, remembering how tired I was, how much like a jet-setter I felt.

"You did?" He laughs with me, and crinkles appear in the tanned skin around his eyes.

"It was the most impulsive thing I've ever done, and people were like, 'Who do you think you are, flying to Sweden for the weekend?' I stopped telling people. I felt a little embarrassed, actually."

I look at his children in the pool and say, "But you know, he died two years later, and that birthday weekend was the last time I saw him."

"Yes," he says, looking at his kids too. "Such moments are important in a family." He smiles at me. "That's a nice story."

It was a stretch to get the money to go, I remember. I was a grad student, no job. But now who remembers the money? So much money has come and gone in my life since then, but that birthday party was spectacular, hundreds of people gathered in the old Gothenburg opera house to wish him a happy sixtieth.

How much he loved me. How much I loved him. That's what's important. That's what will stay with me forever.

Dinner is outside on the patio behind the kitchen at ten large round tables. The sun sets to the left behind the apple trees; the pool is empty now, behind the trees to the right.

There is roast chicken and prime rib and salads beyond counting. Italian bread. Whipped butter.

I hang back, looking for Michael, who hasn't made an appearance again. But I begin to feel ridiculous standing on the outskirts and decide to just get in line, figuring he'll show up eventually. Once I'm through, I walk out onto the patio and begin to look for Anders and Anya, thinking I could sit with them. But as I crane my neck around, I notice that Michael is already at a table, motioning me toward him. I keep looking for the Swedish couple, thinking they could come sit with us, but they and their two kids are already seated with our host, closer to the orchard.

Sitting at the table with Michael is the pregnant lady from the kitchen and a very tall man I'm assuming is her husband—he's a good foot and a half taller than she is, and I can understand now why her belly is so very large. I groan a little inside when I see her, particularly when I realize that the only free seat is next to hers.

Heather and Bill are their names. Michael does a lot of talking, and I throw in a comment or two. I do find out, after a few very carefully posed questions, that she is due in two weeks, that she and Bill have just bought an apartment in Manhattan.

I refuse wine and feel self-conscious, but no one seems to notice. Michael and Bill drink heartily. Heather drinks a sip or two of white wine, a little defiantly, it seems to me. She picks at her food and I think, *I hope I'm like that when I'm pregnant.* Disinterested in food. Disdainful.

I say in my head: *Dear God, please let me be that way. Don't let me gain all the weight back when I'm pregnant. Please, God, don't let that happen.*

But God? Make sure I'm actually pregnant first. That's the first order of business. We can talk about the weight later. Sorry to spring so much on you at one time.

I find myself looking at Heather a lot, covertly, so as not to weird her out. Even with her shiny face she's gorgeous, and her tall husband is too. I wonder if they have any idea about how privileged they are, with their talk of nannies and their new West Village apartment (it's a townhouse, really, with three stories) and their February vacation to Barbados. "I think we'll go again this February," Bill tells Michael, although Heather doesn't look very enthusiastic. I suddenly feel a little queasy about all the money around me, as I catch snatches of conversation about how this one's Bentley is "like a tank!" and how hard it is to find a nanny who "speaks proper English."

Or maybe I'm just being cranky because I feel so unwelcome. Reggie was dismissive when Michael introduced us; Heather was curt in the kitchen, and even now the back of her shoulder is turned toward me as she focuses on her husband. The man to my right spoke with me for a moment at the beginning of dinner but is now engaged in a heated discussion about the stock market with a man beside Michael across the table. I'm a little cranky with Michael too, that he didn't save a seat beside him. What was he thinking?

I look to the west, where the orange ball of the sun is slipping below the apple trees. How very spectacular. Imagine being able to just walk out and sit here in the sunset whenever you want. If this were a Harlequin romance—and wasn't I just thinking I was finally the heroine of my own Harlequin romance?—I would meet Reggie's older, more brooding brother, the true heir to all this magnificence, right about now. Or Reggie and I would have had a spark, would meet each other's eyes now across the crowded patio.

But that isn't happening, which is maybe why I feel kind of deflated. I am at my skinniest, at my prettiest, and the man I have assigned the role of the hero doesn't notice me. The way he looked at me, or rather didn't look at me, is as familiar as rain. I just didn't think it would keep happening after I lost weight.

Maybe that sort of thing happens to normal, pretty girls too. I always thought only fat and ugly girls knew what that felt like.

After dinner I help with clearing the tables, because Michael has taken off again, to smoke some pot I think, judging from the wink-wink, nudge-nudge dance he did before he left. Back and forth from the yard to the kitchen, I tote plates and cutlery. I make a couple of jokes with a woman I'm assuming is Reggie's wife, and she is kind enough, though she initiates nothing. When we've almost finished, I come in and see Michael and Bill and Reggie and a couple of well-built, tall men leaning over a bowl of chips from the appetizer portion of the evening, munching and waiting for a fresh pot of coffee to brew.

They are laughing the giddy, silly laugh of people who have just smoked some good pot, and Michael pulls me over and introduces me to the new folk. I can't remember their names. Then I step back because they are pushing each other and laughing, making kissing sounds and slapping one another on the bum, and, as sometimes happens with me, my mouth lets words out before my brain has actually vetted them and I say, laughing, "Whoa, do you want me to leave you gentlemen alone?"

In the sudden silence that follows, all eyes on me, the coffee pot squirts a very loud burst of steam and Reggie frowns, about to say something, when Heather waddles in from the yard, stops in the doorway, and, holding her back, says into the steam-filled silence, "Bill, are you ready to go? I'm really tired."

As he goes to her, the conversation resumes, and I slip away, thinking, *When am I Ever Ever Ever! going to learn that you can't tease straight men about their sexuality?* No way, no how. I think back to the I Teased Him

About Being Gay and Consequently Never Heard from Him Again Guy, and I remember that he was rich too. Hmm.

I hang out on the screened-in porch on the side of the house and look at the purplish-red horizon turning blue-black in the gaps between the apple trees. I think about the evening and my hopefulness as I was getting dressed this afternoon.

I think I'm done with this hero stuff. There's no such thing. Okay, I knew that before, but I also know something else now: This isn't my crowd; these aren't the people I'm interested in talking to.

Later it will be clear to me that this moment is the beginning of the true end of my hero/heroine, prince/princess fantasies, the rescue kind. This is where that part of the mansion's stone wall, as opposed to a white picket fence, falls into the moat, never to be put up again.

After about half an hour, Michael sticks his head into the porch, sees me there, and sits on the adjacent couch. "There you are," he says.

"Did Anders and Anya leave?"

Michael nods.

"That's too bad. I would've liked to say goodbye to them."

"Almost everyone is gone," Michael says. I think about getting up to go too, but I don't.

We talk as the evening grows cool. We talk about everything: politics, depression, alcoholism, all the biggies. He takes Luvox and says it works for him. He's in Freudian therapy four times a week. He's battled alcohol and drug addiction but feels he's got it under control now. I nod and look away from his bloodshot eyes. *Is this a man I can fall in love with?* My critical faculties are jumping up and down to be heard: Clinical depression! Drugs! No real job!

There I go again, I think. *No wonder I'm still single. No wonder I've never been in love.*

But he does have the smart, witty thing going for him. I dig a man who can make me laugh. He reminds me a little of Jon Stewart from *The Daily Show*—same kind of humor and slanted look at politics and life in the United States today. He doesn't have a job, per se, but he's been helping out with a global warming conference scheduled for mid-September; it's taking a lot of time but paying very little. He also writes essays and such for cash, but that hasn't been very lucrative. I ask him how he's surviving, and he says, with a little smile, "I have a very understanding mother."

"Hmm," I say.

At around eleven o'clock, he walks me back to my car in the pitch blackness. There is no moon and certainly no streetlights out here in the country. I stumble a couple of times, and he catches me, and finally he just holds my arm the whole way. We kiss a little at the car—not enough for me to even decide whether it's a good kiss.

"I'll call you," he says.

"Great."

Driving home, I think again about the obvious trouble spots: no money, no job (what is it with me and men who don't have jobs?), and the drug and alcohol addiction stuff I glimpsed (I might also ask, what is it with me and men with addictions?). Against these factors, I weigh my attraction to his wit and humor.

It's too close to call, so I'll leave this one up to fate. Let's just see if he even calls me after that rather embarrassing display of foot-in-mouth disease in front of his friends in the kitchen. As I turn off the dark back road onto the Taconic, I vow *never* to joke with a straight man about his sexuality again.

Dr. McGroary draws some blood on Monday to check my HCG levels, though he's a little amazed that I saw anything on the pregnancy test so soon after we did the injection. Nevertheless, he takes me into his office and pulls out a little paper wheel. "Based on the insemination date—August twenty-ninth, right?—you would be due on May twenty-first."

That date sounds significant, so I pull out my planner and see that the twenty-first is commencement. *Oh, man! That would be super convenient. School will be done; nothing to worry about at my work except the summer programs, but my boss can handle them. Great great great. Easy to remember my due date too!* Still, I can't quite believe I'm really pregnant, since I'm as skeptical as McGroary about the faint positive. I decide not to tell everyone until the blood test comes back.

Ilona smiles and says to me as I leave, "I'll call you as soon as I hear anything!"

Back at the office, school is now in full swing. Orientation was last week, and this is the first week of classes, so no one can find the right classrooms. I spend the day sorting out double bookings and students who come back from their first class hating the professor, a fellow student, the room they're in, or how far they have to walk from the parking lot to the classroom.

By the end of the day, despite my vow of silence, I've told everyone in the office about my faint positive, feeling both fraudulent and pregnant.

People get really excited by the idea of pregnancy. I mean screaming-jumping-hand-clapping excited. Some I haven't even told about trying; others, like Crystal, have been with me the whole way. Pat nods sagely from the edge of the room, since she almost always knows things as soon as I do. Sometimes she guesses about things before they've even happened.

I can't sleep that night, and in the morning I call Ilona, because I can't wait anymore.

"I was just about to call you," she says. "They came in this morning. You're pregnant!"

"Pat! Pat!" I jump up and scream out my door toward her office. "I'm pregnant!"

"Alexandra! Alexandra!" I hear Ilona's voice calling me from the phone as Pat comes in and hugs me, phone and all. "Dr. McGroary wants you to come in again tomorrow," I faintly hear her say, "for another blood test. The HCG level was a little low, so we just want to make sure it doubles over the next couple days. Can you come in?"

"Anytime!" I say, Pat and I jumping up and down in each other's arms. Then the low-hormone comment registers and I pull away. "It's low? Is that bad?"

"It's probably just because it's early. We always have people come in again in two days to be sure that the hormone levels double."

After Pat and I stop laughing, I sit down and call Margaret at the office. "This is it!" I tell her. "I'm pregnant!"

"Mrs.!" she screams so loud, I have to pull the phone from my ear. "Only you, my Mrs., would get pregnant on the first try! That's amazing."

Linda screams too when I call her, and I lean back in my office chair and stare at the peeling paint beside my tiny window. *Well,* I think, *here we go!*

It's another thirty-minute drive up to Mount Kisco the next day, and another long day and night of waiting for the blood-test results. Michael hasn't called me or emailed me. He usually sends me a joke or a manifesto of some kind every few days, so I'm guessing I blew that one.

School is chaotic, but my runs in the morning with Lyde and Pat keep me grounded. It crosses my mind that I may be harming the baby by breathing so hard and heating myself up like this, so I order a book on running and pregnancy from Amazon and sit around waiting for that too.

That night I call Mom and Dad. Dad answers the phone. "So," I say, "I'm pregnant."

"Oh, good for you, kid!" Dad says, and then I hear him say, "Mimi! It's Donna."

I hear the other extension pick up, and I say, "Mom, the doctor's office called me today. We did a blood test yesterday and I'm pregnant!"

Mom starts to laugh and she says, "Is this the Danish place you used?"

"Yes, I used a Danish donor."

Mom laughs. "The first try. That's amazing."

"That's good, Donna," Dad says. "I'm hanging up now; you two can talk."

"How do you feel?" Mom asks.

"I don't know. Sort of the same, just dizzy once in a while."

"I always knew I was pregnant when my breasts got tender."

"No changes there yet for me."

"Wow, the first try." I can hear the smile in her voice. "It was meant to be."

After I hang up I wonder if I should tell anyone else. I want to, but several women have warned me not to, saying they did call everyone, only to have to do it all over again in reverse when they had a miscarriage. But I remember a conversation I had with Bev when she was going through disappointments in her adoption journey—mothers choosing to parent their babies after all, leaving Bev to start again and wait to be chosen by another mother. Twice this happened, and in the midst of this, Bev told me it was as important for her to have her friends and family with her in sadness as in happiness. They were a comfort to her. Perhaps it was even *more* important that they be with her then. She shrugged and said, "Why be sad alone?"

So I do call everyone I know to tell them I'm pregnant, and, happily, it takes up a lot of the waiting time for the results of the second blood test.

Late in the afternoon the next day, Ilona calls me for Dr. McGroary. The numbers are fine, nice and strong now, she says. No need to worry. He wants to schedule me for an ultrasound in a month to take a peek at the heartbeat. I make like I'm busy that week and finagle an appointment the week before. (One of the friends I called last night mentioned that she didn't wait for the eighth week to get an ultrasound. Her midwife did it at six weeks, and they saw the heartbeat no problem.) If I have to wait a whole month, I will lose my mind.

The weirdest thing about pregnancy, which no one told me about, is that once your pregnancy is confirmed, you get two bonus weeks added to your total pregnancy weeks, which means they measure how pregnant you are from your last period, not from when you were inseminated. I can see the rationale for that, since most women are not as certain as I am when they were inseminated. So even though I know I've been pregnant for only two weeks at this point, they've given me two extra weeks, so ta-da! I'm four weeks pregnant already!

Now that I am a bona fide pregnant woman, my most overwhelming feeling is of being normal—well, mostly normal. What I mean is, I feel like I'm finally swimming in the same stream as every other woman (except my stream had no man in it). After so many years of feeling different and out of it—with friends dating and marrying and being normal, and my feeling normal only intermittently, usually when I was thin—I am pregnant. I am going to be a mother.

I also feel tired and nauseated all the time. Into my third real week (or my fifth week in the land of bonuses), I'm having trouble sticking to my no-sugar, no-flour routine. I crave white food. I've had pregnant friends who craved only fruit, particularly watermelon. That was the kind of pregnant woman I wanted to be. But it looks like I'm more of the white bread/rice/pad Thai kind of pregnant woman. Pad Thai is what I crave more than words can express. I dream about it. Late one night, when I should be sleeping because I'm so tired, I scatter all my cookbooks looking for the low-fat pad Thai recipe I've used before, and I make plans to go to the Chinese grocery store on Central Avenue to get fish sauce. In the morning, though, I put the books away. I will not ruin my three years of good health now; I will not jeopardize my passport into the land of normalcy. I will not surrender.

Still, the nausea worsens, and I'm so very tired.

I drive to Mount Kisco for my ultrasound appointment, drinking a big bottle of seltzer. I think back to my university days of handing cup after cup of water to Margaret before her ultrasound to see if she was pregnant, and our disappointment that the scan showed no baby. *Now I get to have something exciting in my life too,* I think. But now I see that for what it was: a false thought driven by a kind of self-pity. I've done plenty of exciting things in my life. Why must I always denigrate what I have, and what I have done?

I'm a little early for my appointment, so I sit on the couch in the waiting room, looking at all the photos on the bulletin board of Bakas and McGroary, holding the babies they have delivered. There are parenting magazines all over the coffee table in front of me, and I can't resist. I grab one at random and start to flip through it. I'm a part of this fraternity (or would that be maternity?) now. *I'm one of them. That's me,* I think, looking at the pretty pregnant women in the magazine, although I'm amazed at how spindly some of their arms are. Their bodies are crazy thin, and they have these huge beach balls blowing out from their bellies. They look a little like the pictures of the starving, drought-stricken Biafran kids with distended bellies that I used to see when I was a kid.

Sylvia, the ultrasound technician, calls me in and gives me a moment to change into one of those paper gowns again. I lie back on the examination table and remember all of us laughing such a short time ago. *Let's make a baby!*

I'm smiling when she comes back in, and when she asks how I am, I tell her the story of my last visit to this room. She says, "They're great doctors here. Bakas delivered both my kids. I've never met a doctor who was so close to being a midwife. He'll never force anything on you. He'll listen."

As she spreads cold jelly on my belly, she tells me about how all the nurses at North Westchester hospital—down the road where Bakas and Mc-Groary have privileges—use these doctors too.

I lie back, smile at the ceiling, and say a prayer of thanks to Pat for introducing me to Dr. Bakas five years ago.

Sylvia runs the ultrasound apparatus over the skin of my lower pelvis and looks intently at the gray and black images on the screen. She's all serious and professional now, pressing the wand down into my belly and my very full bladder. I have to focus in order not to pee.

"Hmm," she says. "Here's the sac," she says, pointing to something that looks vaguely circular. "I'm not seeing a heartbeat."

She presses and looks some more. I think about what I've read on the web about "empty sac" pregnancies that never evolve, babies that never grow or develop a heart, even though the placenta and everything is in place.

"Is it empty? Is there nothing there?"

"How far along are you?"

For a moment I'm not sure how to answer. Should I say five weeks or seven weeks? "Seven weeks along," I say.

"Oh, well, that must be it. It's just too early. I'll talk to Dr. Bakas, but I think you should make another appointment and come back either next week or the week after." I nod. I think, *Oh please don't let this be bad. Don't take away my baby now.*

"Your HCG numbers have been going up, right?"

"Yes, so far."

"That's good. Okay, I'll let you go to the bathroom now. Remember to leave a urine sample as well. You'll need to do that every visit from now on."

"Okay." I go into the bathroom and dwell on the idea of an empty sac. I see empty burlap sacks for some reason, flour scattered out of them.

I leave the sample, get dressed, and walk to the front with my planner in hand. I arrange to return the following Friday at nine-fifteen, then walk out of the office in a kind of trance, averting my eyes from the parenting magazines and the baby pictures on the walls.

Clearly it's not time to celebrate just yet. I think I need to lay low a little now, focus on making the little zygote inside me grow into a heart-beating fetus. *Please, God, give me this and I won't bug you about gaining weight during pregnancy. I'll not bug you about other, more petty stuff if you just give me this one big thing.*

SEVEN

Maybe I'm Not Pregnant

I've been stepping down off the Wellbutrin, trying not to go too fast, worried all the time about the multiplying cells deep inside me. Am I perverting the course of their multiplying? This is my last week on the medication, at fifty milligrams a day; then it will take a few weeks longer still for it to be completely out of my system.

I worry about the no-heartbeat evening, and that the heaviness I'm feeling is the beginning of depression brought on by withdrawal. This is what it starts out like: can't move, dark thoughts, heavy listlessness.

But perhaps this is what it feels like to be pregnant.

I think about my mom then, her four pregnancies and three children.

Is this how she felt? Worried, heavy, even a little hopeless? Wow, if I feel like this after going through the mere possibility of an empty-sac pregnancy, how must Mom have felt to go months and months with a baby, only to lose him at term? To have him die inside her womb and then stay there for days—until she asked a friend, "Why is the baby not moving anymore?" To go to the hospital and give birth to a dead baby boy she and my father named Gordon and buried quietly at the edge of the cemetery just outside of town.

I put my hand to my belly. I have always felt sad that I never got to know this older brother, Gordon, but now I feel something else altogether: a kinship with my mother. The turmoil I've felt over the last weeks—the mood swings, feeling crazy, feeling suddenly angry—must have been what it was like for her too.

This morning, after leaving Jackie and making a new appointment, I get into my car, still trancelike. It seems to me, as I sit there with the car running and the air-conditioning on, that the nausea I have been feeling the last week is suddenly much worse. So much worse, in fact, that I can't take it. I don't want to eat spelt toast anymore; I don't want fruit, grilled chicken, or salad. When I think now about eating all these foods, which I have been eating without hesitation for three years, it is like imagining a large stone in my stomach.

All I want right now is a soda cracker.

I drive back toward school but detour into the Stop & Shop a block from the doctor's office. I feel something let go, like an anchor chain breaking. There's a slight tug, and then the ship just floats out to sea.

I go in and buy soda crackers. And rice noodles and oyster sauce. Perhaps I can use it instead of fish sauce in some pad Thai tonight. And a box of cookies. And a bottle of seltzer.

I eat two of the cookies sitting in the car in the parking lot, fast, like it's not actually happening. Then I feel sick. Too much sweetness too fast.

I sit with my head on the steering wheel and close my eyes.

What have I done?

When I get into the office, Pat follows me upstairs and sits in my visitors' chair.

"What happened? You look terrible."

I glance at her and wonder which is worse, the empty sac or the cookies in the parking lot. Pat and I have pulled each other along these last few years, and those cookies make me feel like I've betrayed her.

"There was no heartbeat."

"What does that mean?"

"Well, either it's too early or there's a problem." I bend down to turn on my computer, and the low-grade nausea intensifies for a second but then lets go as I sit up. "I guess we'll know next week. I go back on Friday."

Pat says, "You're just assuming it's bad, aren't you?"

"Kind of."

"Don't do that to yourself."

"But it's weird—I'm not. Inside I feel tense and anxious, but in my head I'm totally calm, like, *Don't jump to conclusions!*"

"Exactly—don't jump to conclusions!"

"I'm just really tired." I feel my face quiver and stop myself from crying. I think back to the cookies and how I ate six more of them as I drove back to the office, even though they made me feel shaky and awful.

Pat stands up and gives me a hug. "Oh, Alex, I'm sorry." I close my eyes, because this only makes me want to cry even more.

I'm doing it again—I'm lying about food. I'm not going to tell her, and it's going to sit there between us.

"I went in there so unprepared," I say when she stands up. "Like a kid, sort of, who still doesn't expect bad things to happen. Then, when she showed me the dark empty sac, I felt . . . I don't know. Alone."

"I'll go with you next week," she says.

I nod. "That'd be great."

"And don't go by yourself to any more of these appointments."

"You're right." I nod. "I guess it was all going too well," I say.

"What do you mean?"

"Nothing." I shake my head. "It's okay. It will be okay."

"What are you thinking? You're thinking this is your fault or something, aren't you? Well, it's not. Don't jump to conclusions."

I nod and Pat lets it go and walks into her office, and I turn and stare at my computer screen.

I guess I actually think, deep down, that I don't deserve to be pregnant. I'm trying to fast-track myself somewhere I'm not supposed to go. If you can't get a man, you can't have a family. End of story.

A few days later I feel better, but still kind of crazy, wanting to eat all the time.

I sit on my favorite chair, a wingback that I rescued from the curb on garbage night and refinished, and I rest my pulsing legs on the black coffee table I found at a different curbside on a different garbage day. I think about making pad Thai, but I can't seem to move. I eat half a sleeve of soda crackers instead and drink a quart of seltzer.

When the phone rings, I put aside the crackers and check the phone number on the living room extension, but I don't recognize it, so I don't answer it. I wait for the machine to pick up. And when it does, Michael's voice fills the room.

It's been over a month since the Labor Day party, and I have been assuming that since he hasn't called, he's not going to. And part of me has been relieved. There were issues, it seems to me. Risks with him, the drugs, the not working, the way he said, "I have a very understanding mother." I can imagine, somehow, being in the position of a caregiver. Besides, there's this uncertain pregnancy. When would I tell him? What would I tell him? "I think maybe I'm going to have a baby"?

But I am curious enough about his calling that I pick up the phone. "Hey there, I'm here. I was just screening my calls."

"But you picked up for me. I'm flattered."

"Well, what can I say?"

Michael doesn't say anything for a moment, and I don't either, mostly because I can't think of anything.

"I'm sorry that I haven't been in touch. I've been working on this global warming conference, and I've been in D.C. for the last two weeks. I didn't bring your number. I'm sorry."

"Oh, okay." *I guess that's a valid excuse.* "How is the conference going?"

"It's a lot of work. But we've got some senators coming and some high-profile activists. It's going to be good. I have to write a bunch of press releases and stuff right now. I'm kind of procrastinating."

"Well, that's a good time to call someone you haven't talked to in a while." *Ew. Did that sound as bitchy as I think it did?* I try to think of something to say to recover, but my mind is blank.

"So, are you still planning to come up and visit your friends in North Adams?" he asks.

That's right, I had told him I was going to visit Jenn and Dave at the end of September. "I talked to them a couple of days ago, and unless something changes, I'm going up this weekend." I'm perfectly happy that we have skipped right over talking about the Labor Day party.

"So, do you want to come up to Brandon at some point too, so we can have a real date?"

"Well." I think about it for a second and realize that I don't want to. What I really want is for him to come down to North Adams. It'll be a long haul for me to go to him on top of the drive to North Adams, especially with how tired I have been. Besides, I went to Poughkeepsie to see him, so it seems to me that it is his turn.

"Can we play it by ear?" I say, wishing I could just tell him directly that I would like him to come to me, even bring me flowers. "It's kind of a long drive. To then drive up to you seems like a lot right now. Maybe we can talk when I get there, see if I have the energy."

"Sure, and I'll try and get a lot of work done before then too, so I'll feel less stressed."

Michael calls me on Friday and says he would really like to see me on Saturday. He knows about a cute restaurant in a cute little town about fifteen minutes from Jenn and Dave's place. Can I see myself making that drive?

I look out the tiny window over my desk at work and wonder how much I care about this. The struggle over where we will meet next is beginning to feel like a power play. Do I want to make him come the whole way to North Adams just to make a point?

After thinking about it, I realize that I've made my point already. So I say sure, that's fine. I can drive fifteen minutes. Because I can, and to make any more of it would feel petty.

I get to Jenn and Dave's place around eight, while Dave is still putting Sophie to bed. Jenn is in the kitchen, bending sideways to put dishes in the dishwasher because her belly is so far out in front of her. She still has four weeks to go, but she says she's already busting out of all the maternity clothes she wore last time.

"It's that second pregnancy. You have no stomach muscles left, so the belly goes out forever."

"Oh, it's good to see you, Jenn," I say, and we hug awkwardly around her belly and laugh.

"Do you want some seltzer?" she asks, opening the fridge.

"Of course."

We sit in the living room, listening to the rumblings of David's deep voice telling Sophie a story. I lie back on the couch because I'm feeling nauseated again, though the seltzer helps. I mention my date the next evening, and tell her I hope they don't mind my taking one of our evenings to do this.

"Don't worry, Alex," Jenn says. "I think it's great." Upstairs Sophie says loudly, "I want Mommy to read me a story too!"

We look at each other as Dave's voice gets a little louder to talk over Sophie's high-pitched one. I can't hear what he's saying, but I imagine it's something soothing about Mommy coming later to kiss her goodnight. But Sophie does not give up, and before long, Dave comes down to the living room and shrugs at Jenn, who hauls herself out of her chair and goes upstairs. Dave plops down in her seat and begins to drink her seltzer. "The joys of parenting," he says.

We smile at each other, and I say, "I'm pregnant."

"What!" He leans forward out of his chair and puts down the seltzer.

"Ha!" I laugh. "I am!"

"That's great!"

"Yes."

He looks at me and says, "You don't waste any time!"

"It was fast," I say. "I went this week for the first sonogram, and there was no heartbeat, so there's a little worry about that, but we're hoping it's just too early.'"

"You were just here!" he says, gesturing out to the porch where we had dinner that night on my way to the lodge. "This was just an idea a few weeks ago!"

I laugh. "I know. I'm a little stunned." I lean back into the couch. "I'm a little nauseated too. All the time. It's a lie about morning sickness; it's really all day sickness."

"Yeah, Jenn had it bad the first time, with Sophie." He looks up as Jenn comes down the stairs in her rolling pregnancy walk. "Hey, Jenn, Alex is pregnant!"

"No way!" Jenn says, falling onto the couch beside me to give me a huge hug. "Look at us, Dave. Two pregnant ladies!"

The town where Michael suggested we meet is indeed cute. Wildflowers sprout out of every corner, and the smell is heady and exotic. After five minutes, though, it's almost too much. This is the first olfactory anomaly

I've experienced. I remember my sister couldn't stand the smell of basil during her first pregnancy.

I park a little down the street from the restaurant, in front of a house that is selling corn and pies and tiny wooden cardinals. They sit on a table, waiting to be bought, but no one is there to take the money. *A trusting town,* I think as I click on my car alarm.

I walk back to the restaurant, where Michael gives me a kiss on the cheek. "Listen, I just checked it out and, well, it's kind of dark and smoky. How about we walk around and see what else there is?"

"Sure," I say, happy to not have to sit in a smoky restaurant.

We walk along a pathway that runs by a river, and then we pass over a flower-covered pedestrian bridge to the other side. This was a mill town once, and along the river are buildings rising up from the concrete that was set down to hold the river in place.

We come across a sweet little restaurant with a patio built over the river, and though it is late September and a little cool, we decide to eat out there.

We chitchat. I order white wine, though I'm not sure why. It's like I don't feel pregnant right now, the empty sac looming over me, even though I spent all last night and today talking to Jenn and Dave about what it's like to have a baby. I listened intently to Jenn as she talked about gaining tons of weight in the third trimester with Sophie, gaining and gaining and then developing preeclampsia, which led to a miserable delivery. "With this pregnancy," she said, "I swam every day. I am not going through a delivery like that again."

As we sit together, looking at the menu, I decide that I'm not going to tell Michael about the pregnancy. This dinner is about getting to know him without all the distractions of the Labor Day party—to see if I want to keep going with this, or if my hesitation is warranted.

Our wine arrives, and I order lamb and roasted potatoes and steamed veggies. No sugar, no flour. We settle into a nice conversation. I take a sip of wine and realize I don't want it after all. It tastes like metal. And the smell, together with the scent of wildflowers brought in by the occasional breeze, turns my stomach.

He's a little more smart-alecky than I remember from the party, but also genuinely smart, and he knows a hell of a lot about global warming. He confesses that he still hasn't written the press releases that should have gone out yesterday, but he will get back tonight and work on them until they're done. He also tells me he is stressed about money; two magazines owe him big checks, but he's been too busy to get after them.

For some reason, I order cheesecake for dessert. The idea is to share, but he only has one bite. I leave three bites on the plate and push it away. I glance back at them as we leave, and I wonder why I did that. I want those bites. I think about those bites as we walk through the scented village. Even as Michael and I talk during this little walk, I am thinking about food and my obsession with it. It is not over for me, obviously. I don't have it licked. The last three years appear to have been a hiatus, not a recovery.

Somehow we have a lot to say to each other. He puts his arm around me as we walk. I slip my hand under the waistband of his pants and let my fingers rest on his hip. I stop thinking about food and listen to him properly.

We kiss enthusiastically and passionately at my car. He presses his long body into mine, pushing me against the driver's door.

"I'm coming to Manhattan soon to visit my mom," he says after we kiss for a while, leaning back so he can see my face. This gesture pushes his pelvis into mine, and I catch my breath just a little. In a good way. "Can we see each other then?"

"Sure, that sounds like a plan," I say, kissing him quickly on the lips and slipping out from between him and the car. I pull my keys from my purse. "So call me when you come down."

He opens my door once I've unlocked it, and I roll down the window. "Good luck with the conference," I say as I pull away.

He smiles and waves, nodding thanks. In my rearview mirror I notice him wander over to the yard sale to pick up one of the carved wooden cardinals. I still don't know what I think about him. We have a lot in common, and I enjoy talking with him. Well, I can be uncertain. I don't have to decide now. I'll go on one more date.

On Friday I arrange to meet Pat at Dr. Bakas's office for the second ultrasound. "See you at nine-fifteen," I say as we leave each other at 6:00 AM after our run. Pat lives just down the street from the office in Mount Kisco, so she'll drive over later in the morning. I get home, take a shower, and go back to sleep (I've been doing this instead of writing when I get back ever since I got pregnant). I wake up still exhausted, thinking I've only slept for half an hour.

But when I roll over to look at the clock, it's 9:00 AM, and I leap out of bed with my heart pounding. I run to the phone and call the office to tell them I'll be fifteen minutes late.

"You'll be more than fifteen minutes late," Ilona says. "You know we're in the Brewster office on Fridays, right?"

Oh my god. Of course they are. How could I have forgotten?

"Well, don't worry, we have an opening at ten, so take your time and drive up here safely. Remember to drink lots of water too."

I call Pat on her cell phone and hope to catch her before she leaves the house.

"Alex, I'm really sorry, but I have a meeting at eleven with Susan and the registrar. There's no way we'll get back from Brewster by eleven."

"That's okay," I say slowly. *That's okay. That's okay.*

"Can you make the appointment for Monday? I can come then."

"I could, but I don't think I can stand not knowing for that long."

"Well, call me right afterward. Tell me exactly what happens."

I drive the hour up to Brewster and drink a two-liter bottle of seltzer on the way.

Jackie brings me back into an exam room and leaves me alone to change. I lie shaking on the bed beneath my paper gown—cold and terribly nervous. And I have to pee so badly, my eyes are swimming in my head. I jump down to cover myself in my T-shirt, and then lie shivering on the exam bed.

"How have you been feeling?" Jackie asks as she comes in, putting on rubber gloves.

"Queasy. It's the weirdest feeling, like I'm always just a little unbalanced."

"That's a good sign," she says, squirting jelly on my belly.

"Really?"

"One theory is that high levels of hormones in your body make you feel nauseated. And high hormone levels are what you want."

She presses the wand into my pelvis and gets that professional look on her face again. I watch her for signs of bad news.

She looks and makes some adjustments to the keys on the machine, then turns the monitor toward me a little more. I crane my head to see, using my left arm to lift and hold my head up and to the right.

"There, do you see?"

"See what?"

"There, that pulsing light. That's your baby's heart beating."

"Oh my god." Spontaneously my eyes have gone prickly, and that wonderful, lovely, miraculous pulsing light wavers through my tears. "Wow. I'm pregnant."

"Yes, indeed. You are pregnant," Jackie says, turning the monitor back toward her again. "Now, I just need to take a few measurements here for Dr. McGroary, and then I'll let you pee before he comes in to talk to you."

"Oh, wow," I say, lying back. The tears roll down and pool in my ears. "Wow." I use the paper gown gathered up over my breasts to soak them up. "Wow, wow, wow."

So this is it, I think as I'm driving to work. *This is really it. Fully the real thing.*

Olaf, you are the father of my baby. Thank you.

I think of Ken and wonder now if he would ever have come around. I'm a little sad that my dream of two families for my baby is now over.

I also remember a conversation with a friend of a friend at a picnic the weekend after I bought Olaf's sperm, which sat on the couch, waiting for me to get home from that picnic. Rachel, a colleague and friend, had invited me to the picnic because she thought Sarah and I might have a lot to talk about. Sarah had had a child through artificial insemination four years before.

"My dad left my mom before I was even born," she said after we had talked for a while and had grown comfortable with each other. "I always wanted to know who my dad was. I just wanted to see him, even just a picture. But

Mom had thrown everything away." Her daughter ran to her from across the grass to show her a feather she'd found. Sarah looked at me over her daughter's head. "I didn't want that for her. I think that knowing your father is, well, embedded. Unavoidable. I needed it like breathing."

I felt my face flush as I thought about Olaf, sitting in the sun on the couch in front of the window.

"So how did you have her?" I asked quietly, looking at her daughter, who was now pulling away and running to get some watermelon. "Did you ask a friend?"

"No, I used an open sperm bank."

"A what?"

"An open sperm bank. You know, like an open adoption. . . ."

"Oh."

"I thought you said you had researched this."

I nodded and let Sarah be distracted by her daughter again. Who knew there was such a thing as an open sperm bank? Your kid can have the option of knowing their father, getting in touch someday?

I walked away from the party to a quiet space in the trees where I couldn't really hear anyone anymore. I sat on a stump and tried to deal with this news. I would have done that. I would have gone with an open sperm bank if I had known about it. I want my kid to have a chance to meet his or her father—at least see his face and have a conversation.

But now I wonder—if it had come down to choosing between my baby's knowing his or her father and my choosing the Danish sperm bank, would I have gone with an American donor who was willing to be known?

I remember my sperm-search uneasiness. I had trouble finding a specific guy, but the Danish thing was never in doubt. I wanted a baby who looked like me, like my family, my sister's kids. I remember the cozy feeling of knowing that Olaf's blood and mine, when joined, would go back through Danish generations to the Vikings, even as far back as the cave dwellers. That linking was important—it included my aunt whom I lived with at fifteen, my uncle whom I saw sing at the Gothenburg opera house.

Now I don't know what I would have done if I had known about this other option. And I don't know what it says about me that I don't know.

Now that I am really pregnant and the baby is down there, I settle in a little. The terrible uncertainty, the back and forth, is over. When I walk into the office after the ultrasound, carrying a little bag of soda crackers for my endless nausea, Crystal follows me out into the hallway after I pick up my messages. "Everything okay?"

"Yes, it's all great." I give her a hug. I feel calm and happy. "I'm going to have a baby."

I go running in the morning. My book on running arrives from Amazon, and I strategize about how to keep running until the very end. I eat white food all day to stay as unqueasy as I can, and I indulge my pad Thai craving often.

My weight gains are miniscule, and my next visit to Dr. Bakas is routine. He uses a little machine on my belly, and I cry as I listen to the lovely *whoosh*ing sound of my baby's heart beating.

At sixteen weeks, I go for the amniocentesis at Northern Westchester Hospital, where I'll actually have the baby. Pat is with me.

I go with a degree of certainty. I know, in my heart of hearts, though I won't necessarily say it, that if they discover something like spina bifida, or some other terrible child-suffering disorder, I will have an abortion. But things get a little murky when I think about something like Down syndrome, where the strain is more on me as a parent than it is, per se, on the kid.

How would I handle something like that financially, emotionally, and physically, being a single mother and all? In my head I take the cowardly way out and say that I don't have to make a decision about that until I have to make a decision about that.

As Pat and I sit down with the genetic counselor, I face what I am sure is just the beginning of people's wondering what is going on with the baby and me. When I introduce Pat as my friend and birthing partner, the genetic counselor nods, but I can see she's wondering what the real deal is. It gives me a pang; I want to be here with a husband. The fact that I am so different from what I imagine most of her patients to be like makes me uncomfortable.

And Pat gave me a look when I said "friend" *and* "birthing partner," and I realize I haven't actually formally asked her. I've always just assumed she would be.

There are questions and more questions, and the upshot is that I come from a healthy family. Although I have printed out Olaf's particulars too, his extended profile isn't nearly as detailed as the questions she asks, so she says, "Well, we'll just leave his side blank and focus on you and your family." She waits for me to nod, and then she continues, "So he's Danish, you say?"

"Yes, and so am I. Well, half. My dad is Norwegian."

"You know that the Scandinavians have fewer genetic disorders than any other genetic grouping."

"Really?"

"Yes. So, in terms of donors, Scandinavian is a good idea."

"What do you know?" I think back to the closed– or open–sperm bank issue and think, *Well, chance takes with one hand but gives with another.*

Autoimmune issues have cropped up in my sister's kids, but perhaps those are more from her husband's side of the family. I am under the impression that we don't have autoimmune problems in our family, but I find out later that my mother had asthma that was really bad when she was a child, although she hasn't suffered from it much since she moved to Saskatchewan.

Our counselor takes us across the hall to a large room with the biggest ultrasound machine I have ever seen. It is very new, she tells us. It doesn't quite do the new 3-D images that are now possible, but it does provide a fabulously accurate picture of the placenta, the baby, and the umbilical cord. I am nervous. A long needle is about to be pressed down into my uterus, where the baby floats in amniotic fluid, to take a bit of that very fluid. A fluid that is filled, the doctor tells me, with baby pee. It is precisely from that pee that they will grab a spiral or two of DNA to test.

"Pee?" I say.

"Yes," the doctor says, grabbing the needle, and I look away and hold Pat's hand.

I am still getting over the grossness of my baby peeing all over inside me when the nurse starts the sonogram, squeezes gel onto my belly, and presses and slides the wand around. She and the doctor talk quietly to each other, but I look at Pat and hold her hand and say, "How are you feeling now?" This morning, on our run, she told Lyde and me that she and her husband are in a difficult spot again—not necessarily fighting, but distant, strangers passing on the way to the kitchen or living room.

She smiles at me. "Okay." She shrugs. "Things will get better. My brother gave us tickets to a show in the city and a voucher for a hotel. He and his wife will take Ali, too, so we can get away. Maybe we can talk about stuff then."

I nod and think how hard it must be for her, living in her mother's house, Ahmed not working, their son, Ali, with them all the time.

"But I love him, you know. He's my best friend. I want things to be better."

I nod and she says, "He loves me. We'll work it out."

As we talk, the doctor puts in the needle and I feel it, but no more than a little pinch, and then it's done. For something that was so full of potential to be painful and frightening (I only glanced at it, but I'm sure that needle was at least a foot long), it wasn't so bad.

The nurse keeps pressing the wand around my pelvis and stopping to take measurements. Then she says, "Want to see?"

Pat and I strain to make out something human in the light and shadows on the monitor. This is a much better machine than the one in Dr. McGroary's office; it's actually in color. "The baby is really moving," the nurse says. "Look! There are the feet. They're crossed at the ankles; can you see?" She presses a flurry of buttons, and a picture prints out.

"Feet?" I say. "There are feet already?"

The nurse laughs. "Yes, there's everything already—all the baby has to do now is grow."

She hands over the picture and, sure enough, my baby's little feet are crossed over each other, as though they are resting on an ottoman. Even the little toes are visible. "Holy crap, that's cute!" I say, instead of crying.

When I get back to my office, I fax the picture of my baby's tiny feet to Margaret's office, and she calls to say that she thinks the picture is the cutest thing in the entire *universe!* After work I run to Staples and make color photocopies and send them to Mom and Dad.

In all the excitement of realizing that my baby is actually finished making all its parts, I have kind of forgotten that I went for the test to see if there were problems, not just to get cute pictures taken. It will be at least a week for the results to come back. As I wait, I talk about my amnio experience with the memoir-writing class I am teaching, and during the free-write that day, one of the women writes a piece about her experience a few years before. Her husband is an obstetrician, and he came with her for support during the amnio but was helpless afterward when a slow leak developed from her uterus to her stomach cavity. She lost the baby over the next week; her womb slowly dried out. Her husband was crazy with grief because, even with all his training and experience, there was nothing he could do.

I check the web and realize that the complications from an amnio are quite serious, and one in three hundred women experience them. I remember that both Bakas and the doctor who performed my amnio said something about complications, even detailed them, but I didn't really listen. I had already made up my mind. I let my eyes glaze over as they talked.

For days I wander around, touching my growing belly, pressing to be sure it feels like there's still something down there.

I don't hear from Michael for weeks after our dinner in Massachusetts, although he does include me in the mass emails he sends around every day about global warming and Darfur and such. But two weeks or so after the conference, he leaves a message on my machine, and we play phone tag for a while before we finally talk. It is nice when we do. He makes me laugh.

I think to myself, remembering us kissing at my car, *I may just go right ahead and have sex with him. I'm not sure about the long-term prospects, given the drugs and joblessness, but yes, when I see him next, it will end in sex.*

But I will not go to him. If he wants another date, he has to get himself down here to New York. And finally, in December, after I do the amniocentesis but before my results are back, he calls to say he is coming to New York. We decide to go to dinner and see what happens.

I suggest a Thai place because my obsession with pad Thai has not gone away. If anything, it is stronger than ever. My nausea, though, has gotten much better. It's less and less all the time, and recently I have noticed that I can go whole days without feeling queasy.

Michael likes the idea of a Thai place and suggests Thai-Tastic, which seems cheesy, he says, but it is apparently very fashionable and tasty. It's on the east side. Sure, I say, wondering what I have that I can wear to a fashionable restaurant. It's time to go shopping, I think. My pants don't fit anymore, and my tops are getting tight around the boobs. I have started wearing my running bras all the time, mostly because they are looser and have more give. I've taken, in fact, to wearing them to bed. My breasts are so sensitive now that when I roll over in bed, the movement of fabric against my nipples hurts so much, it wakes me up.

That Friday I find a great parking spot around the corner from the restaurant. As I walk to the restaurant in my high heels, I think, *This will be the last time I wear heels until I give birth.* My balance feels off and I feel myself totter, but with sex on my agenda tonight, the shoes seem right.

I lurch through the front door, catching my heel on the mat, and look around to be sure no one has seen this. Michael is at the bar, looking down at what looks like scotch. The maître d' takes my coat and I walk to Michael. I'm wearing a new striped shirt with a new black camisole underneath. I've left the shirt untucked and open, and I'm a little self-conscious of the bump now visible below the waistband of the new stretchy black pants I've begun to wear each day.

"Hey!" he says when he sees me. "You look great!"

"Thanks, so do you." And he does. We look each other over until the maître d' comes to take us to our table.

In all my certainty about our impending sexual relations, I've forgotten that I should tell him I'm pregnant.

I order pad Thai, and he touches my hand casually over the white tablecloth. "So, Michael," I say. "There's something I should tell you."

"Oh," he says carefully, pulling his hand away to shake out his napkin. "Okay."

I look at him and feel myself blush. "I'm pregnant."

He blinks and runs his hand over his jaw. "Oh. That wasn't exactly what I was expecting."

"Really? What were you expecting?"

"I don't know. Something . . . else." He moves the cutlery around beside his salad plate and then looks up at me. "So, is there someone else in your life?"

"No," I say. *Actually, I guess there is someone else in my life,* I think, as I explain what has been happening in these last months. There *is* someone else, because this baby has become a person to me. Those tiny toes are connected to a real person, who has begun to take up room in my awareness as more than a pregnancy.

Michael nods and listens as I talk. He asks a few questions. Our food arrives, and as I use my chopsticks to eat the lovely noodles, I tell him that even so, I'm interested in, well, "advancing" our relationship. I leave it ambiguous, but he gets it.

He smiles at me and cuts into his steak. "There's something I need to tell you as well." He doesn't bring the piece of steak to his mouth, but puts down the cutlery, crosses his finger over his plate, and leans toward me. "I have herpes." He sighs and sits back again to resume eating. "Yes, so that's my big revelation."

"Right," I say, and nod and keep eating and think, *I may as well take off the high heels.*

"I don't have an outbreak now, and it's been quite a long time. It's usually when I'm stressed." I nod again. But even with condoms, I can't bring myself to take that kind of risk with this other person inside me, who already depends on me to keep him or her safe.

He seems to sense this and says, with a sad half smile, "So we know where this evening is *not* heading, right?"

"Right," I say sadly, and we are quiet for a while.

"So," he says jovially, "there's a Frank Capra movie playing down in the Village. Do you want to head down there after dinner?"

"Sure," I say.

We go to the movie, and then to a little place around the corner from the theater for drinks. More seltzer for me. I'm waterlogged by now, and even in the best of times these days, I'm always rushing to the bathroom. I'm also bushed, my stamina all gone. I'm usually in bed by nine.

Michael would like another drink, but I suggest we head out. We walk to the car and he grabs my hand and I feel suddenly awake again. At the car he presses me against the door and kisses me, and now I'm really awake. I forget the people walking along the sidewalk beside us and let the kiss get deeper and heavier. I pull his shirt out from his pants underneath the leather jacket he is wearing and run my hands up his back. It crosses my mind: *Fuck it. Invite him home. Drive him to Westchester. Use the condoms in your purse.*

But he pulls away, and I wave the lapels of my jacket to cool off.

"This is too bad," I say, and pull the keys from my pocket. "If I weren't pregnant . . ." I trail off.

He nods, looking sad.

"Can I drive you somewhere? Where does your mom live?"

"On the West Side—26th and 8th."

"No problem. I can drive you."

We don't touch each other again in the car, though I want to put my hand on his leg or through his very nice hair. I may be a little worried about his drinking—he's had quite a few this evening—but I still want to touch him.

He turns to me as I pull over to park in front of a fire hydrant on his mother's block. We look at each other; though we tend to talk and talk, right now we have nothing to say. He gives me a peck on the cheek and opens the door. I watch him and his leather jacket walk away and I think, *I will never see you again.*

And I am right. We email for a while; then I just get mass emails. And then it is nothing.

EIGHT

It's a Girl!

It is the week after the amnio and my date with Michael. I'm in the office with a student who is asking about changing thesis advisors. He's a nice guy and not the type to complain. We brainstorm possibilities and seem to have settled on a better alternative when my phone rings.

"Just a second, okay?" I say to the student.

"Alexandra?"

"Yes?"

"This is Alison from Northern Westchester Hospital."

"Alison?"

"The genetic counselor."

"Right! Okay, do I have to close my door for this?" I ask, thinking I may have to send the student outside.

"No, everything appears to be A-OK."

"Really? Oh, wow. That's great." I let out a huge sigh. That *is* great.

She goes through some specifics and says she will send the details to Dr. Bakas, who can give me copies, which is good, because it's kind of distracting to talk about this with a student in my office. I probably should have just sent him out. "Wonderful," I say as she is about to hang up. "Uh, Alison, I did say I wanted to know the sex."

I can hear Alison shuffling some papers around. "Okay, yes, I see that here. It's a girl."

Jacob jumps back when I leap up screaming, then laughing. I had come to accept that I was probably having a boy, since artificial insemination is supposed to produce more boys (though I'm not sure that's actually true). But here we are: a girl. "Thank you thank you thank you!" I say to Alison.

"I guess you wanted a girl," she says. I can hear her smiling.

"Who knew? I guess I did!"

We hang up and Jacob says, "Congratulations. I didn't even know you were pregnant."

"Thanks!"

Pat has come out of her office because of the noise, and I say, "It's a *girl!*"

We laugh and hug. Then I catch my breath, and Pat says, "Let's talk in a little bit; I'm actually on the phone," and I say to Jacob, "Okay, okay. Back to work."

Jacob says, "I think we were almost done anyway. I'll talk to the director about switching, like you said."

"Okay, that makes sense," I say, floaty.

"Congratulations again," he says and leaves.

I pick up the phone and call Mom and Dad.

"So," I say when Mom picks up, *"it's a girl!"* Mom and I scream together, and she yells out to Dad, "Norm! It's a girl! Donna's going to have a baby girl!"

We laughed together, and I am happy. This is one of the purest moments of joy I remember from my pregnancy—hearing how gleeful Mom is, and my own glee about telling her. Why did I call them first this time? I wonder now. There was nothing deliberate about it; it was just the first thing I did. *This goes back to the toes,* I think.

Seeing the picture of my baby's toes, I felt so happy and so proud, the kind of pride that I wanted to share with my mom and dad—which is why I went to Staples and made a color photocopy of the picture. I wanted to share how amazing it was to know that those toes were growing inside me, and that I had made her, and I wanted them to be proud of me too. And I think that feeling carried over to knowing it's a girl and made it real.

This was the beginning of a change in my relationship with my parents, a shift that would come to full fruition later, when my daughter was finally born.

The nausea is completely gone these days, but my craving for white food isn't. If anything, it's worse. I think about food all the time. In the evenings it's especially bad—I feel propelled into the kitchen. It all starts with white food: rice, crackers, potatoes (especially chips, if one can even call chips "potatoes"), then moves on to anything else—most inexplicably, KitKat bars.

My eating, in the last few days especially, has been erratic and binge-like, in a way it hasn't been for years.

One morning at work, I go into Pat's office, I move her purse and carryall bag onto the floor and say, "I've been eating again." I look at my hands. "All the time."

Pat puts her pen down and turns toward me in her swivel chair. "Do you know why?"

"No. I mean, I started eating flour again, crackers and stuff—you know, we talked about that—for the nausea. But then there would be these spurts where I would devour sugar and chips, which I haven't told you about. In the grocery store, chips and cookies seem to just appear in my cart and find their way into my house, and then I eat them at night."

Pat smiles at me a little and takes a breath to say something, but for a change, I'm the one cutting her off. "I kept thinking that I would pull myself together, and when I was all good again I would tell you. But I can't seem to make myself good again."

"This has been going on for a while?"

I nod.

"It's hard being pregnant. Everything is out of whack."

I nod.

We look at each other and I feel helpless. Here I am again.

I find it harder and harder to run. Because of my constant peeing, we change our route to stop at Lyde's house halfway through so I can go. This morning I say to Pat and Lyde, as I struggle to catch my breath, "Last night I ate Cheerios with cream instead of milk."

My legs and body feel heavier and heavier with each run, although, according to my visits to Dr. Bakas, I've only gained about seven pounds. After last night I'm sure I'm up another three.

"Listen," Lyde says, "I gained thirty pounds my first trimester with the twins. My doctor made me cry on my third visit. He said if I didn't stop gaining weight, I'd put the lives of my babies at risk."

"I can't believe that's true. Doctors are so insensitive," Pat says. To me she says, "Bakas won't say a thing about that to you. He's wonderful."

"No, he didn't say anything. But the nurse did. I'd never seen her before, and there I was, feeling proud that I'd only gained seven pounds in the last four months, and *she* made some comment about slowing down on the food, that I still had a long way to go."

"Don't worry about it," Pat said. "Look. You're running, swimming, doing yoga. You're doing the right things."

Yeah. But what I don't say is that I have come to hate exercising and have to force myself every morning to get out the door to meet them.

I have been so determined to not do what I would expect myself to do, given my history with weight and food: gain all the weight back during my pregnancy. I will not do that. I say it to Bakas. I say it to McGroary. I ask what normal weight gain is for the entire pregnancy, and they say twenty-five to thirty pounds. With seven gained already at four months, I've got only eighteen pounds left, and the baby has hardly started growing yet.

But I am a new person now. I am the kind of person who trains for a half marathon. Who feels sexy. Who gets dressed for a date and plans to have sex. The kind of person who hasn't binged for three years. A normal person who is having a baby, flosses her teeth every day, keeps her house clean. I am not going to go back to feeling like Old Alex, the one who graduated from Sarah Lawrence but felt like shit, and whose body hurt.

"I feel like I've given up on men," I say suddenly, in what feels like a non sequitur, but I wonder if it really is. We've just started running again after stopping at Lyde's house for a pee. It hardly seems worth the effort, so little pee comes out, but it does help a little with the discomfort of the baby bouncing on my bladder.

"Because you got pregnant without a man?"

"No, not that. It's more about Michael, and last week." I wonder what I'm trying to say. "As long as Michael was there, it seemed like a possibility. I felt like I was still dating, still looking for a guy, even with the baby and all. But it feels like that part of my life is over. I'm not going on any blind dates now that I'm showing." We turn a corner and start up the high hill behind Lyde's house. "It feels like just me and the baby now."

"Okay," Pat says. "That may be true, but it doesn't have to be forever. Just for now."

Yeah, but . . .

I have a bad feeling about this weight gain. I won't be the skinny chick I was when I got pregnant after I'm done being pregnant. And to me, meeting a guy is totally contingent on my having a skinny(ish) body.

"And if you wanted to, you could still go out on dates," Lyde said. "Some men like pregnant women."

"Maybe," I say. "But I don't like the kind of men who like pregnant women."

We finish our run in the dark, which is how it has been these last weeks, and we get into our cars and drive home. As usual, I go back to sleep.

It saddens me how my struggles with eating and my weight have stayed with me even when I'm pregnant. The food and my fight with myself over food have sucked so much of the pleasure out of my pregnancy. These struggles have colored, and probably always will color, every corner of my life, and they raise the question: *How do I manage not to pass this on?*

Despite my determination, the weight creeps up. I go to my sister's in Toronto for Christmas and only go out running one morning. There is snow and ice, and I use that as an excuse, saying it's too dangerous. When all my restraint around food disappears during the holiday, I think, *Well, it's just the holiday.*

It is the same at the Hashimoto Christmas, which is at Jeff and Susan's cottage again. I spend a great deal of time trying to finish the pink blanket I'm knitting for this baby girl of mine. The youngest Hashimoto sister, Lisa, is pregnant too, a couple months ahead of me, so she and I sit together and knit and talk about morning sickness and our doctors and our plans for the delivery. Emily's youngest kid is now crawling, and I pick him up once in a while and look into his round, happy face. "I will have someone like you very soon," I say.

I hide how much I am eating and how distressed I am by Susan's deterioration. We all hide it, I think. No one talks about the fact that she is in her room most of the time, on oxygen. How she has to sleep sitting up in order to keep breathing. There is a halfhearted night of karaoke, but no one really feels like it. It is a pretty somber few days, and I try not to compare it with the fun and excitement of the Christmas before, or the wedding in August.

When I get home I go back to running with Lyde and Pat, but I cancel one out of three runs. By the end of January I stop pretending and don't go at all anymore.

Pat tells me, "Well, you made it to five months; that's pretty impressive.

You can still walk now, though, and swim. You don't have to stop exercising. In fact, you shouldn't."

Bakas says the same thing. But by the time I'm six months pregnant, I've gained thirty pounds, with a burst of gaining in February when I'm not running anymore. I've got to stop this. I've got to stop this.

Margaret calls me on a Wednesday in the middle of February to say that Susan is in the hospital. On Thursday she calls me at work to say she has died.

I sit looking out my small window and think, *I'm not surprised.* But that doesn't make the sadness any easier to take. I feel my stomach burn a little, and I feel queasy. I put my head down on my desk. Tears drop onto its gray surface as I think about the wedding and the tulips spread end to end in the park where we took pictures. I picture Susan walking up the aisle with her dad, then down the aisle with Jeff.

Goodbye, brave Susan, I think.

Then I pull myself together and go to talk to my boss about being away for a few days for the funeral.

It seems strange to say this, but Susan looks beautiful in her casket. Like herself, even.

The night before the funeral, there is a viewing at the funeral home. The room quickly fills with the people in Susan's life. All her siblings have come, of course, and her mom and dad. People she has known here in Ottawa and during her time in Quebec. Some people from back in Saskatchewan too. Jeff's kids are all there. His daughter's baby is crawling now, making her way among the guests across the carpeted floor.

There are six or so photo albums with pictures of Susan, all the way back to when she was a baby. As the room grows more crowded, I find a seat and look at the pictures. Susan was incredibly photogenic, and the aliveness of her in the photos is disconcerting and upsetting as she lies in her casket a few feet away.

The next day I help out where I can. Margaret gives me the job of taking care of the food—setting it all out in the basement of the church, then covering it, so that when the funeral is over we can all just walk downstairs. Jeff has set up a photo tribute to Susan at one end of the basement—pictures from their time together. I look at them as I get everything ready with Lisa, who is now due in two months and whose belly seems very self-contained to me. She has not gained any weight in her face or arms or legs—it's all in her belly—and I cringe inside when she tells me that she is still running. I am comparing myself with her—negatively, of course—as I look at the photo tribute and find myself battling a feeling of outsiderness as well, when I notice that there is not one picture of me in the Susan tribute.

Everything piles on top of me, and I have to go to the bathroom to cry.

A little later Lisa asks me to come with her to talk to the priest, to help choose a reading for her to do during the service, and I almost cry again, this time because I feel suddenly reassured about my place in the Hashimoto family. As we look through the readings and try to find one to capture who Susan was, it feels futile. How can you possibly do that? Especially with Susan, who was so open and lively.

Upstairs at the funeral, I sit with the family in the front pews, not sure if I should. But Margaret gestures for me to, and as I sit I notice Linda and Glenn and the kids sitting a few pews back. In the midst of Susan's funeral, when I should be thinking about her life, I sit and ponder my own. Where do I belong? Why is it so important to me that I belong up here with the Hashimotos in the front pews? Why is their love and acceptance so crucial? The service feels strange to me, as the priest talks about Susan's coming back to the church in her last months. I look at Margaret with a frown; that doesn't seem right to me. And Margaret gives her head a little shake. I look around and realize that the real Susan is here in everyone's memory. Jeff gets up and talks about their romance and the joy he got from their short time together. Lisa does the two readings.

I wish someone from the family would speak about her life, give us the other aspects of her, the mischief maker, the social convener, the karaoke singer. But no. And then it is all over. We stand and follow the casket out the front doors and watch as it is loaded into the hearse that drives it away. It is bitterly cold, but the sun shines so brightly, it almost blinds us as it reflects off the snow.

It is later that evening, as the family eats together, that Jim announces he and Margaret are going to try to have another baby. I didn't realize Margaret had made so much progress in getting Jim to change his mind. Last I heard, he'd said he would rather throw himself off a ten-story building than go through diapers and sleepless nights again. But this is exciting news. And it is that bit of aliveness I think about as I go home—that and Lisa's pregnant belly and getting to know Jeff's granddaughter as she crawled around the basement of the church after the funeral. Life in the midst of death is a bit of a cliché, but it really is a comfort to me.

March is a hateful month. Where February is short, and somewhat brightened by the fact that it is my birthday month, March is long. February is undeniably winter. But March, well, March contains spring break, which fools me into thinking we are near the end of winter. I'm always too hopeful, and March always disappoints me. It is never spring enough, and as I lug my big pregnant body around in heavy winter pregnancy clothes, I can't wait for the month to end and spring to begin.

The one bright light is that Margaret calls me a little way into March to say that she and Jim are already pregnant. She stopped taking the pill the day of Susan's funeral, and here she is, three weeks later, pregnant. She is due in November.

"My baby will be almost six months by then," I say, imagining the drive up to see her and the new baby. "I am so happy. It's just like we talked about this summer." It so often doesn't go that way. But here we are, pregnant together.

Margaret's pregnancy makes me look around my apartment and realize that I have done nothing to get ready for my baby. I have not painted her room. I have not arranged birthing classes. I have not found a doula, although I'm thinking I would like to have someone with me during the labor.

Not a midwife, exactly, because I have McGroary and Bakas—whom I grow to love more each visit—but a comforting person who has attended other births and is trained to help me get through my delivery, step by step.

I have officially asked both Pat and my friend Megan to be my birthing coaches, and they've agreed to attend a class with me once I've found one. It is true what they say, though: The second trimester is the liveliest. Now that I'm in my third trimester, I wish I had made better use of those months in the middle of my pregnancy.

I come into the office one day to find a huge piece of white paper on my desk with a name and number. "The woman who taught my birthing class," it says underneath.

No need to guess who "my" is, since Pat has been gently, then not so gently, pushing me to get this scheduled. "And don't forget the hospital tour," she says.

The woman who taught Pat's birthing class is named Janet, and she sounds nice when I call her. And she's cool with the idea of two friends, rather than a husband, being birthing partners. She has a class starting in a couple of weeks, and I sign us up. It is once a week for six weeks.

Birthing babies must be very complicated if we have to attend six two-hour classes to get ready.

At the first class, I am horrified to see that we are expected to sit on the floor. I look at Megan, who has driven here, to White Plains, from her apartment in the Bronx.

There are floor chairs we can use, which are cloth and give us something to lean back against, thank God, but getting up and down off the floor while being this pregnant is a horror show for me. Megan helps me down and flops beside me.

Megan is the perfect choice to help me with this—she is calm and loving and just the kind of person I want to have with me when I am screaming in pain. I first met her on our trips to Nicaragua years ago, at my previous job. She was working with street kids there and had been hired to lead our group of students around the country. She has been back in the States for a while now and is getting her master's in social work. She and her girlfriend,

Luz, moved in together after leaving Nicaragua and have a great, cheap one-bedroom apartment in Knightbridge. But it is a big deal for her to drive all this way on a Sunday afternoon, much less six times. I have told her she can miss a couple of classes, and she says she might have to do that.

The first class is really about introductions. Of course, the other six women are there with their husbands. All the women are older, about my age, thirties and forties. Most are high-powered professionals—lawyers, a couple of doctors (Why doctors would feel the need to be in a birthing class, I don't understand. Don't they cover that sort of thing in medical school?). I keep my story short during introductions; I just say I'm a single mom, and these are my birthing coaches, but I feel self-conscious nevertheless.

Janet outlines the structure of the six classes, then has us do trust exercises with our birth coaches: catching us as we bounce on a ball, holding us up as we lean over the ball and pretend to have contractions. Megan's arms tremble as she holds me up, and she and Pat switch off. I've now gained forty-five pounds; I feel terrible for them, and vow that I will not give birth in such awkward positions if I can help it. I also think it's a brilliant idea to have the two of them there so they can spell each other off.

It doesn't feel like we cover much in the two hours, and we leave the Y in cold, wicked March rain.

That Saturday I am standing in line at Pathmark. It's a store I've never been in, but I was driving a different way home and was struck by a sudden need for cheddar cheese. I drive into the parking lot, knowing that I won't rest until I get some mac and cheese.

Behind me in line is a woman with her daughter. The woman sees my big old belly—I'm undeniably pregnant now—and she smiles at me. This happens a lot. If I'm feeling shy or tired, I can't meet people's eyes in public or this sort of thing will happen. Strangers now touch my belly or help me carry my groceries or offer to put gas in my car. It's nice.

I feel like a delicate flower. I have never been treated this way before in my life, and a part of me never wants this baby to be born, so I can enjoy the caring attention from strangers forever.

This woman's daughter seems about five years old. She is sitting in the cart, singing a song to the Cheerios box. I am aware of a ruckus a little way over and look up to see a man bearing down on us, pushing through the crowd. I wonder who he could be. Is he this girl's father? The woman's husband? My little singing friend looks up and stops singing, and I can see her get tense. He yanks her out of the cart and, through tight angry teeth, says, "I *told* you not to sit in the cart." The mother watches him carry her away, all the while hissing at her in rage, shaking her. I look at the mother—she casts her eyes down now—and I put my hand to my belly and turn toward the cashier.

I am never letting any man near you, ever, I say to the little girl inside me. I can never get married now. I can never put her in jeopardy. All men are violent and unpredictable, angry and hurtful.

I think how I am happy to be doing this alone. Really happy, but also really confused.

As I walk out to the car, I wonder where in the world I've gotten the idea that all men are angry and hurtful. The men in my life have been good, kind people. My father is a lovely man. I've never had a boyfriend raise his voice at me, much less a fist. With the exception of the guy in the boathouse when I was little, I've had positive experiences with men.

It makes me think of the conversation I had with my mom months ago, when I told her I thought something was broken inside of me. I think it again. Something fundamental is cracked, and if this is what I really think of men, is it any wonder I'm single?

Pat and Megan and I make it to the second birthing class. It's a windy, cold Sunday, unnaturally dark so early in the day. Pat drives with me, and I have to haul ass to get there in time. Megan is a little late because of an accident on the Deegan. We are all finding this a bit of a strain, and there are four more Sunday afternoons to be lost this way. Megan and Pat are being nice about it because they love me and want to be there for me. And feeling as vulnerable and touchy as I do these days, I *would be* hurt if either of them complained, even when I feel the same way.

Today's class is about fear—primarily any of the birthing partner's fears that may come up during the birth. It becomes clear that what Janet really means is the father's fears. I feel a blush of self-consciousness start up my neck the further we get into the class. Janet moves into territory such as a primal fear on the father's part that his wife is going to die during this process, especially when she starts screaming; when the pain gets intense, it is natural to feel, deep inside, that this is a death experience.

So she sends the men to a different room to write out, as a group, a list of their fears. She has Megan and Pat stay with us. Megan says to Pat under her breath as the men leave, "I guess we have no fears," and Pat says, "I guess not." I love them both so much in that moment, I can't look up from the floor, because I'm scared my love will spill out of my eyes like tears. Here in the main room, Janet has the wives come up with a list of what they think their husband's fears will be.

I glance at Megan—we are sitting a little apart now—and I say to her, "Oh, brother."

"Not having a penis is really awkward sometimes," she says.

Pat and I decide to go out to the washroom across the hall while the wives continue their discussion. We each take a stall, and I look at the tiled floor and focus on peeing. I can go almost anytime these days. From her stall I hear Pat say, "Oh, shit."

"What?"

"I'm bleeding again." I hear her unwind toilet paper from the dispenser. "You don't have anything on you, do you?"

"I might have something in my purse left over from last summer." I haven't, of course, had to use tampons or pads since August. "Megan might have something."

"I think I'm okay for a bit," she says. I hear her stand up and flush the toilet. "I wonder if it has anything to do with the Clomid," she says.

She and Ahmed recommitted to their relationship months ago and decided recently that they would try to get pregnant again. Because she had irregular periods and difficulty getting pregnant with Ali, Bakas put her on Clomid to help with ovulation. She has been checking her hormone levels this week to see when she should start taking it.

"So you've started the Clomid?"

"I took the first one this morning."

I look at the door, where graffiti has been painted over. It is a darker blue than the rest of the stall. I wonder for a second what it said—JOANIE LOVES CHACHI?

"That is so weird," she says. "I'm not supposed to have my period for ages. It couldn't be the Clomid, could it?"

"That doesn't seem right." I unravel toilet paper and say, "Pat? Do you think you might be pregnant?"

There is silence from the other stall. I flush my toilet and say over the noise, "You bled right through your pregnancy with Ali, right? And you didn't realize you were pregnant for quite some time."

"That's right."

"It could be." I smile thinking about it, and we emerge together out of our stalls and smile at each other.

"This could be very cool!" I say as we wash our hands.

Back in the birthing class again, I keep an insincere smile on my face as the other women finish up their lists. What can I add, since I have no husband, no one who loves me in that way or will be there experiencing the primal fear Janet is talking about?

I feel stiff and uncomfortable. I want someone to love me so much, he is afraid I will die. Mixed up in these emotions is another related sadness: I was living in the land of normal for a while. There was potential for love. I was running. Fit. Dating. Having sex.

Now I am slip-sliding back into being the person I have been most of my life. Outside. Different. Alone.

I see Bakas or McGroary every other week now. In these last six weeks before delivery, I'll go in every week. They explain that either of them could be at the birth, depending on who is on call when I go into the hospital. Each visit my weight goes up, and so does my blood pressure.

Normally I have stellar blood pressure: 120/80, 110/70. But each week it creeps up.

McGroary says to me this week, "Can you get more rest? Can you take time off work?"

The idea is astonishing to me. "Well, there is no one to do my job if I'm not there."

"Alexandra, your blood pressure is steadily rising. This could mean you are developing preeclampsia, which is very dangerous. It could threaten both you and your baby. It's not terrible now, but it is creeping up."

"I'll talk to my boss," I say, getting up awkwardly from the table.

On Monday Pat goes in to the Bakas/McGroary office too, and Bakas draws blood for a pregnancy test. She, like I would have done, ran home after the birthing class on Sunday and bought a home pregnancy test. It was positive. She called me, and we talked about taking our babies to the park together.

On Tuesday I decide to tackle the birthing-class issue. I hate having to do this sort of thing—stand up for myself, make waves, leave a class early. Complain.

I take a deep breath and call Janet. I tell her I can't continue the class. It's just too painful. There is a silence. I rush in to say that I don't blame her—though in my heart I do, for being insensitive. But then again, the world doesn't revolve around me, and the majority of the class was couples, so should she have changed her curriculum to spare my feelings? Anyway, what's done is done. She suggests that the doula she has paired me with could cover the remaining information in a one-on-one session with us; Janet will just turn over half the tuition to her. We make that arrangement. My girls are relieved, and so am I.

That afternoon Ilona calls Pat to say the blood test came back positive, confirming the home pregnancy test. We jump up and down and scream in the hall outside our offices. She is to go in the next day for another blood test to see that her HCG levels double.

"Wow, that is going to be so great," I say, thinking about the two of us with young kids. "Both my best friends will have babies with me. Wow."

I think how everything feels so complete. I couldn't be happier. My best friends are pregnant too. Our lives of motherhood stretch out in parallel lines. I am so lucky I can hardly believe it.

The numbers for Pat's second blood test are a little low, but Bakas says not to stress. We'll do an ultrasound in a week or two, he says, and see where we are then.

I talk to her on the phone, sitting on my favorite chair in the dark. I look at the lights across the valley from my apartment and listen as she worries about this baby. Ahmed is worried too, but more about what kind of an impact this baby will have on their lives. Now that it's a reality, he's worried about money. He wonders how they can even afford the child they have. But Pat wants this baby. I can hear it in her voice, how attached she's become to this tiny zygote of a being.

I realize after a while that the reason my apartment isn't painted, that the baby's room isn't done, and that I have not bought a crib or set up the changing table, is that I've been hesitating to ask my friends to give up a weekend day to come to my house to paint. But nothing else can happen until the painting is done. When I confess my fear to Pat, she gives me one of her looks and I hear how silly I sound. I get on the phone and ask people to come to a painting party in two weeks.

The two upstairs rooms are a kind of grayish, dirty cream, and I would like the baby's room to be a lovely soft yellow. I'll move things around and put her in my old bedroom, which is over my living room, and move myself into my current office. That way, any crying is less likely to disturb my neighbors.

It seems straightforward enough, but the problem is that both rooms are jam-packed with junk—paper stuff, books, an extra bed in the office, and a mix of secondhand baby stuff in my bedroom and other furniture or junk I haven't known where to put. (I haven't slept up in my bedroom for months; I've been downstairs in the spare room. Going up and down the stairs three times a night got old a long time ago.)

So in my eighth month, with rising blood pressure, I work on cleaning out my office. It strikes me now as insane—or, worse than that, irresponsible—to be removing shelves and shelves of dusty books and putting them in boxes, then carrying them down the stairs to hide them in a space I have created under there. Hundreds and hundreds of books, and I work night after night doing this, totally ignoring McGroary's warnings.

I clean and pack or throw away the entire contents of those two rooms, until all that is left in them are the big dressers and bureaus that will have to stay in there while we paint.

I buy paint and brushes and rollers and an extender, because the ceiling over the stairs is at least fifteen feet high.

It is only after seeing Bakas on my next visit, and hearing him *also* saying that I'd better rest or there is going to be trouble, that I get up the nerve to talk to my boss about taking some time off work. I'm thinking that I'll ask to take afternoons off or something, but she jumps in and clears the schedule so that I can take the whole next week off.

So. Oh my god. Here's where I admit that I love bed rest. I love not having to go to work. I love sitting with my feet up, watching bad TV or reading books.

What *is* hard is sitting and thinking about the painting party happening the coming weekend. How I forgot to buy drop cloths, how I haven't picked up drinks or beer or anything yet. I lie on my couch and make lists in my head, because I'm too tired to get up and grab a pen and paper.

I'm so terribly tired.

At my next appointment that Friday, my blood pressure has gone down. "You had more rest this week," McGroary says, looking at my numbers. And I say, "Yes, I took the week off work."

"Great. Keep up the good work." He makes a note on my chart. He doesn't say anything about the fact that I've now gained almost fifty pounds.

That weekend we paint. Or, more accurately, my friends paint. Ahmed comes; Pat stays home because of the pregnancy. Christina and her son Daniel come. Crystal comes too, and that about fills the upstairs with people. Halfway through the day, it is clear we are going to run out of paint, so I leave for the second circle of hell—Home Depot on a Saturday afternoon—and stand in line for an hour with my aching, swollen feet and sore back.

When I return to the house, they are on the last drips of paint, and friends from work arrive with soup, so we go outside to eat in the warm April sun. I feel guilty that I wasn't helping them with the painting.

"Don't worry, there is still plenty left to do," Christina says. After lunch I go up and see that this is, sadly, very true. There is no way we will finish the two rooms by the time it's dark, and I envision myself alone in the morning, painting by myself the whole day.

My friends are troupers and stay until it is too dark to see. Daniel has done a great job with the high hall area over the stairs, but now he is sprawled on the couch, tired and ready to go home. Christina follows behind me as everyone clomps down the stairs to the living room.

"I'll come again tomorrow," Christina says. "Kyle is going to his father's again, and Daniel has a game out of town."

"Oh, Christina, that's so great. My bedroom still needs a whole other coat."

"We'll have fun!" she says, trying to cheer me up.

All that next week, I go upstairs after work, turn on all the bald bulbs, and lie on my side to scrape the paint off the wood floor with a plastic flipper—or, when that doesn't work, a razor. Getting up off the floor to move to the next bit of floor is too hard, so I just drag myself around. I remind myself of a dog I saw in Nicaragua who had lame back legs that he dragged behind himself with his two good legs.

It feels strange being alone in these rooms that were full of people and life and sunlight just a few days ago. They're empty and stark now in the bare-bulbed light.

It crosses my mind that I should ask for help with this too, but I don't. Who would want to do this? So I drag myself over to the next bit of floor.

It seemed like a good idea at the time, but I wonder suddenly if I haven't just cast myself out of normalcy forever. Have I perhaps institutionalized my aloneness? I talked a good game about simply bringing a child into whatever relationship I find after she's born, but how am I ever going to find that relationship if I'm always taking care of a kid? It's been hard enough all these years to find someone when I *could* jump out on a date any old time, without having to find and pay for a baby sitter.

I stop scraping paint for a moment and look up at the freshly painted ceiling. Is this how Mom felt when she was pregnant? Awash with doubt? Is this the hormones? Am I depressed? I'm so all over the place, I can't tell. Maybe I shouldn't have gone off the antidepressants. Maybe I've made a terrible mistake.

The next weekend is the doula substitute class. There are two of them, Jennifer and Sadie. Jennifer is the more experienced; Sadie is in training. I pay them $350 in addition to the money that Janet forwarded to them. This will get me what we are doing today and their presence at the birth—for however long that takes.

Jennifer does most of the talking; it's interesting, but it goes on and on. Meg and Pat droop, and I push her to wrap it up. Finally we end, without really finishing, but I figure it will all be clear soon enough.

Pat and I walk into Bronxville at lunch a couple weeks later and talk about her sonogram, which is scheduled for the next day. Her first sonogram last week showed no heartbeat, but Bakas wants to give it another week, just like he did with me, thinking it is probably just too early.

"Do you want me to be there?" I ask Pat.

"That's okay. Ahmed is coming."

"Okay. Good."

"I've been eating flour," Pat says after a brief silence. "I had some pasta last night."

I touch her arm, and we look at each other, a kind of mutual helplessness on our faces.

Things have changed a little with Pat and Lyde since I stopped running with them. They have cut back a bit, and because of that, Pat has gained a little weight—which looks good on her, actually. She looks quite healthy and robust.

"You know, it's been a real struggle to stay out of the food these last few weeks. After years of it just being a way of life to not have sugar or flour, about a month ago, it got hard," Pat says. "I bet it was the pregnancy. I didn't realize I was pregnant, but it was still making my food crazy."

"I bet you're right," I say, thinking back to that day in the parking lot when I ate two cookies real fast, breaking the no-sugar, no-flour barrier quickly, like ripping off a Band-Aid, thinking it wouldn't count or hurt if I did it fast. Nothing was going to stop me from eating those cookies. "I bet it's the hormones."

"It was the same with Ali, now that I think about it." She pushes the hair out of her eyes and looks up at the late-April sun. It is finally a warm day, the main reason we are out for a walk. "I had the same feelings, but I didn't know I was pregnant, so I just thought it was me."

NINE

The Homestretch

The day of Pat's second ultrasound, I am restless. I can't stay in my office, and I find myself downstairs a lot, thinking that way I will see her as soon as she comes in. When she does, I can see right away that the news is bad.

I follow her upstairs to her office and close the door. I sit in the guest chair and lean toward her over the desk.

"It's an empty sac," she says to me, her eyes tearing up. They are already red, and I watch her face quiver as she tries not to cry. "Bakas said I could wait to see if I miscarry on my own, or they can schedule a D&C."

"I'm so sorry, Pat." I get up and give her a hug, and she gives in and cries. "I'm so sad, Alex," she says into my shoulder. "I really wanted this baby. I wanted it for me and for Ahmed and for Ali. I want him to have a brother or sister."

We stay like that for a while, and I rub her back. I feel tears in my eyes as I remember how scared I was when I thought my baby might be an empty sac. How attached I was already to the baby I felt sure was growing there.

I want to tell her they can try again, but that seems like cold comfort, so I say nothing except, "I know."

"Anyway," she says, pulling away and wiping her eyes, "I'm not going to wait around for a miscarriage. I scheduled the D&C."

"Oh, honey," I say. "I am really sorry."

She shakes her head. "So am I."

I am so sad for Pat, and sorry for myself and the loss of that lovely vision of the two of us having kids together, like sisters with our babies months apart, watching them grow up together, friends forever into the future. And on top of that, Margaret would come to visit too, and all three children would play together. What a cozy dream.

When I tell Margaret about the empty sac, she is silent for a long time. Over the years, Margaret and Pat have come to know each other through me. "Do you think she would mind if I wrote to her and told her how sad I am?"

"No, I think that would be nice."

Margaret's voice quivers a little as she says, "I don't know why this is hitting me so hard."

A few Saturdays later, I have promised Pat I will go into the office to help her out with some stuff, but then I plan to come home and finish setting up the baby's room. Things are almost ready. A friend from Toronto came down to help. She and I cleaned, and she moved boxes around and put books in new shelves downstairs. She did a ton of work. Without her I would never have been ready.

This morning, as I get dressed, part of me wonders if my baby shower is going to be today. There have been a couple of hints. So, to be safe, I put on makeup and clothes that I wouldn't be embarrassed to be seen in.

Everything seems normal and quiet at Slonim, and I think, *Oh, I guess I'm wrong.* There are no cars parked around; even the parking lot across the street is empty. So when I open the door to the living room of our office building, I am shocked to see the room filled from end to end with friends. "Oh my god," I say, and I start to shake. "Oh my god."

"So you're surprised," Pat says, watching my reaction, and I say yes, because it's too complicated to explain how a part of me knew that perhaps it was happening, yet when I walked into the room I was overwhelmed by the sight of practically everyone I know sitting there, waiting for me. Yes, I'm shocked and overwhelmed more than surprised. I'm moved to shaking.

I look around the room. Jenn and Dave have come down from Massachusetts. Friends from grad school, current students, faculty I work with, and many staff people are here: Bev and her girlfriend, Maureen, with Jaiden; Lyde and all her kids; Crystal, Christina, and everyone from the office. On and on. I look around and see other friends I haven't talked to in a while. There are probably a hundred people in the room, and at the far end is a six-foot table overflowing with presents.

There are games, of course, and I have to wear a hat made of bows from the presents I open. Pat has everyone take a piece of paper and write down a bit of advice for me, advice for when I'm in the midst of it and looking for some guidance. I have them still, those yellow pieces of lined paper. I take them out once in a while to read when I feel sad. They make me feel loved and cared for. In that collection of papers is also a poem Lyde wrote and read that day—a funny, lovely poem about her and me and kids and love. I cried in front of God and everyone as she read it. And I had a fleeting thought then, which I forgot, only to recapture again later: *This is my family. This is the family I have made. Here are my people. This is my life. And what a wonderful life it is.*

The Wednesday after my shower, my office mates in Slonim House throw me another surprise shower. They set it up while Crystal takes me out shopping for an outfit for the baby to come home in.

This time I am not only overwhelmed, but truly surprised. I have not been expecting another shower at all. They give me a jogging stroller, and I vow as I open it that I will get myself back into running shape as soon as the baby is born.

One of the women in the office writes the baby and me a song.

I have decided to call her Kaj (it rhymes with "eye"), after my grandfather. She will be Kaj Grace Abildgaard Soiseth. Grace is for my sister; it's her middle name. It would also be nice for the baby to have another name to fall back on if she finds Kaj too unwieldy.

The song goes like this:

Little K, little a, little j, little Kaj. Even before you joined the world, you were the apple of your mother's eye. And as you make your way, we will shout it to the sky. The name we love to say, little K, little Kaj. The name we love to say, little K, little Kaj.

After the two showers, there are only three weeks left in the semester, then a week for graduation, and then my baby is due.

My blood pressure keeps climbing, and I'm not surprised, because the last two weeks of school are crammed with thesis readings and end-of-year parties. I have to organize them all, and I can't bring myself to ask for any more time off to rest, even though I'm unbelievably tired. I go every Friday for a checkup and watch my weight and my blood pressure rise.

The week of graduation, I call to move my appointment to Thursday afternoon, because I will need to be at commencement on Friday.

Finally, during the week of commencement, I can take it easy. My work is done, really, except for cleaning up. I come in late, and even lie on the couch in the empty office next door. At home the baby's room is organized and finished, as well as my bedroom upstairs, though I continue sleeping in the spare room by the bathroom.

The downstairs is a total mess. Every night I ignore my pulsing nesting instincts and sit around and rest. Then I find myself crawling into bed by nine. All of commencement week, I plan to get off my butt and clean, because Margaret and Linda are coming on Thursday night—it's the Victoria Day long weekend in Canada, so they thought they would help with any last-minute stuff—but I figure I'll have time to clean on Thursday, after my doctor's appointment. By the time they get to me after driving from Canada, the place will be spick-and-span.

On Thursday I drive up to my appointment, thinking that, with all the resting I've been doing this week, my blood pressure should be down today. And with all the heartburn, I've really not eaten much, either.

I also realize, as I drive, that tomorrow is the baby's original due date. Ultrasounds since then have moved the due date to the twenty-second, which is Saturday. But I have a feeling I won't hit either of those dates. There have been no Braxton Hicks contractions, nothing to suggest to me that the baby is near coming out. She is low, and her head is engaged, they tell me, but I feel the same as I've felt for weeks. It'll be a week or more yet, I'm convinced.

Because of Mom's experience with Gordon, I am hypervigilant about the baby's movements. If she is still for too long, I poke around to make sure she is okay. I'm usually only satisfied when she gives me a good kick. What a roller coaster pregnancy is. I don't know how women continue being mothers while they're gestating another kid.

It's Bakas at the office today. They call me right in, but I snag a cup of water from their cooler before walking to the back. It's wicked hot and humid today. I'm wearing as little clothing as possible. With only four summer outfits that still fit me, I'm limited.

The nurse takes my blood pressure, as usual. I watch her frown as she listens through her stethoscope while she releases air from the pressure cup.

"It's 146/96," she says, and I sigh. That's not down at all. That's up even more. I step on the scale for her next, and I turn my face away. Enough with the bad news today.

"Two hundred and twenty-three pounds," she says.

Wow, I've gained fifty-three pounds with this pregnancy. Fifty-three fucking pounds.

This kid better come out weighing twenty pounds, and the placenta, another fifteen. Otherwise I don't know if I can live with myself.

As the nurse leaves, I drink up the rest of the water and then lie down on the examination table. I fall into a sleepy daze while I wait for Dr. Bakas. I'm half dreaming about Linda and Margaret at my place, the three of us waking up late and spending all morning at breakfast. They will take care of me, and I will let them.

Bakas knocks, and it startles me. I feel a shiver ripple over me, and suddenly the air-conditioning is too cold, blowing on my wet, sweaty clothes. Bakas walks in, holding my file. He has a pen out and is reading as he walks, clicking the pen open and closed. "It's up again," he says.

"I know." I sigh. "But I can really rest now," I say. "School is done." He is still reading. Then he's flipping through the pages.

"When's your due date again?"

"Tomorrow is the original due date, based on when we did the insemination. The ultrasound date is Saturday."

"Hmm."

He usually does a pelvic exam to see if I've dilated at all, but today he looks up at me from the file and says, "You know, I think we should send you over to Northern Westchester for a blood test. We could do it here, but they have a lab downstairs at the hospital, and we can get the results in a few hours, rather than days."

"Blood test for what?"

"I'm just a little worried about your pressure."

"I feel okay," I say. "A little tired."

More clicking of the pen. It's loud in my head, and I realize I feel a bit strange, like I'm dehydrated or have a fever.

"I just want to be safe."

"Okay," I say.

"You can drive over, and I'll call and tell them you're coming. Check in at the desk on the main floor. McGroary is on call there and will supervise the tests."

"Okay," I say again, and he leaves.

I get down awkwardly from the table.

Damn, it's hot out. It feels like July, not May. I sprout sweat the second I step out of Bakas's office. The metal on my seat belt scorches my palm as I pull it around and under my belly. I've had to move my seat back so far that I have to sit a little sideways in order to get the clutch all the way down to the floor. I turn the car on and point the vents directly on me, with the AC going full blast.

The hospital is only down the block, but I drive nice and slow to savor the AC. Once I'm in the lot, I park as close as I can to the ER doors so I don't have to walk very far. As I wait to be called up to the desk, I call my boss.

"Hey there," I say when our receptionist answers. "Is Susan in?"

"No, she's out at a meeting. Can I get her to call you?"

"Sure, she can call me on my cell, but the battery is really low. Just tell her I've been sent to the hospital for tests."

"Are you okay?"

"I think so; I feel okay. Well, a little weird, actually, but I think it's just the heat. The doctor said he was being safe."

"Okay, I'll tell her."

"Hey, can you get Pat for me?"

"Sure, hang on."

I take a quick glance at my battery indicator and see that it's flashing on and off; there's very little juice left. "Hi, Pat," I say when she picks up the phone. "Listen, uh, Bakas has sent me over to the hospital for tests."

"Really? What for?"

"I don't know, exactly. I'm waiting to be taken up to the maternity ward."

"He must have said something."

"It's my blood pressure. But I should be back in the office later today."
I wait a bit, then say, "Um, do you think you could come up here and wait
with me?"

"Sure," she says. Then there is a pause. "But wait, I don't have the car.
Shit. Ahmed took it today."

"Right, that's okay. I'll be fine. They're just drawing some blood and
waiting. It's just waiting."

Above my head, the TV suddenly gets louder. I look up to see why,
but there is no one around. I notice the lady at the reception desk near the
entrance, beckoning me toward her. "Hey, I gotta go. They're taking me
upstairs now."

"Okay, keep me posted!"

There are papers to sign and other business to take care of, and then I'm
up on the maternity ward. Getting off the elevator, I remember the tour I
took with Pat a couple of weeks ago. What I remember most was the nurse
being super irritated about women giving birth in the whirlpool. It makes a
terrible mess, she said, and is a ton of work to clean.

"If your family is with you in the birthing room," she also said, "if they
need to get out for a breath of air, be sure to tell them they must go back out
the double doors to the waiting room. We can't have people pacing around
in the halls outside the birthing rooms."

I am taken by that very waiting room and see toys in the corner and a
TV turned to the hospital channel. The nurse takes me to a room at the end
of the hall. "Great, here's a room you can wait in. I'll send McGroary over
as soon as he's free," she says.

The room is dark, but it isn't as cool as the hallway, which is good,
because I'm chilled again. It's a large room too, almost as big as one of the

labor-and-delivery rooms. I sit at the end of the bed and look around. I decide to call Pat with an update.

"So, Pat," I say, "maybe Crystal can drive you. Maybe Susan wouldn't mind if you both left for a little while. It just feels a little . . . well, I'm okay. Don't worry about it if you can't."

"Hang on, I'll ask Crystal."

"Can you call me back? My battery is almost dead."

I'm aware, as I sit on the edge of the bed waiting for Pat to call me back, that my belly rests on my thighs now. There are bad fat associations with that feeling, and I remind myself that I am pregnant. That's what happens when you have a baby growing inside of you.

To get rid of the feeling, I crawl into the bed and lie on my side. Now that I'm really still, I feel the coolness of the room settle down on me, and I wrap the white blanket from the end of the bed around my shoulders, my cell phone in my hand under my chin. I sleep.

It is McGroary who wakes me up; I'm not sure how. Maybe I just felt him watching me, because when I open my eyes he is there beside the bed, looking down at me.

"You okay?" he asks.

"Sure. Just tired."

He shoves his hands into the pockets of his white lab coat. This is McGroary's habit, to push his hands down into his pockets. He does it so often that the pockets flop outward, sitting open all the time, like they are waiting for his hands.

"I just talked to Dr. Bakas, and I think he's right—we're going to take some blood. Also, I want you to go for an ultrasound so we can be sure the baby is okay."

"Fine." I'm a little dizzy and dry-mouthed.

"A technician will be by soon for the blood, and then someone will take you for the ultrasound. We'll know more when the bloodwork gets in."

"I'm going to be . . ." I pause, not wanting to show him I'm worried.

"Yes?" he asks, turning back from heading out the door.

"Everything is all right, right?"

He smiles at me. "Don't worry."

But I do worry. In my easygoing way, I'm kind of an anxious person.

For example, I'm worried because I haven't heard back from Pat and I wonder what's happened.

When I wake up again, it is to see the tech with her cart of supplies. She tourniquets my arm and draws vials of blood. I don't know how many, because I've turned away and tried to go back into my dream.

I am asleep again when someone from transport arrives with a wheelchair to take me for my ultrasound. I'm worried about Pat. What if she gets here while I'm gone? I want to leave a note but the transport person is more or less tapping his toes, so I take my cell phone and put my purse in the drawer of the bedside cabinet.

"You'd better take that with you," the nurse says from the doorway. "I'm not sure this room will still be free when you get back."

"Okay."

Pat arrives then with Crystal, saying she tried to get through on my cell phone but couldn't. We stand for a moment, debating what to do, and Crystal says she will drive to my apartment and get clothes and my cell phone charger, just in case I have to stay the night. I ask her to bring my knitting too, because I'm still not done with the pink blanket I started ages ago, and suddenly I feel as though I need to finish it before the baby comes.

She gives me a look but says okay. I wish now I had packed a bag, so she wouldn't have to go searching through my messy apartment for clothes.

The transport guy and Pat and I head for the elevator, and when we get outside the ultrasound room, Pat sits in a chair, and I wait in the wheelchair.

"I can't remember when I felt her move last," I say to Pat and start digging around my lower pelvis. Pat laughs. "Stop it!" she says, grabbing my hand. "You'll poke your baby's eye out."

But when she sees that I'm really worried, she gives me a quick hug and says, "It's okay, Alex. It's going to be fine." Pat holds my hand as we wait. I think about Mom and her first baby again. It was only when she and Dad got to the hospital, two hours away, that she knew her baby was dead. The doctors could hear no heartbeat. And only after they saw the decay on his neck, once my mother had given birth to him, did they realize it had been days. The doctor told my dad this quietly in the hallway. "It's the diabetes," he said. "Another day and Mimi would have died too."

"What diabetes?" Dad asked.

"Your wife has diabetes. That's what killed your son."

Mom's doctor back in tiny Punichy hadn't figured it out. Was it because he was a drunk I wonder as I sit with Pat. Or was it the doctors' strike? Something was going on, and I try to remember what. Certainly, my mom was isolated. All her family was back in Denmark. Even Dad's brothers and sisters lived hours and hours away.

Staring up at the ceiling, I feel connected to her like I never have before. I see her in a totally new way. Not as my mother so much as a woman alone, delivering her dead baby. It makes me so sad, I want to cry.

"Good afternoon!" a blond woman with a tight lab coat over an ample bosom squeaks out to us in her rubber-soled shoes.

"Hi," Pat and I say together. I shiver.

"Cold?" she asks. "I know, it's chilly in here."

"Scared," I say.

"Don't worry, honey," she says, without breaking her rhythm. She's chewing gum and smells faintly like cigarette smoke. She is deeply tanned.

"I had issues with my pregnancy, but he's an eighteen-year-old boy now, so don't you worry." She gets me up onto the bed and pulls the white curtain separating my bed from the other one. She makes room for Pat on the other side of me. "Lift your shirt and we'll get started."

I brace myself for the cold jelly and am surprised that it is mildly warm. She drops it back into a gel container–shaped hole in the machine.

"I know," she says, "it's these new machines. They have a little heater for the gel!"

I nod.

"These new machines can take pictures in color and three dimensions!"

"This one?" I ask, excited to be able to see what is inside of me, what this baby looks like, whom I have been waiting on for nine months. It's more than that, actually—she feels so far away, even though she's just inside. If I could see her, I would feel reassured.

"No, it's a good, clear machine but not three-dimensional. Those machines aren't actually all that helpful diagnostically when looking at a fetus. They are more for the parents to get a picture than for doctors."

I wonder if Gwyneth Paltrow went to get a picture like that. I wonder how her pregnancy feels compared with mine, what difference lots of money would make.

Just as in McGroary's office and upstairs with the genetic counselor's ultrasound machine, I have to twist and hold my head up with my left hand to see the screen. Pat peers over my shoulder.

The technician presses the wand into my belly, and shapes pop up on the screen. She presses low near my pelvic bone, all business now.

Oh god, don't let anything be wrong.

She stops and looks at the piece of paper hanging from the back of my wheelchair on a clipboard.

"Is everything okay?" I ask, not wanting to seem like one of those pushy, irritating patients.

"Fine," she says.

"Okay."

"I'm going to take a few measurements; it'll just take a sec."

After she is done, she hands me a towel to wipe my belly. I now have to pee badly; I have a kind of suggestive need to urinate whenever I get an ultrasound.

"I'm going to get transportation to take you back now," she says. "The doctor will talk to you. Don't you worry."

Pat and I wait in the hall for someone to take me up again. We don't say much. Part of me is conscious that Pat's last ultrasound was a very sad one, and that her D&C was only five weeks ago. She is stoic about such things, but I can feel a kind of hurt coming off her.

We are taken up to the same room after all, and we sit and wait for Crystal and the doctor. *It would be nice to have my knitting,* I think. *Give me something to do.*

Crystal arrives with a change of clothes and my own nightgown, my penguin housecoat, and my knitting, although one of the needles fell out in her car. We wait to see if I'm actually going to be admitted.

When Dr. McGroary comes to see me, he apologizes for the wait; he's been doing a delivery that just finished. He has seen the ultrasound, and everything seems fine.

"I'm just worried about your blood pressure. I think we should try to get this delivery going."

"Does that mean you'll break my water and give me Pitocin and all that?" I remember the doula saying that when the baby isn't ready, trying to force it out means women almost always end up with a cesarean. First it's Pitocin. Then the contractions come really hard and fast, so you have to get an epidural, which slows down the contractions, and in the end there is the cesarean.

"No, we'll just start by trying to stimulate labor. We'll insert a balloon in your cervix to urge it to open more. It has been shown to help. We'll admit you and put in the balloon, and hopefully tomorrow you'll be on your way."

TEN

It's Not Called "Labor" for Nothing

The balloon does nothing. By morning there are no contractions and no widening of the cervix. Dr. McGroary moves Megan and Pat and me through the double doors into the inner sanctum of childbirth: the labor-and-delivery area. He is going to break my water and get this show on the road.

None of us sleep well on Thursday night. They put Pat and Megan and me in a tiny room next to the lounge. The balloon in my cervix feels weird—not even uncomfortable, just weird. As the pregnant mom, I get the bed, such as it is, a narrow, plastic-covered mattress. Pat sleeps on a chair whose cushions flop out to make a very narrow facsimile of a bed. Dear Megan gets the floor.

"I can't sleep like this," I say, feeling it is hard to breathe with all of us on top of each other. I can hear the air moving in and out of their nostrils.

They don't say anything, but later they will tell me that I was a total prima donna. I think about it now and wonder why I didn't just send them home to have a good night's sleep. I guess I thought there was a chance I would go into labor during the night. But of course I didn't, and I was very glad for them to be there, because I was scared.

Megan goes to my car for the orange squishy earplugs I'm sure are sitting in the unused ashtray, but when she comes back, she has not been able to find them.

In the meantime Margaret and Linda arrive, having driven straight from Canada to the hospital.

"Mrs.!" I say. "Linda!" I make introductions all around.

"My god, you two look alike," Megan says about Linda and me.

"When I'm skinny you can hardly tell us apart," I say, and Linda and I smile at each other.

Pat and Margaret hug like old friends. "Again, I am so sorry about your miscarriage," Margaret says, and Pat nods.

"How is your pregnancy going?" Pat asks, and Margaret pulls up her shirt to show us her little four-month bump.

I am so glad to have my four favorite people together with me that I just lean back and watch them talk to each other. Would this configuration be possible if I had a husband? I think not, and I'm confused about how I feel, where that understanding fits in with my wanting to have a more traditional arrangement. It strikes me that maybe I don't want that so much after all.

I can't imagine being happier than I am at this moment.

The nurse comes in to give me a mild sedative.

"Here are the keys to my apartment," I say to Linda as I write out directions to my place. "Okay, you know I wasn't expecting this, right? I was going to clean up this afternoon. The sheets on my bed need to be changed, and I know there's shit all over the place."

"Don't worry. Who cares? You're having a baby!" the Mrs. says, and I feel a little better.

As they leave I can feel the drugs gently nudging me to sleep. I go to the bathroom one more time, and the three of us go to sleep.

Once we are moved to the birthing room on Friday morning, Dr. McGroary sends Pat and Megan out, and he and the nurse break my water. Then everyone comes back in, Linda and Margaret arrive, and soon we have the boom box plugged in. We play Gloria Estefan's song "Hoy" over and over again, singing at the top of our lungs.

Nothing much is happening, though I imagine that what I am experiencing every few minutes is a contraction. They are teeny-weeny—practice contractions that stop me from talking for a moment as I focus inside on the pain. Then out I come again and make a joke. But by eleven o'clock, they seem more regular and painful, and Margaret suggests a walk. So off we go, walking down the halls, past rooms filled with new mothers and tiny, squeaking babies. We step to the side as a woman in a hospital bed is rolled by us into a room; behind her walks the father, carrying a baby.

We glance at each other but don't say what we are thinking—*no cesarean!* But I know in my heart that we are pretty much headed that way anyway. Breaking my water puts time on the table—twenty-four hours, or the doctor goes in with a knife to take the baby out. After twenty-four hours, infection is a guarantee.

The room we're in is huge, the size of a small restaurant's dining room. But it feels blessedly like a living room, even though I'm told surgical lights roll out from the ceiling, like landing gear on a plane, when they are needed.

During the walk with Margaret and Linda, my contractions get lackadaisical and sporadic again, so I sit still for half an hour, and they speed up. At 1:00 PM Dr. McGroary comes in and rocks back and forth on his heels, shoving his hands into his waiting pockets. "You know," he says, looking at me and only me, "we might have to think about Pitocin soon."

"I know," I say. "But please let me try on my own for a little while longer."

He nods slowly and speaks quietly to the nurse as he leaves. She's an older woman, efficient and wrinkled, with a healthy dose of perfume to hide the smell of cigarette smoke. It's on her hands mostly, and they make me think faintly about my mother; her thin, permed hair reinforces the similarity. But when she talks, she's all Bronx.

My doula right now is the young one, Sadie, and she jokes with us, but it's Margaret, mother of two and a doctor, whom I turn to when I'm wondering what to do next.

Throughout the afternoon we sing songs and talk. Linda, Megan, Margaret, and Pat are getting along famously. I sit on the ball and zone out as contractions come and go. Linda sits behind me at one point while I'm on the ball and starts to French braid my hair. I ask her if this was what her labors were like, and she said hers went a little faster. With Audrey, her oldest, the water breaking was what sent them to the hospital. Her second and third births went superfast. "And there certainly weren't as many people around when I gave birth," she says, and I laugh, because it *is* kind of funny: Four friends, and now two doulas, are here.

Everyone takes turns going out to eat lunch, and I get ice chips, since I'm not supposed to eat during labor, just in case they have to take me for an emergency C-section.

As the afternoon drags on and there is no progress, I ask for an enema, which I've been told will sometimes get things going. Nurse Bronxie is skeptical, and she's right—it doesn't do much.

I keep changing positions, hoping it will help, but there is no progress.

By 5:00 PM the contractions are much worse, but still nowhere near strong enough to get Kaj out into this world, and this time when Dr. Mc-Groary comes in and rocks on his heels, Margaret gives me a look that says, *Time's up.*

The original IV site attempted by a shaky-handed nurse even before we were moved into the labor room has bruised up my left arm spectacularly. My Bronx nurse is the one who finally got an IV in, and it is through this site that a Pitocin drip is started. As she hangs the bag, she says, "Now we'll see some action," and she pats me gently above my bruised left arm. She straps a monitor around my belly to keep an eye on the baby's heart rate, and my time of walking around or getting out of bed is over. It doesn't bother me too much, because I'd pretty much stopped moving anyway. It seemed to only slow my labor.

"People hate my labor story," Pat says when Margaret asks her about giving birth to Ali.

"Really?" Megan and Margaret laugh.

Linda is behind me, giving me a lovely light massage on my shoulders.

Megan is massaging my feet. Margaret is sitting to my right, where the monitor for the baby is. She reassures me occasionally that the baby is doing fine.

"I had no pain," Pat says. "Granted, Ali was six weeks premature, but the only reason I knew I was in labor was that I had an appointment that day with Dr. Bakas, and when he did an internal, I was seven centimeters dilated."

Margaret talks about her experience with Christian, her oldest son; how she pushed him out while she was actually vomiting at the same time. Linda talks about how giving birth to Audrey was hard, but what she doesn't tell us is that Audrey was stuck, and that Linda screamed in pain for hours because they couldn't give her an epidural, either. There was a slightly nightmarish feel to that delivery, Linda would tell me later, because no one was really sure why the baby wouldn't come out.

It is now, under the influence of Pitocin, that everything begins to get kind of underwater. There is no doubt for me now what a contraction feels like, rippling, ripping, burning, cramping through my pelvis. It is what branding must feel like for cattle, again and again. For hours and hours I breathe deep and *puff puff puff* the air out, through the evening and into the night. I find a place on the ceiling or the wall as I feel a contraction coming. It's just an echo at first, a tingling, and I say with dread, "Here we go again." And Margaret takes my one hand, Linda the other, and I find my comfort spot and stare at it as the contraction takes me over and I breathe in—a long, long deep breath.

No one told me this, but I come to realize that this is the breath that makes it possible to survive the pain—not the *puff puff puff* of the outgoing breath, but the deep, calm, strengthening power of the incoming breath.

I rest during the spaces between, dipping into a hazy dream as Linda and Megan and Pat and Margaret move in and out of the room. I am aware at one point that Linda has been gone a long time.

"Where's Linda?" I ask, looking around stupidly.

"She just went for a break."

Another contraction is on its way when she stands beside me. "There you are," I say, relieved, missing her. But then I begin to panic, because she is standing between me and the light fixture I have been using as my focal point for the last half hour. "Move move move," I say, panicked, because if I can't look at my spot, I won't survive the pain. If I don't start my inward breath at the exact right moment, I will begin to whimper and gasp and suck in short breaths—"Oh my god, oh my god, oh my god I can't take it"—and Linda says, "Sorry sorry sorry, did I hurt you?" And she leaves again and I don't see her for a long while.

About 1:00 AM, I go pee during a break. The doula helps me to the bathroom, dragging the IV pole, but a contraction catches me before I'm seated, and I stand and tremble, staring at the juncture where the bottom of the toilet meets the floor.

"It doesn't have to be this way," the nurse says to me as I sit down. She throws a look at the doula. "There are other options."

I know she means an epidural, and I'm tempted, but not really. I want to do this on my own. I don't want a cesarean. I shake my head and she walks out.

At 3:00 AM, when the doula is out of the room, Margaret stands beside me during the hollow space between contractions and says, "You know, there's no shame in an epidural. You've been going a long time, and there is still the pushing." She looks at me so softly that I want to cry. She brushes the wet hair from my forehead. "You need some rest."

I nod and say, "Oh god, here comes another." And we clasp hands, and I grunt and feel stars exploding in my brain until it passes and I lie back to rest.

The nurse comes in to check on me a little later. "How are you doing?"

I say, "I want an epidural now." Margaret is right. I am utterly exhausted, and I feel that soon even the breathing won't save me. Soon I will die from the pain.

The doula sends everyone out and looks at me in the strangely quiet and empty room. "Are you sure? You asked me during our first meeting to check with you to be sure. Are you sure?"

"Absolutely," I say, resolutely, because I have no doubts now. I have gone as long as I can on my own.

The anesthesiologist is sent for, and this is the period that is hardest to take. I don't know if the pain is actually worse, or if waiting for it to be over makes it seem worse. I don't have any real concept of how long it is before he gets there, and then I sit on the side of the bed, curving my spine as I curl over my large belly and try to stay as still as I can, even as a contraction hits.

The first epidural doesn't work on the left side, so he redoes it. Even the second doesn't work properly, though they turn it on high. But the third try is the winner, and as I lie back in the dark cave of a delivery room, it seems as if a light fills the room as the pain recedes. Perhaps it's so late in the night that it's actually dawn, but when I look at the spaces between the pulled curtains, it is still dark outside. Margaret pulls on my penguin robe, Linda puts on my sweater, and everyone scatters for some sleep. My nurse lowers the lights completely, and I sleep too.

Dr. McGroary has been at the hospital all night, sleeping somewhere, and he comes to see me regularly. But at 8:30 AM, it is Dr. Bakas who comes in to wake me up. He sits beside me on the bed. "So, how are you feeling?"

"Better since the epidural." I smile.

"You got some rest?"

"Yes."

"Well, I think we might want to think about pushing soon."

I am afraid. I don't feel ready. I don't know why I think that, but it seems as if this whole exercise has been about my forcing this baby to do stuff she isn't ready for. Maybe it's because I can't feel the contractions anymore, but I look around for McGroary. He'll understand. He's been here all along and has seen this sluggishness, all yesterday and last night.

The nurses begin to take the end of the bed off, and by 9:00 AM the ceiling panels slide open and lights do indeed swing down like the wheels of a plane before it lands.

"You're still here?" my Bronx nurse asks with a smile as she rigs a bar over the bed for me to pull on as I push. I smile back at her and test the solidity of the bar. "So, do you feel the tightening? The urge to push?"

"I guess so." I say, though I don't really know what she means.

She puts her hand on my belly, waits and waits, and then says, "There. Feel it?" And I actually do now. There's a pressure in the back, as though I'm about to have a bowel movement. Then it is gone.

"Good, well, that's when you want to push."

I nod.

Everyone gathers around. My legs are up and open. "Push!" someone says, and I do.

"No, that's not right," Bronxie says. "You're pushing with your head, holding your breath like that. Feel it deep down. I know it's hard with the epidural, but pretend that you're having a bowel movement; push like that."

"But . . ." I start to say, but I don't know how to express what I'm really worried about. I'm afraid I actually *will* have a bowel movement.

"Don't worry," she says. "All women feel the same, and yes, you probably will have a bowel movement, but we'll wipe it away and on we go."

So I let go fully and push and push, not quite getting it right but trying over and over. After an hour or so, I ask to pull on the bar across the bed, but that doesn't do anything and I lie back again.

Much later Margaret says, "There she is! I can see her head!" McGroary squirts oil around to help lubricate her exit, and for a few moments I have new energy and push harder and harder as Pat yells, "Push! *Push!*" I try, but the baby just doesn't get any further.

The nurses rotate; some kneel on the bed beside me and help by pushing on my stomach. "Try this," one says, twisting a towel and slipping it over the bar above me. "Pull on this."

Somehow four hours pass in this way. I am hot. My head is pounding and my face is burning. Every two minutes someone says, "Push!" and I do. McGroary comes back at some point and Bakas comes in and out, a pained look on his face. I hear him tell Pat that he finds this part so hard; he really hates to see women in pain this way.

This pushing part seems to belong to the nurses, who ask me to try first this, then that. Four different nurses cycle in and out, and I am aware that while I continue in this monotony of pushing, these nurses have moved around the ring of labor-and-delivery rooms and delivered other babies.

At some point, McGroary stands beside me and feels my fevered forehead—he must be thinking about cesareans. It is way past twenty-four hours. I'm thinking about it too now, and it's hard to summon up any of the determination I felt when we walked around and saw the woman wheeled in on the bed. I envy her now—done, like that—and all the women in the adjacent rooms, and their doneness.

He says to me, "Perhaps I should turn down the epidural. I think it might help you to feel the urge to push."

The memory of last night's labor pains jolts me. "I have to be honest—that scares the shit out of me."

He smiles at me a little. "It'll be okay."

I nod because although I am afraid of all that pain again, I also trust him.

He turns down the epidural, and the need to push is much stronger, but I am so tired now that it's hard to conjure enough strength to do much about it. A little more time passes, and I begin to shake uncontrollably and cry. "Can you get Dr. McGroary?" I ask Margaret.

More pushing, and when I open my eyes he is beside me. "I can't do this anymore. I need help." I try not to sound pathetic. I can't actually get myself to say I'm ready for a cesarean, but that's what I mean.

He nods at me and goes over to talk to one of the nurses, and they all leave for a while. Margaret is on my left, and Megan and Pat are on my right. I haven't seen Linda or the doula for a while.

"It's okay, Mrs.," Margaret says. She looks up at the monitors that track how the baby is doing. "She's okay. All this time, she's been okay." I feel the automatic blood pressure cup tighten on my arm, and I look over to see that my pressure is still crazy high: 170/105.

"Okay," McGroary says as he comes back in with all four nurses. Bronxie says, "Sit up a little more," and she kneels beside me on the bed. I can feel McGroary squirting warm water and wiping me clean. I learn later that he was trying to get rid of some of the olive oil he used to make the way slippery.

"On the next push, Alex, we need you to give it everything, okay?" Bronxie says right in my ear, just for me. McGroary has something that looks like a miniplunger, and I can feel him placing it on the baby's head and pulling a little to see if it is suctioned on tightly.

"Ready?"

I nod. I hunch over, taking short, quick breaths to prepare. Then I feel it come, that urge to push, and I take a deep breath and everyone says, "Push!" McGroary grunts a little as he pulls, but I'm hardly aware of it for the rushing in my head as I puuuuuuuuuuuuuuuuuusssssssssssssssssssssssh and something goes *pop*. McGroary stumbles backward and I fall back from pushing. "Too much oil still," he says to the nurse beside him. "Can you get me another clean towel?"

I have a moment or two of rest, when I disappear into myself. Then we are all poised, the plunger attached, and I take a deep breath and push again. Bronxie and another nurse are on the other side of me on the bed, pushing down on my belly, Margaret and Pat help me roll my shoulders forward and hunch over, and McGroary pulls. For the first time all morning, I can feel movement, and I look down to see her emerge, finally, dark wet hair, red with blood, and a long body that comes and comes out of me like a red ribbon. I see McGroary put his finger under the plunger and pop it off, and suddenly she is there, landing crossways in his arms. A nurse is cleaning her up, and I look at her, this baby of mine. How long and thin she is, like an arrow. For a moment I think, *Thank God she has Olaf's build. Good for her. Lucky for her.*

After hours and hours of sameness, everything is moving and changing suddenly. Baby Girl Soiseth is on my chest for just a second as they cut the cord; then she is gone, under the warm lights in the corner of the room.

I can't stop crying. "I did it! I did it! Oh my god!"

Margaret and Pat and Megan are all crying too, saying, "Good job!" Patting my arm and pushing the wet hair from my face.

"Where's Linda? Where is she?"

"I'll get her," Pat says, and I'm quivering and still crying and I can't stop. Bronxie says to me firmly, as she tries to put a thermometer in my mouth, "Okay, that's enough. You have to stop crying now."

I gather my strength to stop, and then Linda is there. "I did it! She's born!" I say around the thermometer, and Linda is crying and holding my hand. "Where were you? Were you here when she was born?" Linda shakes her head.

It is only later that Pat will tell me Linda couldn't bear to be in the room a lot of the time. It was too hard for her to see me in pain; it frightened her. Pat and I looked at each other as she told me this, and, though we didn't say anything, we both thought about the birthing class and the men leaving the room to write out their fears. I remembered how sad I was that no one loved me enough to be afraid.

With Linda beside me, they bring Kaj over, all clean and wrapped in a white blanket. I can hardly see her through my swollen eyelids, and she blinks at me through the vitamin K cream. "She's beautiful, Alex," Linda says.

"Welcome to the world, Baby Girl Soiseth." And Kaj and I squint at each other until the nurse takes her away to the ICU to monitor her temperature. "Don't worry," the nurse says. "She's perfect and healthy. But she has your fever."

ELEVEN

The Long Hollow Nights

Pictures of me from right after the birth show me bloated and red-eyed, with burst blood vessels all over my face and bruises up my arm from the intravenous line attempts. I'm still shiny with sweat, and my wet hair is plastered to my head, although I still have a little of the French braid that Linda did the day before. Word goes out that the baby is finally born, and visitors start to arrive almost before McGroary has finished helping me deliver the placenta. He gives me a few stitches too. I'm elated now, feeling kind of high and light-headed, but disjointed, because my baby is somewhere else.

Not inside me. Not beside me.

Friends arrive from seeing her in the nursery to tell me she is beautiful—with an ever-so-slight plunger-shaped head.

Bronxie shoos everyone out and takes me slowly and carefully to the bathroom. I realize suddenly that I have to pee very badly, because, of course, the catheter has been gone since I started to push, and the saline drip has been slowly pumping me full of water.

My face is shocking to see. It's as wide as a sideways watermelon and as red as the inside of one. "Don't," Bronxie says, guiding me away from the mirror to the toilet. She shows me how to use a squirt bottle to clean myself after peeing. "It will sting a little at first—you've got some stitches."

Back in bed, I can't keep my eyes open. "Take these," Bronxie says. I don't even ask what the pills are for, but I hope they're for my booming headache. She checks my blood pressure one last time before cranking the bed down flat. It's 140/90, already much better. As I fall asleep I think, *Shouldn't I be breastfeeding her? Won't she starve? It's already been over an hour since she was born; shouldn't I be asking about this? Oh god, how is her fever?* But I'm asleep before I can even finish that thought.

The next two days float by in a wonderful haze of visits and talking. I'm moved to a lovely single room facing south, where the May sun shines in almost all day. There are flowers everywhere and more gifts, and people take turns holding Kaj while she sleeps.

I call friends and family as soon as I'm moved and properly awake to tell them about the birth—Linda called Mom and Dad while I was sleeping, but I call them myself to give them the details. Jenn and Dave are ecstatic, and Jenn is very sympathetic to my preeclampsia experience. Megan comes back after taking a shower and sleeping for a few hours. She brings her girlfriend, Luz.

Finally, at about five that afternoon, a nurse rolls Kaj into my room in one of the plastic-walled cribs they use in hospitals. After a few hours in the ICU, my fever left her, and she was pronounced well enough to come to my room. They bring her to me swaddled tightly in a hospital blanket, sleeping on her side. "You can try feeding her now," the nurse says. "If you need help, we have a nurse on duty today who is trained as a lactation consultant."

Kaj is sleeping too deeply to eat, so I give up after trying for a few minutes. Linda and Margaret arrive with takeout. Pat comes back too, after a trip home to shower. Christina brings Kyle, and Crystal comes by with some food. Lyde comes with her oldest son. The room is bursting with people, and I am aware that I am so very happy, safe, and loved. Luz holds the baby, then Megan; Pat takes a turn, then Margaret.

And so it goes all weekend, with rotating visitors bringing more gifts or flowers. Margaret and Linda and Luz and Megan are a constant; Pat comes in and out with Ali. He gets a pin from the nurse's desk that says: I'M A BIG BROTHER. He tells the nurse, "I'm a big brother, and her name is Kaj."

The nights, however, are a dark haze of sleeplessness and confusion about how to get the baby to stop crying. I knew her so well when she was inside me, but now that she's out in the world, I don't get her at all. Her tiny face scrunches up and her bruised lips open wide, crying the squeaky cry of a newborn, when she wakes up that first night at midnight. She has been in this world less than eleven hours, deeply asleep that whole time, but now, at midnight, she is fully awake and hungry. I struggle out of bed to get her from the hospital crib. When I have her in my arms, I realize I have hardly held her all day. I'm scared I'll drop her. I didn't think I would be this awkward. With years of baby-sitting behind me, I thought I was a pro.

The struggle to feed her is comedic. My nightgown gets stuck underneath me, and I'm pinned down for a moment until I get the idea of putting Kaj down in the middle of the bed while I settle myself. I take ages to set everything up, until finally I have pillows around me to bolster her to my breast. When I get her to latch on, I'm not sure it's right. Should it hurt this much?

Breastfeeding will be an ongoing struggle the first weeks, especially on the right side. That first night I hardly sleep, and the next day I ask that she be taken to the nursery during the night. They bring her in every three hours for breastfeeding. I do my best.

If she is crying while she's in the nursery, they don't tell me, and I'm too afraid of the answer to ask.

On Sunday night, after Margaret has driven my car to my apartment, and Linda has brought her back to the hospital, we settle in for the evening. Linda will sleep on the chair that turns into a bed, and Margaret will sleep on the floor, and at 4:00 AM they will get up to drive back to Canada.

When 4:00 AM comes, they are getting their things together when Kaj is brought in to nurse. As I say goodbye to Linda and Margaret, I feel like I will cry and never stop.

How horrible it is that we live so far away from each other, that Kaj will be sitting up with the help of pillows before Linda sees her again. That I will be so far away from Margaret when she gives birth to her own baby.

And when they leave, I am shocked by how afraid I am in the dark, holding my baby alone, feeding her but not sure that it's right, because it hurts so much when she first latches on. I have one of those moments, like when you are standing on the sidewalk next to cars rushing by and it suddenly occurs to you that one step out and you would be dead, hit by one of those cars speeding by. Anything could go wrong now—the hospital could catch fire; I could lose my job; I could trip carrying her and land on top of her.

This is the beginning of weeks and weeks of fearful nights breastfeeding alone in the dark, of shushing and soothing and struggling, while the days stretch open and happy, full of visitors and light.

On Monday, I ask to be discharged. It's a much more complicated thing than I would have thought, including another visit by McGroary. "Are you sure you want to go home today?" he asks me on his early-morning visit. I am a little confused; aren't I supposed to want to rush home?

"You had a very difficult labor. You might want to rest another day." But I say no, I want to go home. Remembering this now, I can't imagine what I was thinking. How much more rested and prepared I would have been if I had slept another night with the baby in the nursery.

The pedestrian who took care of Kaj those first tense, fevered hours drops by for another look and says she's in fine health, though she suggests I take Kaj to our own pediatrician within a day or two for a baseline look at her. Once she leaves, I make an appointment for Wednesday morning.

Both Pat and Megan have to get back to work today after missing Friday, but Megan's girlfriend has more flexibility, so she drives up from the Bronx to take me home.

As I wait for her, I think about the four empty days ahead of me before Mom and Dad arrive on Thursday night. I think back to Jenn and Dave's offer to help out any way they could, and I wonder if maybe Jenn would mind coming to stay with me for a day or so. The thought of days and days of just me and the baby in my empty apartment freaks me out.

"Jenn?" I ask when I call her on my cell.

"Hey! How are my two lovelies doing?"

"Great!" I say. "We're going home today."

"So soon. Well, I guess you're anxious to get home."

"Kind of . . . though I was just realizing that Mom and Dad aren't going to get here until Thursday." My usual hesitancy to ask for help seems to have left me. "Do you think you could come down for a little while?"

"Lovey! Of course I'll come down. But you know I'll need to bring Hatty Bell; she's still breastfeeding."

"That's fine!" Though I wonder how the neighbors are going to feel with two little kids in the building all of a sudden. But then a surge of defiance strikes and I think, *They better darn well get used to it.*

"It will take me a little time to talk to Dave and pack the car and such. I should be there by late afternoon."

Luz and I pack all the gifts and flowers and put Kaj in her car seat. She is shockingly small and hunched over in her pink pointy hat. The wonderful outfit that Crystal bought for Kaj to wear home is way too small. Instead I put her in the size-three-months green dress that my boss brought as a gift, and it floats around her like a tent.

I am shocked by how hot it is outside. It was hot when I went into the hospital, but now it feels like a supersized summer. Everything is heavily green and humid. The air feels like water, and I look at Kaj beside me in the back seat and am worried that pollen or dust is going to get into her pure, clean lungs. Luz and Megan's car doesn't have air-conditioning, so we drive along the highway with the windows down a quarter of the way. Although

Kaj is perfectly sheltered under the canopy of her car seat, I want to put a filter over her mouth and nose to keep her clean and safe.

Luz has to get back to work right away, so she helps me get all the stuff up to my apartment, then bops back down the three flights of stairs to her car.

I look at Kaj in her seat on top of the dining room table. Now that the car seat isn't moving, she starts to jerk spasmodically and work her mouth in her sleep. Any moment now, she will let out a wail. Even after only forty-eight hours of knowing her, I have come to instinctively understand what she will do next; I just haven't quite figured out how to get her to stop crying, other than sticking in the boob. More important, I haven't figured out how to get her to sleep for more than an hour or two at a time at night. I look at her and for some reason think of Bronxie, coming into my room that morning as I was packing up to leave. "Here," she said, handing me my cell phone charger, which we had left in the labor-and-delivery room. "You know, if you had had any other doctor than McGroary or Bakas, you would have had a cesarean before I even came in for my shift on Saturday morning."

"Really?"

"Sure."

I watch Kaj's mouth moving now, and think how much harder this would all be if I were recovering from a cesarean.

My apartment looks beautiful. Linda and the Mrs. have cleaned up. They put a bowl of fruit and a vase of wildflowers on the dining room table. In the kitchen all the dishes are done, in the fridge are plates of pasta and cold cuts and bread, and in the freezer are frozen dinners. There's fresh salad and more fruit in the crisper. When I sit at the kitchen table to cry, there is even a box of Kleenex to reach for.

I wish, with all my quivering, tired tears, that they were with me now. In the dining room, Kaj starts with the squeaking grunt that is the precursor to a more fulsome cry. It is a sound designed, I think, for maximum penetration. It is an *uh, uh, uh,* but high pitched like a whine, clipped and cut-off and rapid, at a pace that reminds me of the sound I've heard on TV of a machine gun rattling—*uh-uh-uh-uh-uh-uh-uh-uh.*

This is the sound Kaj made in the hospital, the sound she is making now, and the sound she makes all through the night. I go now and look down at her spasming face and jerking arms. Her face is getting red, and will get redder soon when she belts out a full cry.

I set up a breastfeeding station in the most comfortable chair I own, a wide wooden one with gold crushed-velvet cushions. I take Kaj out of her carrier. She can smell the milk, I think, because her crying stops, and she turns her searching face and mouth, her eyes squished closed, and whimpers now with a touching kind of infant longing. I feel a heat enter and swell my breasts that actually hurts, and when she latches on I catch my breath because of the pain. As she continues to nurse, the pain fades to a strange pulling sensation and I relax and close my eyes.

This I like. This makes me feel like a competent mom, a nurturing woman doing the right thing.

The phone rings but I ignore it. My head falls back in a kind of half sleep. This breastfeeding thing takes hours. I switch her to the other side, partly to wake her up again to keep going. Before long I have to pee, and her sucking has slowed down to an occasional spasm in her sleep. I detach her and look around for somewhere to put her.

I have a bassinet somewhere that I bought, to use beside my bed for the first while, but I'm not sure where it is. There's the playpen thingy that Meg and Luz got me, but I'm not sure where that is, either. I left a lot of those things here in the living room, but Margaret and Linda must have put them away.

I lift Kaj up to my shoulder to gently burp her. I walk with her around my chair to check under the stairs, and notice that much of what had been spread out all over the living room is now under there, including the playpen.

I don't think I'm up to opening it right now, though. I walk with Kaj through the dining room into the spare bedroom, where I've been sleeping for months. And lo and behold, there is the bassinet. I finish burping her and lay her on her back in the bassinet. I grab one of the receiving blankets I had her wrapped in, coming from the hospital, and lay it over her because, even though it is quite warm, they say that babies have a hard time regulating their body temperature when they are young.

I want to lie down in my bed next to her bassinet, but there is so much to do. I can't actually remember what those things are right now, but there are lots. I wonder if Linda and the Mrs. are home yet. They are at least to Kingston by now, I would think. Margaret is probably in her own car, heading east toward Ottawa, and Linda is driving west toward Toronto.

I go back to the small table in my kitchen by the window and look out at the empty lot next door. Already the grass is out of control. The landlord never mows that lawn, which is fine by me. It is wild and wavy and sends the smell of nature up to my open window all summer long.

I remember I have to pee, and it is while I am on the toilet that I think, *What am I doing? Just go to sleep!*

So I do, after my warm water squirting and my witch hazel compress, and creep by the bassinet to lie on my back for a second before rolling onto my side to sleep, pulling the blanket over me as I go.

We sleep for maybe half an hour before she wakes me up with that hideous *uh-uh-uh-uh* sound. The skin along my skull tingles, and not in a good way. I quiver as I roll out of bed to pick her up. We walk around our apartment as I joggle her against my shoulder to keep her happy. I change her diaper, wrap her up in her blanket. We walk some more.

Jenn arrives around five o'clock in a bustle of food and bags and Hannah, who is eight months and stays close to her side. Gamely, Jenn hoists all her stuff, including a special pillow to help me with my breastfeeding, some clothes for the baby, and some pictures to hang on Kaj's wall.

"I picked us up some dinner!" she says, showing me the bags from Boston Market. "Chicken! Mashed potatoes. All good mama-building food!"

"Oh, thank you so much, Jenn." I feel the tears start up again, and I blink them away.

Jenn admires Kaj as she puts the food out on the dining room table. We eat. Lyde comes by with croissants and other goodies, which we eat for dessert, and then she takes my laundry away. Pat drops by with Ali and Ahmed, who says he sent a birth-announcement email to everyone on the list I gave him. Other friends drop by.

Jenn and I go to bed around ten, after Kaj finishes breastfeeding. Jenn and Hannah are up in Kaj's room, where there is a double bed and the crib. Hannah doesn't seem to want to be in the crib, though she's in one at home. After Jenn puts her to bed in the crib at eight, we sit downstairs and listen to her crying.

I don't fall asleep, I'm so tense knowing that Kaj is going to wake me up again before I've gotten anywhere near enough sleep. I know I'm going to have that awful shaky feeling.

It is a long, hollow night in that tiny room next to the bathroom, not wanting Kaj to wake up Jenn and Hannah. I try rocking her in the glider that Lyde brought me, but it begins to squeak loudly after only a few rocks. So I breastfeed her and stare out the window and watch the sun rise. I hold out until five-thirty, when I call Megan and ask her to come over to take care of Kaj so I can sleep, which Megan does, lying on the couch with Kaj on her chest while I go upstairs to sleep with earplugs. Jenn gets up at eight and makes breakfast for Megan, who eats it on the fly, with Kaj in her arms. She has to go to work, and I come down to feed Kaj. She is starting to *uh-uh-uh-uh-uh* again.

Tuesday more people come to visit, and there is no sleep again. Hannah is not happy at our house, and she cries. It is no more than any eight-month-old baby would cry, but I am crazy from lack of sleep and have no skin. Sometimes it's Kaj and Hannah crying at the same time, and I feel my blood pressure rise. It saws through muscles and nerves. If Hannah cries when Kaj is asleep, it is as though Kaj is crying, and I jump up. By late in the afternoon I am quivering and feel totally insane. I sit beside Jenn, who has just made me an amazing dinner of pasta and salad and turkey burgers.

I have been thinking all afternoon that I need to be in this house alone after all. I don't have the energy to be with anyone but me. I try to say this to Jenn, and it comes out awkwardly. She has been so kind and generous to come here, and has been wonderful to have, and she's been cooking and cleaning and making tea and bringing me water when I breastfeed. But having two babies here is too much.

Some of the resolve I had about calling her in the first place—the courage to ask for what I need—comes back to me and I say, "So, you know, I think I'm ready to be alone now, with Kaj. Mom and Dad are coming soon."

Jenn nods and drinks a cup of tea slowly. "You know we're happy to be here and help," she says and smiles at me, but in a sad way. Hannah pulls on her mother's pants to be picked up.

"And I'm so very grateful that you came down, and for all the stuff you brought and all the food you cooked. It's been amazing."

"Well, perhaps we'll get ready to go," Jenn says as Hannah starts to fuss on her knee, pulling at her shirt to nurse. "That way we can get home before it's too late."

As I help her carry stuff down to the car, I start to cry. I know I have hurt her feelings, and I want to take the words back and say it's okay, but it's too late.

By 7:00 PM they are gone, and I am breastfeeding in the wide wooden chair with the gold, crushed-velvet cushions, the long empty night ahead of me.

When I switch Kaj to the right side, Jesus Christ, it hurts. My whole body tightens, and it doesn't stop hurting, the way it usually does, and I stick my finger between her mouth and my nipple to break the seal and pull her off because it is like burning, cutting sandpaper biting into my nipple. Kaj starts to cry, and I put a pacifier in her mouth, and she falls for that for the moment. I grab the phone Jenn has left beside me on the coffee table. "Pat, I don't know what's going on; it just suddenly really hurts on the right side."

"Really? Okay, call the hospital; maybe their lactation consultant is still there. Let me see if I can find some other numbers too."

Twenty minutes later I have left messages with the Le Leche League and my doula and a couple of other places that Pat has suggested, but I haven't talked to anyone. "There's this white dot thing near the center of my nipple," I tell Pat when she calls me back.

"Wait, let me look that up," Pat says.

I try to use my fingernail to pop out the white thing. It kind of looks like a whitehead on a pimple, but it is surprisingly stuck, and hard.

"I bet you've got a blocked duct. It says in this nursing mother's book that it can hurt a lot."

"Well, that's right," I say, marveling at the understatement.

It is quiet while Pat reads. "You're supposed to drink a ton of water and have the baby continue breastfeeding on that side."

"You mean I have to put her back on there?" I look down at Kaj. Her face has lost that flat, wide, I-just-got-delivered look from the first days, and I notice that her little nose has popped up like a ski slope. "I don't think I can do that."

"Is it red anywhere? Hard?"

"A little hot and hard on the outer side and underneath."

"It says here that continual breastfeeding on that side will kind of pull the duct clean. If you get a fever, though, you have to call the doctor. It might be mastitis."

"Oh god, I don't know if I can do it."

"You'll make everything worse if you don't breastfeed on that side. The milk will get all backed up."

"Right, of course." I think of all the sessions of breastfeeding ahead of me, through the night and into tomorrow, before I can get to a doctor or someone who knows what they're doing. I must have Kaj latching on incorrectly.

"Do you want me to come down?" Pat asks. Part of me wants to say yes, but I have asked so much of her already. She has been away from her own son a lot to take care of me.

"Thanks, Pat, but I'll manage. If it gets so bad I can't take it, I'll call you, okay?"

"Okay, call! It doesn't matter how late. I'll have the phone by the bed."

I pull the pacifier out of Kaj's mouth and take a deep breath. She is angry and starts to sputter, but before she can get too worked up I maneuver her head to my right breast, pulling down her chin so she gets a good large latch, and *yowzers*. I start to breathe the way I did in labor—good, long, focusing breaths and then slow puffs out, tears falling out of my eyes without my really feeling myself cry. And in this way, I get through the 7:00 PM breastfeeding session. When she is done and I lay her in her bassinet, I check my breast again, and the white pimple thing is gone.

We have a 10:00 AM appointment the next day with Kaj's pediatrician, and although I start getting us ready to go at eight-thirty, it is nine-thirty before I'm out on the street by my car with Kaj in her seat. I've got her diaper bag and my purse, and the mirror that I need to install so I can see her while I'm driving and she is facing backward.

Luz put the base of the car seat in my car on Monday but didn't buckle it in, which I do now, no problem. It then takes a minute to get the seat snapped into the base, but that I eventually get too. The stillness is starting to get to Kaj, and she begins to fuss. It is nine-forty now, and I hate the idea of driving and not seeing Kaj, yet I can't figure out how to set up this mirror. I did bring down double-sided tape and masking tape, because even in the house, as I looked at the mirror, I didn't know how it would work. I finally just tape it on the back of the seat and run back and forth from the driver's seat, looking through the mirror, until I can see her from the driver's seat. I feel weepy and stupid, and I hope that my neighbors aren't watching me. Kaj gives in to crying, but I don't, though I go through much blinking away of tears.

We are fifteen minutes late for our appointment. I have only been here once, a month or two ago, when I talked to Dr. Cutler before deciding to choose her as Kaj's pediatrician.

There are forms to fill out, and I rock Kaj's car seat with my foot as I complete them. We are finally called out of the waiting room into one of the examining rooms, and now it's time to breastfeed again, which I do uncomfortably, since I don't have my security pillows and usual chair. My right breast still hurts, but I grimly put Kaj there. It is much better, though. Each time through the night when I put her to that breast, it got progressively easier.

Dr. Cutler comes in and nods at me as I begin to unlatch Kaj.

"No, don't worry, I have a bunch of questions first; you can let her finish."

"Okay." I throw a blanket over Kaj, though, because I'm not used to having my big white breast just hanging out for all to see.

"So, it looks like Baby is eating just fine."

"Yes. I've got a little bit of a blocked duct, but I think it's clearing up." I feel teary somehow, and look down to clear my throat and blink away the tears.

"How is she sleeping?"

"Well, she isn't really," I say, and start to cry. I catch and hold my breath for a second to stop, and then keep talking. "I don't think she likes to be on her back. I got one of those wedges so she can be on her side, but even that doesn't work." I give up on trying not to cry.

She hands me some Kleenex and says, "How are you doing, Mom?"

"Okay. I think I'm really tired."

"Does your husband help out?"

"No, I'm a single mom," I say. I know I told her this when we met, but I guess she must have a lot of patients, and a lot of patients' parents, to remember.

"Are you getting help?"

"Yes. And my parents are coming tomorrow." Oh, how I can't wait for them to come. A pinprick of light at the end of the tunnel.

"Good." She nods. "I'm going to get the nurse, and we'll weigh Baby and take all the measurements."

While Dr. Cutler is gone, I let all the tears out. I don't even try not to cry; it hurts and burns too much to make myself stop. After a few minutes I already feel less congested, and I burp Kaj and walk around the small room, bouncing on the balls of my feet.

I work really hard to not cry anymore as they weigh and measure Kaj. When everything is done, Dr. Cutler charts her numbers on a graph and shows me where Kaj is: ninetieth percentile for height and eightieth percentile for weight.

"She hasn't really lost any weight since she was born, which is good. I know you said she doesn't like to sleep on her back, but it really is the best way for Baby to sleep. And don't use a soft mattress—like a feather mattress, for example—and keep all toys and stuffed animals out of the crib." She pauses and looks down at Kaj, who has fallen asleep with her head thrown back and her mouth open. "She's quite perfect."

I nod, scared to talk because I'll cry.

"It's Mom I'm worried about," she says, looking right at me.

"I'll be okay when Mom and Dad get here." I nod and press my lips together.

"I would like you both to come back next week. You can make an appointment with the nurse out front."

"Next week again?"

"Yes, I just want to be sure you're both okay."

At home again I'm fine until someone calls, but as soon as I try to talk, I break down crying. Lyde calls to say she is bringing over the clean laundry, and when I can't even answer her, she says, "Pat and I are going to be right there."

"Get out," Lyde says when they arrive. She takes Kaj away from me. "Go for a walk with Pat; get some fresh air."

Lyde slings Kaj over her shoulder and pushes Pat and me out the back door. "Don't come back for at least half an hour!"

"But what if she gets hungry?" I can't imagine just leaving her.

"I'll manage!"

I pick my way carefully down the stairs, and we turn left out of the yard and walk north along my street. "I don't know what's wrong with me. I can't stop crying."

"Maybe you're postpartum—I mean, depressed. You know what I mean."

This must be what happened to Mom after Glenn was born, I think. Even

I remember how he cried and cried and cried. It wasn't long after he was born that she went back to Denmark, and Linda and I moved to the farm. He was still a baby. I remember her carrying him away like an infant. I wonder if it was feeling like this that made her want to run away.

I want to run away.

I feel depressed and inadequate, fat and bloodied, bruised all over and red-eyed. One of the gifts someone brought yesterday was a copy of the latest *People* magazine, and there was Gwyneth Paltrow on the cover with her husband, holding their new baby, born at almost exactly the same time as Kaj—"36 Hours of Labor!" How come she gets out of the hospital after a grueling labor looking like a cover girl, while I am so very destroyed?

"You've got to get back on antidepressants, Alex."

"But I don't want to stop breastfeeding."

"Talk to Bakas or McGroary. It can't hurt. Maybe there's something you can take even while you breastfeed."

"Okay."

"You need some sleep too. Isn't there someone who can come for the night?"

"Well, you know, everyone has their own kids, their own life."

Pat nods. "What about Mo or Bev?"

"There's Jaiden. And Bev lives all the way out on Long Island."

"But Mo is right around here, right?"

"Well, I'll call."

This did give me an idea, though. I could call a doula—not a birthing doula, but a mother's-helper kind of doula. I could pay someone to come in and be with Kaj while I slept. Just tonight, because tomorrow Mom and Dad will be here.

Lyde has made us lunch while we were out, and Kaj is asleep in her car seat on the kitchen floor. Lyde has the small TV on the fridge on. There's some cooking show about frying potatoes on PBS. She is singing too, loudly; we can hear it as we walk up the stairs. In the living room, the radio is on nice and loud. Kaj is deeply asleep.

"Wow," I say.

"You don't want to be too quiet," Lyde says. "Otherwise you're going to be tiptoeing around for the next three years."

"Good point."

After they leave I finally find an organization that sends doulas out to help new mothers. The woman I talk to is very nice, but when she tells me that for eight hours the charge is almost $200 I start to cry. I'm stunned. I have some cash that Kaj and I got at the shower. I could use it for this purpose, but I had hoped to get some kind of equipment thing for Kaj with it.

"I don't know if I can pay that," I say. "I just don't have that kind of money."

"Let me see if I can find someone who will come in for a less. Could you afford a hundred dollars?"

"I think so."

I decide to call Bev and Mo too, just to see.

By five-thirty Mo has arrived with beer and food. Bev and Jaiden are close behind. Everyone takes turns holding Kaj. The glider is squeaking again. Lyde did say that it would do that from time to time; I just need to add some oil, she says. But Mo can't take the squeaking and is out the door and back again shortly with tools and a small can of oil with a long red nozzle, for getting oil right on the screws in the hard-to-reach places.

Bev cooks an amazing dinner, and we sit in the living room, eating buffet-style. Kaj is happy as a clam being held by this person, then that.

They stay until eleven or so, and I even get a shower before they leave. I have time to sit and breastfeed Kaj one long time before the doula arrives a little before midnight.

She is a lovely, soft-spoken person, and she takes command of Kaj right away. "Go, sleep," she says. "I'll call you when she needs to eat."

"I'm going to put earplugs in," I say, "so you'll have to come get me." I know already that I won't be able to sleep if I hear even the littlest peep from Kaj.

Blessed be, I sleep for four straight hours before the doula comes up to tap me gently on the shoulder to feed Kaj. Half awake, I stumble down the stairs. The lights are low, and I don't let myself wake up too much. I feed her on both sides, hand her to the doula to burp, and go up for another three hours of sleep before the doula leaves at eight.

When she wakes me up at seven forty-five, I feel like a new person. I stretch and smile at the sun coming into my room and feel excited, for the first time in a while, about holding Kaj in my arms.

TWELVE

Mom and Dad

They arrive at 10:00 PM on Thursday. I spend most of the day clean-ing in a disorganized and puttering kind of way. Lyde has come and gone with the sheets all laundered, and I make their beds. The rooms upstairs are small, so I've given them each their own. Mom will sleep in Kaj's room on the double bed, and Dad will take mine, with the king-size bed.

I've arranged for a car service we use at work to pick up Mom and Dad. Their plane lands at eight, and since they are landing at the Westchester Airport, I'm worried when they haven't arrived by nine. I call the car service, and they say they are on the way.

I can't wait for them to get to me. I want so very badly to be taken care of.

I don't quite know how to explain this, but I can't sleep knowing that Kaj will wake me up. This is true both at night and during the day. Dr. McGroary tells me this is actually a part of the postpartum depression craziness, and that Zoloft will help.

Part of what I'm hoping my parents can do for me is to keep Kaj happy so she won't wake me up, especially at night. But they are in their sixties and seventies, so I'm not sure how much they can do, or what I'm going to feel comfortable asking them to do.

Carrying Kaj on a path that goes from the front windows down through the very clean dining room, into the equally clean kitchen, and back, I see as I get to the front window that the car has finally arrived and the driver is helping my parents carry their bags up my two flights of outside stairs. I walk down to the main-floor landing with Kaj and open the front door for them. They all follow me up the inside stairs, and I step aside to let them come in. "Should I tip him?" Dad asks me quietly out of the side of his mouth as he passes.

"No, I've taken care of it," I say, also using the side of my mouth.

Dad nods and walks over to the driver, who is just putting Mom's bag inside the door. Mom wanders in and looks around the living room. Dad shakes the driver's hand. "Thanks so much. I'm sorry it was so confusing."

"What was confusing?" I ask.

"I couldn't find Onieda to come up here; I had the map but I could not find the street."

"Really?" But then I remember—on my walk with Pat the day before, there was construction on Onieda. The road was completely ripped up. "Right, I forgot about the construction."

As the sound of the driver's footsteps drifts away down the stairs, Mom and Dad and I look at each other in the silent pause, until I feel Kaj stir and I say, "Here she is," at just the same moment as Mom says, "There she is!"

Mom and Dad come over, and I hold Kaj out. Her face is still in that almost universal squished-newborn state, so it's a little hard to see what she will look like, though her nose has popped up some and her lips aren't bruised anymore. I'm happy to see that the plunger shape of her head has begun to disappear.

"Oh, Donna," Mom says. "She's beautiful."

I look down at her, wrapped in one of the receiving blankets I got at the shower, with a pink hat on her head. She is still kind of red—that redness I noticed right after she was born hasn't gone away yet. Everyone says she will fade into more white and rosy skin. Her hair is much darker than I expected. I was blond, so I expected her to be.

"Good for you, kid!" Dad says as he pats me on the shoulder, then gives me a half-body bear hug on the left side, careful not to jostle the right, where I have Kaj.

"Do you want to hold her?" I ask both of them, and Mom says yes. "You might want to wash your hands first," I say.

She looks a little surprised. I'm not usually directive in this way, but I've become quite convinced that I would be endangering my child if I didn't ask. One of my visitors in the last days (I don't know who) brought anti-bacterial soap, the kind in a pump, and set one up in my bathroom and one in the kitchen. Normally I would be a little freaked out, like someone was trying to tell me something—but when I noticed the soap in the bathroom, I was kind of touched and have not tried to find out who brought it.

As Mom holds Kaj, Dad talks about the cab driver and how flustered he was, not being able to find his way; they drove around for almost forty-five minutes until he figured out a back way to my street. I lead Dad upstairs to his room and show him where he will be sleeping, and the fans I have left for them to put in the windows if they need to cool things off.

"This is nice," Dad says, looking at the dormers and the small window.

"It's a little off the radar. I don't pay much rent, if you consider that you *could* call it a three-bedroom. But you notice there are no doors in these two second-floor rooms," I say, pointing out the salon shutters swinging across the threshold of this room and over to the wide-open space that leads into the room where Mom will sleep. "The landlord doesn't want to put doors in, because there's actually no heat up here. It all radiates from downstairs."

"Is it cold?"

"No, actually it isn't—well, not any colder than the rest of the apartment. He pays for the heat, and it's an old boiler, so by the time the heat makes its way to this apartment, there isn't much left. I spent a lot of time the first year complaining, then just gave up and got a heater." I smile at my dad. "He's never raised the rent in the five years I've lived here, so I don't actually complain about much if I can help it."

Dad smiles at me as though he understands, but it occurs to me that he has no idea what it's like to have a landlord. He has always owned his own home, or certainly since he got married and started having kids, and he paid for all his houses with cash that he had spent years saving. I wonder if he's ever had a mortgage. I don't think he's ever had a car loan. He's not the kind of man to buy things "over time."

He makes jokes about people who "don't ask how much something costs, but ask how much a month!" I cringe a little when he says this, because, of course, this is the only way I could ever afford to buy a new car, or pay for graduate school. His life has been very different from mine, both geographically and financially. He's careful with money; I'm not.

I spent so long acting different from him that it has become who I am. Now I see the wisdom of his ways, but it is too late. I can't seem to change into that more careful person.

"The only problem with this apartment," I say to Dad, taking him across to Mom's room, "is that you can't really be up here in the summer without air-conditioning, and there's no dedicated circuit to plug one into. I finally found an air conditioner small enough to fit in the tiny window in this room," I say, pointing to the window above Mom's bed, "and I guess it's also small enough not to blow the circuits—it's been working fine these last couple of years."

Dad nods.

It suddenly feels very small up here with both of us standing in the limited headroom.

Downstairs I can hear Kaj beginning her *uh-uh-uh-uh-uh-uh,* and from the bottom of the stairs, Mom says, "Donna, she's waking up."

I feel kind of shy starting to breastfeed Kaj with Mom and Dad there, though Dad discreetly heads up to his room to unpack when I sit down and lift my shirt. We are a private family; in the same way that we don't have big fights or emotional scenes, we don't show or talk about our bodily functions.

Mom sits with me, though, while I feed Kaj and tell her about the birth. Dad comes down eventually, after I've switched sides, and they both comment on how beaten up I look, my bloodshot eyes, the burst blood vessels all along my face and neck, the huge bruises from the IV attempts.

"I know. I'm a mess," I say. "And not just physically. I'm not sleeping well.

Well, Kaj's not sleeping, so I'm not sleeping." I look at Dad. "I don't suppose you could sit and hold her for a few hours now so I can get some sleep?"

He looks a little apprehensive, and I say, "As long as you're just holding her on your shoulder, she'll be fine." I glance at the clock. "It's only eight-thirty Saskatchewan time, right? So if I slept until two, it would only be after midnight your time."

Dad nods and Mom says, "You can do that, Norm, right?"

"Sure," he says, but I can tell he's worried.

"Just come up and get me if she starts to fuss," I say. "Sorry to just leave you after you get here, but I'm so tired."

As I'm going upstairs I say, "I'll have earplugs in, so you'll have to come up and get me when she wakes up."

Upstairs I put in the earplugs, and as the foam expands, all sound fades except a kind of hissing, like the sound you hear when you place a conch shell to your ear. My usual fears about falling asleep, only to be woken up by her crying, are gone. As long as someone is holding her, I feel like I can sleep.

Dad gets me up at around two. Kaj has been fussing for a little while, but he walked her up and down the apartment. I take her from him, feeling shaky and longing to stay asleep. But I am thankful for those four hours and take Kaj down to nurse.

For the rest of the night, she and I sleep in one-hour increments. I have begun to write down our waking times, because in the mornings I can't quite believe she has woken me up as many times as she has; surely I've just dreamt it.

This night at around three-thirty, when she starts to *uh-uh-uh-uh-uh-uh*, I roll over, quivering and nauseated, wanting just to sleep. I look at her and back away, because I am afraid of myself. I am afraid that I will kill her. I am afraid that I will shake her and scream at her to sleep. The rage bubbles around inside me, and I think, *I want to give you back. Oh my god, get away from me.* I go into the bathroom, leaving her to cry, and think about my mother. *I'm just like her. I'm going to leave this baby. I'm going to walk out of this apartment and leave her with my parents and never come back.*

This is it, I think, *the moment I was afraid of.*

I can't do this. I am like my mother. I know I'm going to leave her. If I can't even make it through the first week without wanting to leave, how am I ever going to get through a whole childhood and adolescence?

Maybe this wasn't such a good idea after all. Maybe I'm not the woman I thought I was.

I cry for a little while, then feel calmer. My breasts start to ache as I listen to Kaj cry, so I go back into the bedroom, pick her up out of the bassinet, and we sit in bed together, my back against the headboard. She turns her face to my breasts and searches with her mouth, eyes squeezed shut.

Everything compresses as I watch her. I feel my uterus contract; the milk releases from both breasts, creating large, dark, wet circles on my nightgown. My heart squeezes tight too, and I think, *So this is love,* this feeling expanding inside me like a balloon, breathless, fearful, heart-breaking.

Did I really want to kill her a few minutes ago? I did. I can almost feel that rage still. I shiver from fear of it. What if I hurt her? Would I really hurt her?

I stare up to where the gray paneling meets the tiled ceiling and think, *This is not what I thought parenting would be.*

Things are a bit awkward the first days of my parents' visit. I have never hosted them before. If I'm not visiting them at home, we are at Linda's house, which is large and suburban. Here we feel a bit cooped up in the small space. Mom, I see now, when I'm not in a haze of sleeplessness, feels awkward not knowing where anything is or what I want.

And what I want, I can't express. I want her, both of them, to take care of me. I want them to know what I need without my having to tell them. I want to be their baby while I take care of mine. But I don't know how to express that, or perhaps more fundamentally, I don't even really know that that's what I want. I simply feel unhappy and ready to cry all the time.

Things build to a crisis by the third day. I'm getting no more sleep than I did the first days, and I feel crazier by the minute. Everything irritates me. When Mom asks what we should have for dinner, I think she is asking me to go to the store to buy it and cook it. When she asks me how I spell Kaj's name and I say with a "j" rather than an "i," she says she thinks that's unusual, and I take her to mean that I've made a mistake, that no one will know how to spell it or pronounce it. My grandfather spelled his name with an "i," she says, and it is for him that I named her, but the "i" seems so male, somehow. I thought the "j" would feel more feminine. As we have this conversation, I think back to the birth-certificate information I filled out at the hospital and wonder if it's too late to change it. I've made a terrible mistake. When Mom asks me where the salt is (on top of the fridge), she gives me a look, and I think she thinks that's a strange place to keep it. When Dad bumps his knee on my breastfeeding chair and says, "My, you have a lot of furniture in here," I think it's a criticism.

Nothing is right.

That third night, I can't fall asleep, even though everyone else in the house is asleep, even Kaj at this blessed moment. But I can't stop thinking about all my mistakes. I cry because I wish I could ask Dad to stay up with Kaj again, but I can't. He never sleeps well anyway, and he's in his seventies, for God's sake.

I lie there and wish I had money for a doula again. At four in the morning, when Kaj does the *uh-uh-uh-uh-uh-uh-uh,* I look down at her in the bassinet and knowing now what I am capable of I head into the bathroom to rage into a towel. But before I go, I hear myself hiss, "Why won't you sleep? You're killing me!" I shake my fists at her and drag myself away, but even as I'm pacing the few steps back and forth beside the tub, I worry that her crying is going to wake up Mom and Dad. It reminds me how worried I was when Jen was here, sleeping upstairs, that Kaj would wake her and Hannah up.

I can't believe myself, really. I finally sit down on the edge of the tub, weeping weakly into a bath towel. I can't believe how uptight I am about everyone else's sleep. I feel like I'm losing my mind, torn between everyone else's needs and my own.

What about me? What about *my* sleep?

But you are the mother, I say to myself. *You took this on.*

Which is all very true. I sober up and walk back into the room and lift her up and breastfeed her in the living room in the big wooden chair. I look down at her and wait for that transcendent feeling of love to come again, but it doesn't. I look out the window at the growing morning light and feel grim.

So this is what I signed up for. This is being a mother.

I feel myself nod off as she nurses. I wish that she could sleep with me in bed; it would be so much easier. But I have tried, and she throws up violently if I have her in bed with me after nursing. She needs to go back into the bassinet, where I have raised one end up two inches so she can sleep on a slant. It seems to help with the vomiting.

On the fourth day, after Kaj's early evening feeding, I leave her sleeping downstairs and go up to sleep in Dad's bed while I can. But my mistakes visit me again, and the fear of being woken up keeps me awake. I want to avoid feeling that awful shaky feeling again—the feeling of waking up when I need sleep so desperately. Soon I'm so worked up that I'm berating my parents in my head. Before I know what I am doing, I'm back downstairs, angry and trembling.

"I need to talk to you," I tell them as they sit and watch baseball on TV.

They turn toward me as I sit in my breastfeeding chair. "You need to help me," I say in a squeaky voice.

"What do you mean?"

"I need help. I need you to help me." This is more forceful—full of the grievances I was feeling upstairs.

Mom has stiffened up, probably because of the accusing tone in my voice. See what happens when you don't talk about your true feelings? They get backed up and then come out like a knife. "I need you to cook for me and do the laundry and, and, and bring me water when I'm breastfeeding," I say, because I always forget to bring a glass of seltzer with me when I sit in the breastfeeding chair, and as soon as Kaj latches on I crave one. I try to think of other specifics—I had a whole list of things for Dad to do, manly things requiring screwdrivers and drills and such—but my throat has kind of closed over, and my mind is blank. "I need you to take care of me" is all I can say, and then I start to really cry—shaking, sobbing cries. It's the taking-care-of-me part that makes me cry. Dad pats me awkwardly on the shoulder. "You're just tired."

But this only makes me angry. "No, it's not just being tired. I feel like I need you to support me. And Mom doesn't like how I spelled Kaj's name, and I can't change that now, and, and, and Dad, you don't like my apartment." I can't go on because I'm crying so hard, and Dad laughs a little but it's not a mean laugh, it's a laugh that comes from not knowing what to say. He pats my shoulder some more. "No, no, that's okay, Donna. Your apartment is fine. It's good."

"I don't know what you're talking about, Donna," Mom says.

"Yes, Mommy didn't mean it that way. You can spell her name any way you want."

Mom gets up and leaves the room. I hear her grab her cigarettes off the table and go outside for a smoke.

Now I feel like I've ruined my case by being so petty. And it's not what I really mean anyway. I think it is here that I finally understand that what I really want is to be a baby myself. To be fawned over and loved, have my unspoken wishes fulfilled, someone to know intuitively what I want without my having to ask for it. And I am saddened beyond belief because, of course, I can't have that. It's too late for that.

What is also striking to me now is how Linda thought I wanted a baby so I wouldn't be lonely, and I suspected this to be true as well. But honestly, I've never felt lonelier or more abandoned than I do during these dark nights, again and again, feeling like I'm coming unhinged. The thought of another night of just Kaj and me, her not sleeping, me not sleeping, the minutes switching one to the other on my clock radio, makes me want to scream.

"Alex," Dad says. "Go up and sleep. It will feel better in the morning, and we can talk about it some more. You really need to sleep."

I nod because he is right. I'm not going to get anywhere like this. I don't even know what I'm saying now.

I go up to bed, shivering when I realize that Kaj will be awake in two hours. *God help me, another sleepless night.*

The next day I emerge with Kaj, leave her in her electric rocker, and have a shower. When I get out Mom has made toast for me, white bread with butter, which is all I want to eat all day, every day. She has made me a cup of decaf tea too, which is all I can have in terms of hot drinks because of the breastfeeding. I miss my coffee. I really do.

"How do you feel today?" Mom asks.

"A little better," I say. Last night I let Kaj sleep on her stomach on my chest with me half lying, half sitting in the bed. It wasn't very comfortable for me for sleeping, but she didn't wake up every hour, so that was a victory of sorts. Perhaps I've found at least a partial answer to the nighttime horror.

Mom sits down across from me, "It's hard being so tired."

I look at Mom for a moment. I recognize an olive branch when I see it. "It is." I take a bite of toast. "Thanks for this," I say.

"So, you'll show me where to do the laundry today?"

"Sure, great," I say.

"And Norm and I will get groceries later. You'll just have to write out the directions."

I rock Kaj a little in her seat, which I have put on the floor. The little movement satisfies her. Then she grunts. Mom and I look down and see her face get red and squishy, and then there is the tremendous wet sound of a poo. Mom and I look at each other, and I laugh for the first time in as long as I can remember. Mom laughs too; we laugh together until tears come out of the sides of my eyes, and I look down at Kaj's happy, satisfied face and think, *Yes, I feel it now again. This is love.*

Later that day, they do go for groceries, and the next day Dad and I go and buy a stand-alone air conditioner for my bedroom upstairs. He spends days setting it up, including putting plastic over the doors to keep the cool air in. Mom goes out of her way now to cook each meal, brings me seltzer and toast when I'm breastfeeding, does the laundry every day. Dad puts up rods across my three east-facing windows and hangs curtains.

We learn to sleep better, Kaj and I. The trick of having her on my chest works, and we sleep together like that for hours. The long nights compress into shorter bursts of lone wakefulness, and by the time I go back to work after three months, she is sleeping through the night.

I am happy that my parents are with me. Happy that I feel clear in the chest, with nothing to get off of it, no hard truth hiding underneath some sweet smile. I was my messiest self, and they still talked to me. I asked for what I needed, and they gave it to me and didn't say, *Ah, she's too much trouble.*

The Zoloft Dr. McGroary prescribed for me is also making me feel better, I think. Even before Kaj begins to sleep better, I feel less crazy.

I'm happy that my parents get to meet my friends too. Megan and Luz come by. So do Pat and her family, and Lyde too, though there is no laundry right now for her to do (once my parents leave, she will go on doing laundry for several weeks, until I'm more on my feet). One day, as Lyde is sitting and visiting, I'm feeling the softness of my stomach as I breastfeed Kaj. It feels kind of rolly and mushy. I say, "Hey, I kind of like this." Normally I would be appalled, but there is something charming about it that I can't explain.

"Really?" Lyde says. "I always hated that."

"No, it's okay," I say. It's where I am. This is the body I have now—the bruises are healing, and I am alive, and so is the baby.

It is the body that made this baby. It is the body that feeds Kaj, and I am happy in it, even though it is softer and squishier than before I had her. It's okay.

Before I know it, two weeks have passed, and it is Thursday again, time for them to leave. I am heartsick. I drive them to the airport for their late-afternoon flight. We have tea and toast while we wait for their flight to be called, and then, too soon, they are standing in line at their gate. Kaj has slept through all this. Mom and Dad kiss her head. "Go," Dad says. "You don't have to wait for us. We'll just be in this line for a moment."

I nod, kiss and hug them both, and walk away with Kaj to the car. I am crying again, though this feels like a real deep cry, not the trigger-happy hysterical crying I've done so much of lately.

As I walk along the glassed-in walkway to the parking lot, I look down and notice that I can see my parents in line below. I stop for a moment to look at them. They are small from this distance, talking to each other. I see my mom's curly brown hair and dad's graying crew cut. They are so dear to me. I want to run and protect them—from what, I don't know. It's like the moment in the hospital with Kaj when I realized that one step off the curb would mean death. Anything could happen to them anytime, and it scares me, because I feel as though I just found them after having lost them for a very long time. And that I found myself too.

I knew that having a baby would make me see the world in a new way; I just didn't realize how much it would make me see myself and my relationship with my parents in a new way. I see now, perhaps, how it was for Mom. How hard it must have been. How much like her I am.

I know somehow that she did her best. And so did Dad.

I remember that time on the farm, the weeks leading up to her leaving, and I can see them as people like me, someone who is both an individual and a parent on whom the "child me" depends on for protection. I see them struggling and not sleeping and perhaps fighting with each other out of stress. Wanting to run away. Feeling crazy. I see them there, trying to do their best—just like I am.

We have a horrendous trip home, Kaj and I. It takes forty-five minutes just to get out of the parking lot, because she wakes up hungry just as I pull out of my spot. I drive a few spots down and pull in again to feed her.

She sleeps fine after that, until we hit stop-and-go traffic and the arm jerking begins, the face twitches and the *uh-uh-uh-uh-uh-uh-uh*.

Desperate to be moving again so she will stop crying, I get off 287 and take a short cut, but many others have had the same idea, and we move no faster. Finally I can't take it anymore and pull into an A&P parking lot. I get into the back and pull her out to nurse again. But really, she's not hungry. She fusses. She does not sleep. After thirty minutes I resign myself to the crying.

Finding my way back to that stop-and-go 287 with my baby screaming in the back, no one with me to rock her chair, give her a finger to suck on, nothing, I wonder, *Is this how it's going to be?* Alone with a crying baby, helpless to do anything because I am driving, or working, or cleaning the house, trying to do everything by myself. Doing my best, but it's not enough. I can't keep her from crying. She's going to be hurt.

THIRTEEN

So This Is Love

There are a lot of visits to Kaj's doctor in the first few months of her life. I go once with Mom and Dad and again two weeks later, when Kaj is a month old. She continues to nurse well and is gaining weight steadily. She is, in fact, in the ninetieth percentile for weight, and her height seems to have leveled off. There's a slight pause as Dr. Cutler charts her development and shows me where she fits in compared with all the other children her age in the United States, and I feel like the doctor is going to say something about Kaj's weight, like the ninetieth percentile is too much, but she doesn't, and I think, *Well, that's my own shit coming up.*

But she is a chunky girl, with deep creases in her thighs and her upper arms, and a lovely round belly. As she grows and moves beyond that ugly, reptilian newborn phase into the rosy-cheeked infant phase, her chubbiness persists.

As for me, my pregnancy weight gain does not come off with breastfeeding, as had been my hope. But the croissants are probably the reason, and the pieces of toast I still eat while I breastfeed, in a kind of homage to Mom and Dad's visit.

I look down as I feed her, and my breast is almost as big as her head. I wonder if I'm feeding her too much. Is there too much fat in my breast milk because of all the croissants? Is she getting all chubby because I ate so much during my pregnancy?

But Dr. Cutler tells me she is healthy and seems to be flourishing, so I tell myself not to think such thoughts and she will be fine. She is a lovely Gerber baby, and I shouldn't let my sick mind infect hers.

I don't fit into the clothes I wore before I was pregnant, so I basically keep wearing my maternity clothes. This works until fall, when I go back to work and can't schlump around anymore. I buy new clothes in the big-girls' store again, and I think back to the times I bounced by Lane Bryant thinking, *I'm never going to shop there again.*

I gain and gain and gain.

I hate my body and can't seem to stop eating. That early feeling I had with Lyde, of loving the softness of my belly, is gone, because I keep gaining weight, and it's not the soft, doughy kind. It's the hard, round, tight kind.

One night as I'm rocking Kaj to sleep and singing her song to her— *"Little K, little a, little j, little Kaj. Even before you joined the world, you were the apple of your mother's eye"*— I am struck, for some reason, by the idea that the price I have paid to have her, to go against convention, is being paid by my body.

That's silly, I think. *You're being melodramatic.* But the idea persists.

Kaj is a fabulous kid. She is a happy kid.

Those early days of sleepless insanity are better by the time she is two months old and gone by the time she is three months old. She eats well, she sleeps well, she laughs. She reaches for sunlight in the morning as it slants through the dust of our living room. I am in love with her.

Truly and fully, I have given myself over to her.

One evening toward the end of my maternity leave, I feel nauseated and find myself rushing to the bathroom to throw up. I haven't done this since I was ten. I hold it together until 10:00 PM, when I put Kaj to bed upstairs in her crib.

I call Margaret, worried that I'll make Kaj sick, but Margaret says to wash my hands a lot, so I do. I lie on a clean towel on the floor in the bathroom. At 1:00 AM Kaj wakes up for her first night feeding, and I crawl up the stairs to breastfeed her, holding down the vomit. But by 4:30 AM, when she wakes up again, I have not stopped throwing up and have been lying as still as possible on the floor. I try to go up to Kaj, but I can't even crawl to the stairs, much less up them.

Because I have not come to her, she is wailing now. If it were just about me, I would figure out a way to get by. But with Kaj it is different—I am able to do things I would never do just for myself.

So I pick up the phone and call Lyde. I know she still gets up early, and sure enough, she answers the phone. She leaves her husband and kids asleep, comes right over to feed Kaj some of the breastmilk I've been stockpiling in the freezer, and gets Kaj back into bed. She gives me Dramamine and tells me to hold it down as long as I can. By 8:00 AM, when Kaj wakes up again, I feel better.

It is much as I thought: My home-built family is helping me to raise Kaj.

For the first year of her life, I set up a wonderful, if slightly complex, system of childcare. Two days a week I have a grad student from my school watch her in exchange for rent-free living in the extra bedroom downstairs. Two other days, I take her to my friend Idania's place, where her sister watches both Kaj and Idania's daughter, who is six months older than Kaj. Fridays I work at home.

For a year this works out wonderfully. Kaj learns to crawl and then walk at Idania's house. She is loved and well cared for. With the student in my house, she gets a little more TV than at Idania's, but good care nevertheless.

Then Idania gets pregnant. I can see that caring for two toddlers and an infant is going to be too much for her sister, and I start to look for other arrangements. Working at home on Fridays has become harder too; with Kaj walking and sleeping less, I can't actually get that much done, and the graduate student is moving back to Kansas.

So for the first time, I am faced with the real cost of childcare. Idania's sister charged me well under the going rate because of my friendship with her sister, but also, I think, because she is a single mom too, getting by with the help of friends and family. I call around and talk to many people about where they send their kids. My first choice is Padmini's, because this is where Lyde has sent all four of her kids. But when I talk to them about how much they cost, they say $1,200 a month. That would be over a third of my take-home pay each month. I am floored and suddenly scared. What am I going to do with Kaj during the day?

Then one day at work, I happen to be talking to a board member of a nonprofit I'm involved with. He tells me about a place his son has been going to for a year. This was the daycare's first year, but his son had a wonderful experience. He took his son out because he was ready for school. "I couldn't recommend Sue more highly," he says.

Four weeks and two interviews later, I move Kaj into Sue's care at the beginning of August. Sue charges $800 a month, which still takes my breath away, but I can imagine actually finding the money.

There are four children under two, and two daycare providers. Sue has set up her daycare on the main floor of her house, so there are three rooms to play and nap in and a kitchen in back.

I transition Kaj in slowly—we spend two hours there together, then I leave after an hour and come back to take her home.

The third day I'm only staying for half an hour or so; Kaj is going to stay through lunch and her nap, and I'll pick her up around three. When we arrive, I take Kaj's lunch to the kitchen, where Sue is getting bottles ready for the two youngest. We chat as I glance into the center room once in a while to see that Kaj is fine. Somehow my conversation with Sue makes its way to dieting, and she tells me she has lost 130 pounds on a raw-food diet.

"What's that?"

"Just like it sounds. Lots of vegetables. I make my own juices. I don't eat meat or dairy. It's good," she says, and I wonder how that can be true.

I want to tell her that I lost 109 pounds once, but that feels like a long time ago as I sit in her kitchen in my size 24 shirt and a pair of my maternity pants. She tells me more about the diet, and I make myself sound interested, even though the thought of living like that terrifies me.

When I leave, Kaj cries hysterically hard for me, just like she did yesterday and the day before that. I glance at her as I close the door and see her red, scrunched face and arms reaching out for me, and my heart breaks. How can I do this to her? I can't drive away until I calm down. *Please let this get easier.* She loved it at Idania's and would run away to play the second I put her on the floor.

Over the next few weeks Kaj seems to get used to Sue's place and doesn't fuss as much when I leave. I experiment with faster ways of getting there, then settle on what seems like the quickest drive. I listen to NPR on my way there and back. This is the fall of Hurricane Katrina, and I am horrified and say to Sue as I drop Kaj off, "Can you believe what's happening there?"

Sue shakes her head and takes Kaj from me, as well as her little bag of food. "You don't need to bring jars of fruit or veggies for now. I have plenty left."

"You do?" I have been bringing what I usually feed her on the weekends. I think then about how Sue will send one of the three small bottles of formula I've made for Kaj back with me in the evenings, saying Kaj didn't want another. I begin to wonder if maybe I'm feeding Kaj too much. Is that chubbiness my fault?

"Yes. She doesn't eat that much."

"Really?"

But then I think about Sue's saying a couple mornings ago, when I had Kaj dressed all in black, "Well, isn't she looking so slim and trim."

The other daycare worker made a joke about black being slimming, and something went kind of rancid in my stomach. "Well, can you be sure she has both a vegetable and fruit at lunch?" I say now, which feels off the point somehow, but I'm not sure what my point is.

"Of course."

Maybe I am feeding her wrong. Maybe I'm infecting her with fatness just by living together. But I feed her well, healthily. I never give her juice or candy, and cookies only rarely.

September slips into October, and food keeps coming back with us at the end of the day. Sue's comments about Kaj's looking slimmer grate on my nerves, especially because I can see that Kaj actually *is* looking slimmer. Sue suggests that as I transition her off formula to milk, I consider using skim milk. "Kids can't taste the difference," she says.

I begin to wonder if Sue is a bit of a fanatic. Is she actually withholding food, or does Kaj really not want more? What goes on there during the day; what subtle and unsubtle messages is Kaj getting about her body and eating? Does she go hungry there?

I sit in Pat's office in mid-October. "What am I going to do?"

"Move Kaj. You've got to get her out of there. You've been worried about this for a month. It's not getting better."

I nod.

"What does Sue say when you talk to her about it?"

"What is there to talk about? There's nothing overt going on. She says Kaj doesn't want all the food I bring her. End of story."

"Tell her to give it to her anyway."

I give Pat a look and wish I were more like her. "I see her looking at me sometimes and I can feel that she hates me, or my body at least. It's like she's afraid to be beside my fat, like she'll catch it."

"Are you sure you're not just projecting or something?" Pat leans back in her chair. "You've been pretty unhappy about your body since Kaj was born. Maybe you're just giving those feelings to her."

"Maybe, but something is weird."

"Then take her out."

"I know, but God, where will I take her? I've called other places, and they're all just as expensive as Padmini's." I rub my face hard, trying to think. "I can't pay $1,200 a month on daycare. Rent is almost that much, too. I make $3,000 a month; how will I make my car payment? What will I use for food, clothes?"

I worry this over and over in my mind. Kaj still makes a fuss when I leave her in the morning, and she is so happy to see me at the end of the day. I become convinced that Sue hates Kaj's body as much as she hates mine.

One afternoon toward the end of October, I'm sitting at my desk and come across Padmini's number on a slip of paper. On a whim I call her.

When she answers I say, "Hi, it's Alexandra, Lyde's friend? I came to see the daycare this summer." She says she remembers me and I ask if she has a second to talk.

"Sure," she tells me, "the children are having a nap." I can hear her open and go through a door. I imagine she is walking onto the closed-in porch at the front of the house.

"Padmini, is there any way you could give me a scholarship for Kaj? I really can't pay the full fee, but I need to get her into a place I trust." I start to cry and am reminded of the days after Kaj was born, when I cried every time I got on the phone. I control myself and tell her about Sue and what I'm suspecting. Padmini is quiet for a moment and then says that maybe she can do a scholarship. "Could you pay $1,000 a month?" She asks.

In my mind I think, *No way. How am I going to do it?* Paying $800 has been an incredible stretch; I can't even imagine where I'm going to get another $200. But my mouth says, "Yes, I'll make it work."

"Okay," Padmini says. "Let's have Kaj come on November first. Okay?"

"Well, I think I'm going to have to give Sue two weeks' notice. That would be November seventh. Would that work?"

"Fine, fine."

I sleep well that night for the first time in months. I tell Sue that a spot has opened up in the daycare many of our faculty use, and it will make my life so much better in terms of carpooling and such. It's all true—there will be many times in the next few years when Lyde will take Kaj with her as she picks up Nancy.

When I take Kaj in for her first day, I kiss Padmini and give her a big hug. "Thank you so much."

Padmini pats me on the shoulder and says, "It's going to be okay."

As I watch Kaj play on the floor with Padmini, I realize that the battle I have been fighting with my body is a danger to Kaj, and that enough is enough.

Time for the self-pity is over. The self-hatred is done.

This is my body. This is my life. I don't have to lose weight, but if I don't accept myself the way I am, it will infect Kaj. Look how it impaired my judgment for two months. For two months I felt uneasy. For two months I knew it was not right, but I second-guessed myself and let her stay there longer than I should have.

No more.

The April before Kaj turns two, I end up in the hospital for two days and two nights with what turns out to be a common bile-duct stone. From my hospital bed I orchestrate a series of five babysitters and friends to stay with Kaj during the days and nights I'm away.

A few months later, in September, I hurt my back when Kaj throws herself around in my arms, and I have to strain to keep her from falling. Again I marshal all my resources to have people take care of Kaj, this time for a week and a half while I lie perfectly still on the couch.

And Kaj takes it all in stride pretty well. She gets used to leaving the house with one person in the morning, then walking to her bedroom with someone different at night, leaving me on the couch. Every day different people, different configurations. At night I listen to each person's style of reading the two or three books she's currently obsessed with, *Don't Let the Pigeon Drive the Bus* being the number-one favorite. I feel sad about how separated I am from her, not able to pick her up or have her sit on my knee.

But we both weather it all pretty well, I think. I don't freak out or cry hopelessly about how difficult it all is. I feel like the model single mom, doing it all and smiling at the same time.

That is, until the crisis is over.

My first morning heading back to work, I buckle Kaj into her car seat and she says, "Mama! My purse!"

"You forgot it," I say in a rushed but sympathetic voice. We are late and will walk into the middle of Padmini's story time again.

"Oh god," she says, in that exact voice I've been using for the last two weeks.

I stand back and look at her. She smiles at me. In my recent moments of diabolical back pain, I've said things I would otherwise never have let her hear.

"Well," I say, deciding to play it cool, "you have your phone."

"Yeth," she says with her endearing lisp. She puts my pedometer to her ear and presses one of the side buttons. "You have walked 242 steps. The distance is .06 miles," the mechanical voice tells her.

In the car after work, Kaj chants, "I want bagel! I want *milk!*"

It takes twenty long minutes to get home from Padmini's. "I want music! I want song!"

So I turn on our Gypsy Kings CD. "*No,* Mommy. No music!"

And so it goes.

It takes fifteen minutes to get up our three flights of stairs, because I can't just pick her up, I have to persuade her not to look at every stray piece of paper or examine every stone and twig.

I cook dinner, having made a deal with her that she can watch *Barney* as long as she does the Nebulizer at the same time (she has a cold, and with the asthma she was diagnosed with around her second birthday, we are cautious). I'm zipping around the kitchen. Pasta! Chicken! Beans! Salad! Frozen roll in the toaster oven as bagel substitute.

I am a healthy cook for the two of us. My turning point over Sue has stuck. We eat well and sensibly—a minimum of processed food; fresh and simple stuff. I've not really lost weight, and I'm not overjoyed with my body, but I have come back to that place I found after giving birth to Kaj. This is the body that made my baby. It works, it's mine. I don't binge, and the self-hatred is gone.

But tonight, with my back, I'm not doing a very good job. The chicken is still cooking, and the pasta is overdone. The only thing that worked out are the green beans, which are perfect.

She's back from the living room. "I want bagel!"

"Okay," I say. "First we eat the veggies."

She climbs into her high chair, and I put beans on a little plate for her, and some on a bigger plate for me. We both eat our veggies first. This is the deal for all the kids at Padmini's, and it's the deal here at home. But tonight she's having nothing to do with it. No way.

She's yelling, "No beans, Mommy! No beans, Mommy!"

I say firmly, over her yelling, "That's the deal. You know that's the deal. Then there is chicken and pasta and bagel." Somewhere in the back of my mind, I know this resistance is all about how she saw so little of me these last two weeks. It's a reaction to all the changes in her schedule and circumstances.

But I'm frustrated.

The chicken breast I have been "frying" in broth is splattering all over the stove and the floor. I ignore the screaming and cut into one of the pieces. It's still pink inside.

"Arghhhh, the chicken's not even *done!*"

And I cry. This is what breaks me. Not the hundreds of dollars I spent on baby-sitting while I lay on the couch. Not the calling and the worrying and feeling bad about how terribly much I have to lean on my friends. Not the stress about work and all that needs to be done.

This is the thing. *The undone chicken.*

I lean over the sink, my back pulsing and stiff and aching, bawling my eyes out while the chicken still splatters behind me. I collect myself and run water over my wrists for some unknown reason. But something has shifted, and it takes me a moment to realize what it is. It is the absence of Kaj's screaming.

I turn to see her smiling at me, a green bean disappearing into her mouth, another in her fingers, ready to go.

What strange mixed feelings I have watching her. I'm happy that she's eating the beans finally, but it's odd that she reacted to my crying that way, wanted to please me.

I think of the moment last week when I was still on the couch, and she came up to me and put her hands on my face. "I kiss it better," she said. And she kissed my elbow (I'm not sure why the elbow), then crawled onto the couch with me and, in a very un-Kaj-like way, stayed there still as you please for ages.

I realize for the first time, here in the kitchen smelling of cooked chicken and beans, that Kaj loves me.

I mean, of course she loves me—I'm her mother. But the love I feel from her now is fuller. When she was a baby, I understood that she needed me, that she loved me with her rooting mouth and fingers twisted in my hair. But this more profound thing—Kaj as a little person, loving me—feels new.

New to me, I guess. I should have known this more deeply, I suppose, but I've been so caught up in loving her, in taking care of her—and of myself and the house and the car and everything—that I didn't get it.

She loves me and I love her, and between us we have all that it takes to be a family.

FOURTEEN

The Here and Now

So, today Kaj and I live together in a future family that isn't exactly what I dreamed about all my life. It is not, of course, the heterocentric "normal" family I strived for. But my choices didn't lead me there. They led me here, to this now.

Kaj is three years and three months old now. I am forty-three. We live together in the same apartment with two floors; she has her room upstairs and I have mine. In the morning she calls to me, through our doorless doorways, "I wake up, Mommy!" in a crystal-clear voice.

Her plunger head with the fine dark hair and her mottled face have come into their own, and she is a curly-haired blond girl whom strangers touch and say, "Isn't she beautiful? God bless her."

We visit our family in Canada as often as we can, and Dad comes to visit us at least twice a year (Mom can't bring herself to fly again). Kaj loves her grandfather, screaming in the car as we drive up to pick him up, "Grandpa!" and kicking her legs and almost leaping out of her car seat.

Margaret's daughter Skye is also a good friend, and we include the Hashimotos in our Canadian travels. It is not quite the dream second family I had imagined, but it is appropriate and right. Skye and Kaj will grow up like sisters, and when we visit they fall into talking again as if we were there only last week.

The daddy question, of course, has come up. And though I think I'm prepared, I'm not really. I have talked to her all her life about how our family doesn't have a dad, how there are many different kinds of families. Kaj has seen this herself—in Jaiden and her two moms; in our friend Mary, who had her son Daniel in the same way I had Kaj. We talk about Pat and Ali too. In the years since Kaj was born, Pat and Ahmed separated and are now divorced. Kaj and I talk about how Ali's dad lives far away now and Ali lives most of the time with his mom, like Kaj lives with me.

On Father's Day this year, Kaj and I are on our way out of the house to go to a playdate, when she says to me, "I have a daddy."

"You do? Tell me about your daddy," I say. This doesn't come totally out of the blue, of course. She has also been telling me lately about her brothers and sisters—what they tell her, what she does with them. Also, last week her daycare provider asked me what I thought they should do with Kaj when all the other kids were doing Father's Day cards in the weeks leading up to Father's

Day. I thought for a second and said that Padmini could tell her she was making a card for her grandfather. That seemed a decent way to deal with it. But it is clear to me that the idea of Daddy has been on her mind this week.

"Last night Daddy told me I could sleep in the big bed," she says.

"Oh? And how was it sleeping in the big bed?" Last night I finally moved her into the double bed in her room. This is something I've been planning and talking about for months. And this morning she woke up very proud of herself. During the night, when I checked on her, it crushed my heart with tenderness to see her tiny body in the middle of the huge double bed.

"I was scared," she says.

"You were?"

"Yes, but Daddy said I could sleep."

"You mean he said you would be all right?"

"Sure," she says, bending down to pick up an empty and crumpled bag of chips. "Can I have this, Mama?"

"No," I say, laughing. "That's garbage."

"But I want!" she says when I make her drop it back on the ground.

"Come on, honey, Melanie is waiting for us."

This pops her out of her little temper, and she skips along beside me as we cross the street to our car.

"I'm a good girl," she says.

"Yes you are. A lovely girl."

"I don't throw the crayons around."

Well, I think, *she did throw them around, but then she cleaned them right up herself without my saying anything.* In fact, she cleaned up all her toys in the living room, danced around the cleared space with her arms spread wide, and said, "Look, Mama! I clean up!"

I say to Kaj as I buckle her into her car seat, "Yes, you put your crayons away and you cleaned everything up!"

"And I slept in the big bed."

"Yes you did. My lovely big girl."

When Kaj made her Daddy comment, I had a twinge about what she didn't have. But hard on the heels of that was a first full thought: *How wonderful! Like the sisters and brothers she tells me about all the time—who are her friends—this "daddy" is a comfort to her.*

I like that she has found ways to comfort herself. We all have to teach ourselves that. My ways weren't always the healthiest. But imaginary fathers and sisters and brothers seem just fine to me.

A few days later, she says to me one morning, "Daddy is coming to visit."

I say, "Really?" in a rather humoring sort of way, the way I respond to all of her fantasy storytelling talk, like when she tells me she's going to the pool with Lyde's daughter Nancy but I have made no such plans.

"Yes," she says. ("Yeth" is what she actually says. She still has a very cute lisp.) "He's coming in three months."

"Really?" There is more surprise in my voice this time. Where does she get this stuff?

We are in the dining room when she says this, and she grabs my hand and says, "Come. I'll show you." So she pulls me into the living room and around to the place under the stairs where we keep her toys. She grabs a little Ziploc bag, where she has lately been keeping a Dora the Explorer wallet Pat gave her. She opens the bag and pulls out the wallet, and inside are the little slips of paper I gave her weeks earlier as money.

"See," she says, pulling out a piece of paper, "Daddy is coming to visit in three months." She nods at me like this is all the confirmation in the world we need.

I say, "Oh. Well."

As I stand there wondering what to say, she leaves and heads off to play with her teddy bear. I think she must sense something in my hesitation, because she says a similar thing to me again later in the day.

Since Kaj moved into the big bed last week, we have developed a habit of my lying beside her at night to read her a story; then we talk about the day, what she did, what I did. In the morning I also lie down beside her and talk about what is coming up. It's the coziest time of day for us. So the next day, when she wakes up, I go to her room and lie down beside her and we talk a little bit, and then I say, "You know, you do have a daddy. Everyone has a daddy."

She interrupts me and says, "Yes I do." She nods her head vigorously at me. "He's coming to live with us."

"No, Kaj, your daddy is not coming to live with us. He lives in Denmark, but we don't know him."

"He's coming to live at our house."

"No, he lives in Denmark. He gave me the seeds I needed to make you. I wanted you very badly, and he was very kind to give them to me."

"Oh," she says. "His name is Taylor."

I laugh and say, "Sure, we can call him Taylor."

"His name is Mumbaram."

"Mumbaram. Okay. Not Taylor?"

"No." She makes no move to get out of bed, and neither do I.

"I want milk and crackers and Little Einsteins," she says finally, looking up from her bear, which she has been picking at.

"Okay," I say, sitting up, happy to be able to give her what she wants (although I will go with a very loose definition of "crackers" and give her Puffins cereal, which looks like crackers and doesn't seem so odd for breakfast). "Let's go downstairs and I'll get you some milk."

In retrospect, the idea that she has a daddy—in the sense that *all* people have a daddy, but hers doesn't live with us—is probably more than she could process. But at least now she has something to hold on to. She has a daddy. He lives in Denmark. He gave me the parts I needed to make her. I wanted her very much.

That night, though, she won't sleep in her big bed, and I look at it and think about our conversation there this morning. *No, your daddy is not coming to live with us.* I wonder for a moment if I should have been so definitive.

Now I've taken away the comfort-daddy who made if possible for her to sleep in her big bed.

Maybe I was too literal, thinking like an adult when she was thinking like the kid she is. An imaginary daddy could be as real to her as my real dad is to me. And I've taken him away from her by insisting that he isn't coming to live with us.

I think about it another way: If she had said her sister was coming to visit, I would have said okay. And let it go.

Still, it breaks my heart to think that if she was being as literal as I thought she was, she would be waiting for a father who was never going to come. I feel like I'm back on the farm, waiting and waiting for my father to come and then feeling the agony of watching him leave. I think about the longing for my mother all those months and months on the farm—so long, in fact, that I gave up. I thought I would never see her again, but I never stopped longing for her.

This is an awesome thing I have done, I think as I say to Kaj, "You can sleep wherever you like, honey."

Tonight she wants to be rocked in the glider, and I do that too, all the while thinking about how I knew the daddy issue would be a big deal for her, but I didn't know how hard it would be for me.

I don't want her to be without a father, and rocking her here, I realize that part of my being able to go ahead and have her was thinking that she wouldn't be fatherless for very long, because I would find a man soon after she was born. Long before now, certainly. Long before she would be aware of her fatherlessness. He and I would have a child together too. And she would know she was born with donor sperm, but she would have a father nevertheless.

But that is not what happened, probably because it's not really what I wanted. If I've learned anything from this journey, it's that things are not always what they seem, and what I think I want on the surface is often belied by the things I do.

So perhaps I am indeed broken, just as I said to my mom years ago. But that doesn't mean I don't have a family, because I do, even if it is a little small.

And I think seriously for the first time, *Perhaps it's time to expand this family.*

Perhaps I should have another one.

Weeks later we are in the car coming home from Padmini's, and I ask Kaj, just for the heck of it, if she would like to have a brother or a sister.

"A brother," she says without hesitation.

"Oh," I say. "Okay."

"No," she says then, looking out the window at the wildflowers in the lot beside the red light we are stopped at. "No. Two brothers."

"Really? You want two brothers?"

"Yes, two brothers for me and two brothers for you."

"Oh," I say as the light turns green, "I don't know about that."

And though I don't know for sure if I *will* have another one, I do call Claus at the Scandinavian Cryobank (although they've changed their name and are now called Cryos International), and I buy two vials of Olaf's sperm—just in case.

It has been clear to me for a while now that it was never just a baby I wanted. It was a family, probably a slightly larger family than this. One with siblings for Kaj. And one that I can do on my own. That I may very well do on my own.

And who knows? If I keep working on my intimacy issues, I may not stay broken forever.

Epilogue

Looking down the long telescope from my first thoughts of having a baby to the moment where we are now, I think sometimes I did rush to have Kaj. I may even have had her for some not very selfless reasons. But because all those decisions and impulses led to her being in my life, the exactness of her—I wouldn't change a step. As with my uncle's sixtieth birthday, when I flew to Sweden to surprise him, it was the right thing to do.

I don't think about all those machinations much anymore. I think about this child of mine, this girl who wakes up full-blown each morning, who calls across to my room, "Mommy! I wake up!" This girl of mine who is always in the middle of living. "Look Mommy! I'm dancing! Isn't it beautiful to dance?"

She has taught me to live in the moment—to know what it means to fall in love. Because of her, I understand what it means to live and to love and to be afraid but love anyway.

Acknowledgments

First of all, thank you to Olaf for the precious gift of Kaj's life. Wherever and whoever you are, thank you. My writing group: Patricia Dunn, Jimin Hahn, Gloria Hatrick, Deborah Laufer, Kate Brandt, Crystal Greene, and Anne Wenzel, thank you for pushing me to write more and deeper. To my editors, Brooke and Krista, thank you for your belief in this book. And to my agent, Barbara Hogenson, and to Nicole Verity, your first enthusiasm gave me such heart.

To Sarah Lawrence College: Susan Guma, Vijay Seshadri, Mary LaChapelle, Kate Knapp Johnson, and Barbara Kaplan, thank you for your support in my writing and my life. To Slonim House: Crystal, Christina, Denise, Manny, and *hermanas* Alba and Shirley, you've made going to work fun. Anne, you rock! To my mentors and teachers: Myra Goldberg, colleague, friend, and coteacher, Kathleen Hill, Lindsey Abrams, Joan Silber, and Mary Morris, an embarrassment of riches. Fanchon Scheier and Sarah Kate Robbins, thank you for your unwavering support these last ten years. Thank you, Lyde Sizer, for all the running (we'll get at it again) and for reading the book so closely. Bev and Maureen, a million thanks, over and over again, for your help these last months. To my first writing teacher, Joe Kertes, I want to say thank you for making me feel like it was possible to be a writer.

Thank you to Robin Sauve, Anne-Marie McElrone, and Alexandra Samuel, who were my center of gravity back in Toronto, and to Helen Walsh, my fellow traveler, and Megan Park, my great friend.

Jane and Peter Hoyle, your unknowing patronage of the arts by not raising my rent these last ten years has made it financially possible for me to not only keep writing, but also think about having a Kaj at all.

Thank you, too, to Claus and Trine at Cryos International (formerly Scandinavian Cryobank).

To chubby-girl group I send a big fat thanks!

And then there are all those who have taken extra care of Kaj these last six months (or perhaps three and a half years would be more accurate): Padmini, Shanthi, Anusha, and Shakira, and the wonderful babysitters of Sarah Lawrence. And Idania Gonzalez: Without your help with Kaj, and your feeding us once in a while, I could not have finished this book.

Megan and Luz, I wish you lived closer. Jennifer and David, I can't wait to come up to see you again. Dr. Bakas and Dr. McGroary and staff, I've said it before and I'll say it again: You are the best.

Michelle Wildgen and Steve O'Brien, you have been such great friends and support in writing and life.

Thank you to my first family: my mom and dad, Mimi and Norman Soiseth; brother Glenn; and brother-in-law Glenn and sister-in-law Eva. Thank you to Uncle Ralph and Aunty Alice, Carol, Brenda, Barbara, and Kevin, my second family, and to all the Soiseths: I am proud to be one of you. And to my Danish family: Hanne Stokholm, I've often said that my time with you in Denmark saved my life. Erna and dear Alfred (how I miss him), Aunty Rut and David. Uncle Per, I miss you like crazy too. Thank you to all my families: the Hashimotos, Poniatowskis, Oseskis, Hanleys, Dunns, Petillis, and Cullen-Sizers. Finally, to my beautiful sister, Linda, and to the sisters of my heart, Pat and Margaret: I don't know how to tell you how much I appreciate you, except to say I would give you a kidney.

And last of all, to the women who have thought or are thinking of embarking on this journey (you go, Mary Knight!), God bless. It's an amazing journey. Hold on tight!

© JIMIN HAN

About the Author

Alexandra Soiseth received her BA from the University of Saskatchewan, her BAA from Ryerson University, and her MFA from Sarah Lawrence College. She is the assistant director of the MFA writing program at Sarah Lawrence, where she also teaches. She is the former managing editor and communications director of *Global City Review*, a New York City–based literary magazine, and her work has appeared on Babycenter.com, *Literary Mama*, and the radio show "Life Rattle," and in *Lumina* and *McGill Street Magazine*, among other publications. She is the recipient of a Canada Arts Council grant and an Ontario Arts Council grant. She lives in Yonkers, New York.

Selected Titles from Seal Press

For more than thirty years, Seal Press has published groundbreaking books. By women. For women. Visit our website at www.sealpress.com. Check out the Seal Press blog at www.sealpress.com/blog.

Deliver This! Make the Childbirth Choice That's Right for You . . . No Matter What Everyone Else Thinks by Marisa Cohen. $14.95, 1-58005-153-7. A smart, informative book that helps expectant mothers explore traditional and alternative birthing choices.

The Maternal Is Political: Women Writers at the Intersection of Motherhood and Social Change edited by Shari MacDonald Strong. $15.95, 1-58005-243-6. Exploring the vital connection between motherhood and social change, *The Maternal Is Political* features thirty powerful literary essays by women striving to make the world a better place for children and families—both their own and other women's.

Rockabye: From Wild to Child by Rebecca Woolf. $15.95, 1-58005-232-0. The coming-of-age story of a rock 'n' roll party girl who becomes unexpectedly pregnant, decides to keep the baby, and discovers motherhood on her own terms.

The Stay-at-Home Survival Guide: Field-Tested Strategies for Staying Smart, Sane, and Connected When You're Raising Kids at Home by Melissa Stanton. $14.95, 1-58005-247-9. The essential how-to book for stay-at-home mothers, written by a media-savvy former "working mom."

It's a Boy: Women Writers on Raising Sons edited by Andrea J. Buchanan. $14.95, 1-58005-145-6. Seal's edgy take on what it's really like to raise boys, from toddlers to teens and beyond.

It's a Girl: Women Writers on Raising Daughters edited by Andrea J. Buchanan. $14.95, 1-58005-147-2. The companion title to *It's a Boy*, this anthology describes what it's like—and why it's a unique experience—to mother girls.